PILLBOXES

OF BRITAIN AND IRELAND

PILLBOXES
OF BRITAIN AND IRELAND

MIKE OSBORNE

The History Press

First published 2008

Reprinted 2010, 2012

The History Press
The Mill, Brimscombe Port,
Stroud, Gloucestershire, GL5 2QG
www.thehistorypress.co.uk

British Library Cataloguing in Publication Data.
A catalogue record for this book is available from the British Library.

ISBN 978 0 7524 4329 4

Typesetting and origination by The History Press

Printed and bound in Great Britain by
Marston Book Services Limited, Didcot

CONTENTS

ACKNOWLEDGEMENTS

I have, as ever, drawn on the knowledge and expertise of a large number of people. These include those such as Colin Alexander, Bernard Lowry and William Foot, for instance, operating at a national level, and countless individuals such as Fred Nash, David Burridge and Mick Wilks, working more localised patches. I have tried to acknowledge as many of these as I can in the references in Chapters 5 and 6. My apologies to anyone I have omitted. References to published materials are listed chapter by chapter in the bibliography. My wife Pam has been a supportive and long-suffering, impressed concrete-spotter for nearly 40 years now, and I am immeasurably grateful for her continuing enthusiasm and encouragement.

GLOSSARY

abbatis anti-personnel obstacle of sharpened stakes, tree trunks with sharpened branches left in place, tangles of thorns etc.

broch round residential stone tower, possibly defensible, built in Scotland from around 600 BC to the first century AD

caponier/cappanato loopholed structure for commanding the ditch, either free-standing or, more often, attached to the curtain

chevaux de frise logs with stakes through them, used to seal a breach or path

glacis cleared land sloping away from a fortification to provide a field of fire

machicoulis /machicolation outward extension of wall-head, to allow defenders to fire on, or drop missiles through slots, onto attackers below

nuraghe pre-historic round tower found in Sardinia

trou de loup camouflaged pits with sharpened stakes embedded in their bases, used to defend approaches against, especially surprise, attack

panzerwerk(e) an armoured bunker of one or two storeys with concrete walls 1.5m thick and roof-top cloches containing machine-guns, mortars and flamethrowers. A group of such structures is known as a 'werkgruppe(n)'

ABBREVIATIONS

AA	anti-aircraft
AR	anti-ricochet
ARG	Airfield Research Group (journal *Airfield Review*)
AT	anti-tank
BEF	British Expeditionary Force (First and Second World Wars)
BHQ	Battle Headquarters
CBA	Council for British Archaeology
CRE	Commander Royal Engineers
DFW (/3)	Directorate of Fortifications and Works (branch 3)
DOB	Defence of Britain Project (1995-2000)
EXDO	Extended Defence Officer i.e. minefield control post
FSG	Fortress Study Group (journals *Fort* and *Casemate*)
GHQ	General Headquarters (First and Second World Wars)
HAA	heavy anti-aircraft
IWM	Imperial War Museum
LAA	light anti-aircraft
lmg	light machine-gun
MAP	Ministry of Aircraft Production
mg	machine-gun
OP	Observation Post
PRO	Public Record Office, now TNA *qv*
PSG	Pillbox Study Group (journal *Loopholes*)
RE	Royal Engineer
ROC	Royal Observer Corps
ROF	Royal Ordnance Factory
TNA	The National Archive, formerly PRO *qv*
UKFC	United Kingdom Fortifications Club (journal *ALDIS*)

INTRODUCTION

About a mile from my house on the Lincolnshire/Cambridgeshire border, a line of World War II pillboxes extends southwards through the Fens. If one walks any stretch of the east coast between John o'Groats and Land's End, or around the Severn estuary, Milford Haven, Cardigan Bay, Holyhead and the Lancashire coast, one will find more. Travel Britain's waterways and still more will appear along rivers such as the Thames, Medway, Boyne, Dove, Severn, Ouse and Avon, and canals including the Kennet and Avon, Coventry, Oxford and Trent and Mersey. Venture into the countryside beyond Epping Forest, onto almost any one of Britain's 800-odd wartime airfields, or near the dozens of depots, radar sites, experimental stations and once-secret bunkers, and usually a pillbox or two will be revealed. These cost-effective but essentially flawed structures were built in their tens of thousands to solve particular problems at particular times. They were relatively easy to build, but more difficult to remove. The humble pillbox, however, was neither a British invention nor a local phenomenon and can be seen across much of the world. Virtually the whole of Europe, much of Africa and Asia, and the Commonwealth countries have been the setting for pillbox-building programmes. Belligerents and neutrals, Allies and Axis, colonies and sovereign states have all built them. In relatively recent times, paranoid Albania insulated itself from its neighbours of all political hues with 70,000 pillboxes. Both the Egyptians and Israelis defended their Suez interface with lines of pillboxes, facing each other across the canal. The French in Indo-China, the British in the Gulf, and the Americans in Afghanistan have all used small, defensible strong-points variously known as sangars, or hedgehogs, bunkers or dugouts, all essentially based on the same principles as pillboxes but constructed in less permanent materials.

This book seeks to do two things. Firstly, it traces the use in warfare of small, free-standing defensible structures from ancient times to the present, placing the pillbox in a historical continuum and seeking to identify both its antecedents and its course of development. Secondly it provides a typology of British pillboxes through a catalogue of known types and also of individual examples, finishing with a look at the tactical use of such defences.

Only with Henry Wills's ground-breaking book of 1985, and the associated publicity which went with his winning a BBC *Chronicle* award, did the study of pillboxes become firmly established. Subsequent fieldwork by a number of individuals and groups, boosted by the *Defence of Britain Project 1995-2000*, has resulted in a greater public awareness of the significance of these structures. Documentary research funded by the CBA and Britain's major heritage organisations, and carried out mainly by Dr Colin Dobinson in England and Neil Redfern in Wales, Scotland and Northern Ireland, has generated enormous amounts of data to be verified by fieldwork. Some detailed fieldwork has subsequently been undertaken by William Foot, whilst many other individuals have continued to explore evidence on the ground. There are still large gaps in the record, and structures in the field are being destroyed daily, but there is still information to be gained. Amongst the news of losses comes the occasional more positive story – the Staffordshire Regiment Museum has recently taken delivery of a pillbox, removed from beside the rail tracks north of Tamworth.

1

ORIGINS

Since the beginnings of recorded history, conflict has provided a need for groups to defend themselves against each other. Whilst citadels, fortresses and walled cities, being both more extensive and more substantial, have tended to predominate and in many cases endure, there has always been a need for the free-standing, independent and self-defensible strong-point alongside these. Such fortifications have taken a number of different forms, often dictated by purpose, location or available labour and materials. Urgency has sometimes made temporary works necessary, perhaps as a response to a sudden external threat. At other times, the danger has been from within a society, so that factions have perceived a need to assert themselves through the construction of essentially private defensive works. There are examples of the application of both tactical and strategic considerations in these contexts, initiated by state or individual alike. Sometimes individual strong-points combine to provide an inter-dependent network of mutually-supporting works forming a coherent defence system. At other times, there is no underlying cohesiveness, merely discrete structures existing in isolation. This chapter will explore many of the examples, worldwide, which appear to meet some or all of these criteria.

PREHISTORY

Some of the earliest defensive structures must be the *nuraghi* of Sardinia, dating from the Bronze Age. Whilst some form the heart of quite sophisticated fortresses, incorporating huts within concentric defences, in their simplest form each *nuraghe* consists of a tall conical stone tower, between 20 and 50ft (6-17m) high, and 20 to 50ft in diameter. Many are built in dominant but remote positions in order, one must imagine, to exploit the defensive properties provided by their inaccessibility, height and visibility. Many of these towers are provided with parapets, loopholes (*1*) and defended entrances. Although some 8000 *nuraghi* were built in Sardinia, the only possibly analogous structures to be found elsewhere from this early period might be the *talaiots* of Minorca.

In many ways similar to the *nuraghi*, but from a much later period and confined to the mainland and islands of Scotland, are *brochs*. These date from around 600 BC onwards, with a final building phase in the Scottish lowlands in the first century AD. The main feature of the *broch* is a circular tower, up to 40ft (13m) high, and between 22 and 44ft (7-14m) in diameter, with mural stair-passages. The latest opinion appears to favour a steep, conical

1 Orroli, Sardinia; arrow-loops in the defences of the Nuraghe of *c.*900 BC

thatched roof, springing from the top of the cavity wall, thus precluding the presence of a wall-head fighting platform. Neither are there loopholes present, and it would appear that *brochs* were developments of the Atlantic roundhouse, intended to provide added living space under a single roof. The only feature possibly characterised as defensive, is the slotted bar which secured the door, often placed part-way along the entrance passage. Small flanking chambers off this passage have been described as 'guard-cells', but it is difficult to imagine what effective defensive function they might have fulfilled. The best known example, at Mousa in the Shetlands, has a wall-base which occupies over 60 per cent of its area. It is difficult to accept that so massive a structure was intended merely to keep out the elements, however inhospitable its location may have been. Like many *nuraghi,* the *broch* was often the centrepiece of a hut-group, but there are also instances of them being built in isolation, without a surrounding complex of subsidiary structures. However, it must be noted that the definition of the *broch* is far from settled, and this has led to wild fluctuations in estimates of their population, ranging from a generous 500, to more recent figures around the hundred mark or fewer.

THE ROMANS

The two previous examples were from contexts of clans or extended family-groups. Our next examples come from a very different setting. Here, the structures to be examined are little more than units in a strategically-motivated defence system, the fortified boundaries of the Roman Empire. During his six years of campaigning in Scotland (AD 77-83),

Agricola built a defended northern frontier between the Tay and the Forth, which ran along the Gask Ridge, highground running more-or-less parallel to the River Earn and the Allan Water. Whilst the north-south glens were defended by large earth and timber forts laid out in the traditional Roman way, the line along the ridge was defended at intervals of a Roman mile, by two-storey timber watchtowers, each within a compact enclosure constructed of turf and wattle-work, and with an outer bank and ditch. Each tower was manned by eight men detached from a garrison based at the nearest fort and there were probably 18 of these towers distributed between the five forts and two fortlets of the system. The line apparently had only a brief existence, for within a few years of its construction it was abandoned and the Antonine Wall to the south was to become the intermittent northern frontier of Rome. Under Trajan, a line of defence similar to that on the Gask Ridge ran to the east of the Rhine between the rivers Lahn and Main, defining the north-eastern frontier of the Empire. In the next century, a concentration of hostile forces along the Danube saw these chains of watchtowers replicated. Their general appearance is confirmed by scenes on Trajan's Column in Rome.

Unlike the turf and timber towers on the *limites* of Scotland, Germany or Dacia, the continuous stone barrier of Hadrian's Wall enjoyed substantial masonry constructions from the start, two categories of which concern us here. The *milecastle*, as its name suggests, occurred every Roman mile along the Wall. This consisted of a rectangular projecting bastion with wall-walk and raised turret, and contained accommodation for 16 soldiers and their equipment, as well as cooking facilities. In addition to an entrance from the rear of the Wall, there was also an exit which would act as a sally-port. Between each pair of *milecastles* there were two *turrets* which acted as both signal stations and OPs. Although Hadrian's Wall is significantly different from the other Roman defences we have noted, in that its defences were continuously linked, there is evidence that, in at least one case, a *turret* was built as a free-standing structure, only subsequently being incorporated into the Wall proper. The *limes Germanicus* was itself re-routed and rebuilt in stone in the second half of the second century AD under Antoninus, who introduced stone watchtowers at half-mile intervals. The timber-built free-standing tower, however, continued in Roman military use as the signal-tower and the remains of one has been excavated on the cliffs at Scarborough Castle (North Yorkshire).

THE MIDDLE AGES

It has been suggested that Roman timber towers were the inspiration for the stilted timber towers built into Norman mottes in the eleventh century. Excavations at a number of Norman earthwork fortresses, notably Abinger (Surrey) and South Mimms (Hertfordshire) revealed the existence of timber posts sunk into the motte, supporting a platform, which carried a timber tower. Close examination of the Bayeux Tapestry may possibly provide corroboration for such design techniques, illustrated by Norman castles in Brittany, but the connection, if indeed there is one, may be tenuous. Another medieval application of the free-standing timber tower can be found in the *chertas* of Russia, initially loose lines of defence built south of Moscow to defend against Tatar incursions.

Eventually, by the seventeenth century, these were fully-developed lines based on strong fortresses, but in earlier times they were little more than timber towers or gateways, intended to block major routes of potential invasion.

Also from the medieval period, but constructed in stone, are a number of examples of single-family towers in a variety of contexts. The Upper Svanetia region of Georgia, in the Caucasus, contains a number of villages with large numbers of both tower-houses, and houses with adjacent war towers. The tower-houses are usually of three storeys, with thick walls and few openings at ground level. Often the entrance is on the first floor and there may be machicolations at roof level. War towers are usually free-standing alongside houses. They are five or six storeys high, entered at first- or even second-floor level, and have barrel-vaulted lower levels to counter the danger of fire. Their roofs too, are battlemented, loopholed and machicolated. The tower-houses mainly date from the sixteenth or seventeenth centuries, whilst the war-towers had their origins in much earlier times, but continued to be built into the nineteenth century. Most surviving examples, of which there are dozens in each of a number of separate villages, were apparently designed for the use of firearms. The remote location of this region and its height above sea-level (2500m) have combined to preserve this ancient landscape.

There is evidence that a number of pre-Columbian villages in the south-west USA also used towers as a defensive measure against neighbouring, but not necessarily neighbourly, tribes. Some of these structures, such as that at Mesa Verde (Colorado) may date back to the thirteenth century.

In an entirely different context, the family towers of many Italian cities, most famously San Gimignano (Tuscany) and Bologna (Emilia), served a similar function to those in Georgia. They provided a refuge in times of civil strife, a secure vault for the family's portable wealth, and a focus for the family and its adherents. In some instances there appears to have been some rivalry between families as to who might build the highest or the most impressive. The *Torre degli Asinelli* is just short of 100m high, and is one of the few survivors of the 180 towers standing in Bologna when Dante was writing. The city authorities of San Gimignano (2), where 13 of an original 76 survive, enacted legislation limiting the height of private towers to the 51m of the *Torre della Rognosa* in order to prevent an escalation in what they must have regarded as a wasteful and potentially dangerous competition. What this reveals, however, is another factor coming into play in medieval times, which is the status of such structures as public relations exercises, much as twenty-first century corporate ambition is not above a little friendly competition in the skyscraper stakes. When push came to shove, the Capulets and the Montagues would have retreated to their towers, pulled up the drawbridge, and sat out the crisis until it was safe to emerge.

If thirteenth- and fourteenth-century Italian cities were dangerous places, then so were contested border regions, and the Anglo-Scots marches were as dangerous as any. A strong tradition of cross-border cattle rustling, extortion and general mayhem had grown out of the official business of continual warring between the two countries. A local response on both sides of the border was to build tower-houses (3), known as *peles*. These generally consisted of a barrel-vaulted, fire-resistant basement, with two or three floors above. Entry was gained through a first-floor doorway, defended by an iron grille or yett, and

2 San Gimignano, Tuscany; the Torri Salvucci, two of around a dozen medieval towers, inside the town walls

openings were confined to arrow-slits. On the roof was a wall-head fighting platform behind battlements. Sometimes a corner-turret held a staircase spiralling clockwise to give an advantage to the right-handed defender over his similarly dextrous attacker. Thus, according to George Macdonald Fraser, the left-handed Kerrs built an anti-clockwise stair in their tower of Ferniehurst outside Jedburgh. *Peles* were built from the thirteenth century onwards and remained popular and necessary in parts of Scotland until at least the Act of Union. Poorer folk built *bastle-houses*, a barrel-vaulted basement for the beasts, with a living space on the single floor above. These latter are normally associated with Cumbria and Northumberland, but a group of them has also been identified in Clydesdale.

ARTILLERY FORTIFICATIONS OF THE SIXTEENTH AND SEVENTEENTH CENTURIES

As the use of artillery became more widespread, innovative forms of fortification were developed to counter this threat. Two examples of these new forms meet our criteria here. The first is the *caponier* (Italian: *capanatto*). This was designed to defend the ditch

3 Kirkhope Tower near Selkirk, Scotland
(NT379250); the late sixteenth-century
tower-house of the Cranstouns, now
restored and once again inhabited

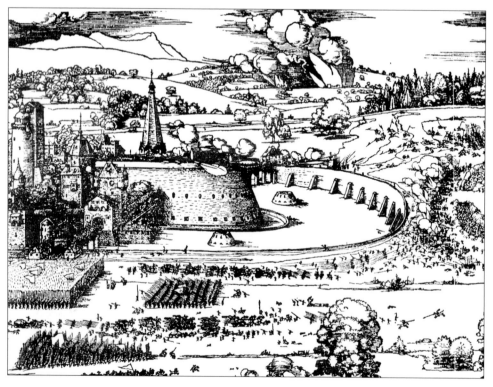

4 Durer's design of 1527 for free-standing *capanatti* in a city's dry moat

of a fortress against enemy attack and became an essential part of fortress warfare up to the end of the nineteenth century. An early example can be seen at Craignethan Castle (Lanarkshire) where a covered stone passage, with loops for handguns, crosses the ditch below the great artillery wall that was built in the 1530s, following the teachings of Francesco di Giorgio. Giorgio's *capanatti* were usually built into the walls at both ends as this was his method of closing off the ditch to attack. Durer, on the other hand, writing in 1527, proposed free-standing, circular *caponiers* in order to command the full width of wider ditches (*4*). It had been found that wet ditches were usually as much of an inconvenience to the defenders as they were an obstacle to attackers. Yet dry ditches, while allowing the defenders to redeploy in order to mount a counter-attack, could also provide the attacker with direct routes into the fortress. Thus the *caponier* was designed to prevent the enemy's free movement in the ditch. Durer's drawing shows a circular building, about 30ft (9m) across, with possibly two tiers of loops for handguns. The sides are battered and appear to have chamfered parapets in line with his usual ideas, utilised in Henry VIII's forts for deflecting cannon-shot. This little building would appear to be the true forerunner of the pillbox. At Franchimont, between Liège and Spa in south-east Belgium, Erard de la Marck, around 1530, converted his castle with its thirteenth-century *donjon* into an artillery fortress by the addition of *caponiers* at each of the five angles of a new pentagonal curtain (*5*). His *caponiers* were low circular towers with coolie-hat roofs. It is interesting to note that a virtually identical *caponier* was built at Delle Grazia Battery (Malta) more than 300 years later. The other type of building constructed exclusively for the use of firearms is the gun-tower, which appeared in Tudor times as part of Henry VIII's coastal defence scheme and was designed by the Bohemian engineer, Stefan van Haschenperg. There are numbers of these small, free-standing blockhouses or gun-towers around Britain's coasts, notably at Dartmouth, Falmouth, St Mawes, Dover, Plymouth and Gravesend (foundations only). These towers were generally circular or D-shaped and, although they had loops for handguns at ground level, usually mounted their cannon on the roof, firing over a chamfered parapet, often through open-topped embrasures. The defences of Plymouth contain several examples. One, at Mount Edgecumbe, is square, whilst the two at Firestone Bay and Devil's Point are more D-shaped. Two Tudor fortresses guard the entrance to the deep-water anchorage of Falmouth, at Pendennis and St Mawes, each having a D-shaped Henrician blockhouse on the rocks below the main fort (*6*), mounting cannon both in casemates and at roof-level. A similar gun-tower at Douglas (Isle of Man) was demolished in 1816, but Derby Fort on St Michael's Island, guarding the approach to Castle Rushen, survives. This is circular but on a larger scale than many of the blockhouses, with a central courtyard and an arc of casemated cannon-loops to seaward. Examples of free-standing gun-towers from this period have been recorded at Youghal (Co. Cork), one linked to Reginald's Tower at Waterford, both in Ireland, and at Dunbar (East Lothian) in Scotland. It is worth noting that examples of such blockhouses, while standing in isolation in the British Isles, as they once did in the English Pale of Calais, do appear elsewhere on the continent of Europe, but often only as components of large fortified complexes, such as the cylindrical Tour Sainte-Agathe at the chateau of Porquerolles (Toulon, France) built in 1531, and measuring 65ft (20m) in diameter, or the slightly later round tower at the heart of Fort Carre at Antibes. The exceptions

5 Franchimont, Belgium; one of the early sixteenth-century artillery casemates added by Erard de la Marck to the earlier donjon

can be found in the strings of free-standing towers which girded much of the northern Mediterranean coastline, in order to discourage corsair raids from (mainly) North Africa. These towers were often placed at an appropriate distance apart to be able to pass signals between them using beacons. Towns or particularly vulnerable or strategically-important places would have fully-developed forts, but the long stretches or remote coastline in between would be defended by solitary towers, often square, sometimes circular, but always of at least two storeys, with cannon mounted on the roof and an elevated entrance reached by ladder. Such systems, from the later 1500s, may be seen all over, but were especially well-developed in southern Italy, on Malta and Mallorca, and around the coast of Spain (7).

By the seventeenth century, the notion of the free-standing artillery tower was firmly embedded. A number of examples appear in the context of coastal defence: Cromwell's Castle (Tresco, Isles of Scilly) of 1652-3, Mount Batten Tower (Plymouth, Devon) of 1650, and the Krudttarnet at Frederikshavn (Jutland, Denmark) of 1686 (8), for instance. It has been suggested that the two English examples were the inspiration for a number of three-storey towers, mainly around 36ft (11m) square, incorporated by de Gomme, the military engineer employed by Charles II, in his coastal defences in the Medway and at Portsmouth and Gosport (Hampshire). These were on a much smaller scale than most of the similar, contemporary works by Dahlberg, particularly in Sweden. The island of Bermuda was defended by a number of masonry gun-towers, both square and hexagonal, the Devonshire redoubt of 1621 still standing at the heart of later works. It is a hexagonal tower, part-hewn out of a rocky outcrop and part masonry. It forms a solid platform with five cannon embrasures.

Although Vauban is probably the military engineer of the Baroque period most closely associated with the bastioned systems of defence, he was also responsible for developing the use of the free-standing gun-tower, both integrated into extensive schemes of defence

6 Falmouth, Cornwall; the Tudor artillery tower known as Little Dennis, below Pendennis Castle

7 Torre de Mola, near Malaga, Andalucia, Spain; one of dozens of such towers built in the sixteenth century to a standard design to defend against corsairs

8 Frederikshaven, Denmark; the Krudttarnet or Powder Tower of 1686-90, with artillery casemates, was the centrepiece of the Fladstrand port defences

and as isolated entities. Several coastal forts around La Rochelle and Rochefort on the west coast of France, have centrepieces comprising either gun-towers built from scratch by Vauban or earlier towers which he reworked. Examples include Fouras (1480-1693), Fort Lupin (1689) and Fort Chapus (1690-1712). Other examples from this period are the fort at Socoa near Biaritz, and several forts in the Toulon defences such as Port-Man and l'Estissac. On the Channel Coast there are examples at Port-en-Bessin (Calvados), and Ile-de-Tatihou and St-Vaast-la-Hougue (Manche). Probably the most spectacular example of this genre is Balthasar Neumann's Maschikuliturm of *c*.1725 at Wurzburg in Bavaria (*9*). Examples of Vauban's bastion-towers, developed in 1687, can be seen incorporated in the town defences of Belfort and Besançon in the Franche-Compte (*10*). These are square two-storey towers, mounting cannon both at ground-level and also under the pyramid-shaped tiled roof. They are usually set on the diagonal, giving them the appearance of being diamond-shaped.

THE EIGHTEENTH AND EARLY NINETEENTH CENTURIES

Occupying a strategic site where the Niagara River enters Lake Ontario, Fort Niagara was consistently modified and updated from its French beginnings in 1687 as Fort Denonville, until its final release by the US military in 1963. During British occupation

9 Würzburg, Bavaria; the Maschikuliturm, designed by Balthasar Neumann *c.*1725, to strengthen the defences of the Bishop's castle

10 Besançon, Doubs, France: a Vauban bastion-tower on the city walls

in 1770 there was a need to strengthen the defences in order that a reduced garrison might still be secure against possible attack from the local tribes. The solution chosen as an alternative to costly ramparts, which would have needed increased numbers of troops to man them, was the construction of two stone two-storey towers, known as the North and South redoubts. The North redoubt was surrounded by a ditch and stockade, while the South redoubt's ground floor was pierced by a passage with gates at each end, thus forming a second gatehouse behind the main gate. Both redoubts mounted cannon at first-floor level and were able to command the entire landward rampart and outworks. A tiled pyramid roof was raised on posts over the open roof-platform, to shelter the gun-crews. The earliest French structure of 1726 has long been known as the French Castle, but it was intended by them as a 'house of peace' to meet Iroquois demands for trade, not military occupation. Whilst purporting to be a provincial manor-house, it nevertheless incorporated machicolations in the dormer-windows, a magazine and a guard-room next to the main door. This building, possibly designed by de Lery, has been cited as a forerunner for the next development in this type of structure, the *tour-modele*. Another of de Lery's probable works at Fort Frederic (Crown Point, Lake Champlain) shared none of this coyness, incorporating a no-nonsense, four-storey, octagonal tower, doubling as a gate-house, with cannon-ports on two storeys, and sited in that corner of the fort most vulnerable to attack.

The *tour-modele* is a mainly French development of the end of the eighteenth century, whose first acknowledged example was a redoubt for 25 men built during Napoleon's disastrous Egyptian campaign around 1800. The plan shows a square, bomb-proof tower carrying two cannon on its roof, surrounded by a deep ditch. Over the doorway is a box machicolation. This design, along with subsequent additions which produced a suite of five models, was adopted as the pattern for future defensive works, but few were built owing to the cost. A set of 46 watercolour drawings found in the papers of the Duke of Wellington appear to represent a scheme for the defence of Paris which included a range of fortifications, but was predominantly based on the use of towers of all shapes. As well as the three larger *tour-modeles*, there were circular, D-shaped and Greek cross-shaped towers. One of these plates shows a design for a revolving floor, by which means a complement of fewer guns could each be given 360 degrees of traverse, a great economy at no sacrifice to effectiveness.

Prior to the development of the *tour-modele*, both Montalembert and Maurice de Saxe had separately advocated the use of circular gun-towers as outlying defences for cities. These ideas had been taken up, in ways unintended by their proponents, by the Spanish on their Atlantic and Mediterranean island dependencies and by the Russians in the defences of their naval bases. By the 1770s, when France appeared to be developing hostile intentions toward Britain, these towers, in a smaller form, were used as the basis of the Channel Island defences. Subsequent experience of the attack and defence of French towers in Corsica, at Fort Tigne (1792) the last work of the Knights of St John on Malta, and an awareness of the work of d'Arcon at Mont Dauphin (1792) in the Alpes de Haute Provence (*11*), for instance, pushed British engineers into using the round tower for coastal defence through the years of the wars with France. A number of different styles were developed, from the proto-Martello designs in Jersey and Guernsey through

11 Mont Dauphin, Alpes de Haute Provence; the Lunette d'Arcon of 1792

the two sizes of tower used on Minorca, to those used to defend Halifax (Nova Scotia) and the Simonstown naval base in South Africa and the well-known Martello Towers of England's south coast (numbered 1-74) and east coast (lettered A-Z + AA-CC), built between 1804 and 1812. During this time only a single square tower was built by the British, at Trincomalee in Ceylon (now Sri Lanka), although there had been a proposal for four trapezoidal redoubts to be built on the Corradino Heights in Malta, never realised. All these towers, despite differences in dimensions and profile, clearly shared a number of defining characteristics. They were circular, elliptical or cam-shaped, with a taper to a roof-top cannon mounting. They were entered at first-floor level over a vaulted basement and defended by musket loops and machicolations. Some had ditches or moats crossed by bridges. It was often the intention that these towers would be combined with other elements such as batteries and fieldworks to achieve integrated defence schemes. Similar towers continued to be built by the British, at home and abroad, into the 1860s. Examples can be seen at Pembroke Dock (South Wales), Leith outside Edinburgh, at Hackness and Crockness on Hoy (Orkneys), the Isle of Grain and Sheerness in Kent, along the coast of Ireland, both of the Republic and Northern Ireland (*12*), on the Adriatic coast (Korcula), at Kingston, Ontario, in Sydney Harbour (Australia), on Mauritius (two dated 1830), and in the Caribbean. The US military built others at Savannah (Georgia), Charleston (South Carolina), Bayou Dupre (Louisiana) and two later square towers at Key West (Florida). A single British square tower from this slightly later period was Fort Cockbourne at Georgetown, Ascension Island. As late as 1882, a square, two-storey, machicolated tower was built at Fort Queenscliff, south-east of Melbourne, Australia.

A separate thread at the time of the Napoleonic Wars can be followed in Ireland. Although there are around three dozen Martello-type towers in Ireland, there was also

12 Baginbun, Co. Wexford, Eire; a Martello Tower, one of 20 or so built *c.*1804 to defend against a threatened French invasion

a string of signal towers built around the coast from Dublin to Malin Head. Some 81 in all were built between 1804 and 1806. Each tower was 13ft (4m) square and 34ft (10.5m) high, with an entrance at first-floor height and another floor above with a flat roof. There were three sets of box machicolations, one over the door and two on corners. Much of the network was abandoned by 1809; some of it was re-activated for the 1812 war with America and then again used as a basis for coast-watching activities in the Republic during the 1939-45 Emergency. A number of towers remain, including Malin Head (*13*) and Carrigan Head (Co. Donegal), and Black Ball Head (Co. Cork). Some of the details differed from area to area, and the costs also varied according to the relative inaccessibility of locations. Each tower was commanded by a naval officer, generally on half-pay, and was manned by three Sea Fencibles with a military guard of half-a-dozen local volunteer infantry. The Admiralty also maintained a chain of signal-towers on the English mainland from Land's End to Yarmouth, but the difference was that the Irish towers were very definitely considered to be defensible.

When the French revised their coastal defences in the 1840s, they returned to their earlier designs of *tours-modeles*. A number of predominantly square examples were built around the Rochefort area. The batterie de Coudepont, the redoute de Chef de Baie, and the *tour-modele* de Saint-Jean-Chatelaillon, are all reworkings of earlier examples. In the Toulon area, the *tours-crenelees* de la Cride and du Cap Negre are examples of new builds from around 1841. Outside Collioure (Pyrenees Occidentale) there is a square *reduit-modele* and a neighbouring circular tower. A similar square tower at the Belgian fortress of Namur, known as the Tour Carree, is reputed to be connected with Wellington,

13 Malin Head, Co. Donegal, Eire; the signal tower, built *c.*1805 as part of the network of anti-Napoleonic invasion measures

14 Exilles, Piedmont, Italy; 'casamatta del blokhaus' added in the nineteenth century to guard one approach to the fortress

and may date from the same time as the neighbouring Dutch Fort Orange of 1816. It is interesting to note a similar structure, albeit less well-preserved, at Fort Concepcion near Cuidad Rodrigo (Castile and Leon, Spain), and also associated with Wellington. An example in the Netherlands is to be found at the Fort de Hel near Willemstad. The three terms used above appear to be fairly interchangeable at this time. An additional structure is the corps de garde defensive de Chauffaud of 1852, to be found guarding the road below the Chateau de Joux, near Pontarlier (Doubs, France). On the other side of the frontier with modern Italy is the fortress of Exilles, where the 'casamatta del blokhaus' fulfils a similar function on the valley floor (*14*). Another similar structure may be seen at Ulm's Wilhelmsburg citadel, a Prussian work dating from the 1840s. Larger variations on these gun-towers were built throughout the nineteenth century, especially by the Austrians in the Italian Tyrol, in Poland and elsewhere, examples include the Malakoff Tower at Sevastopol, Russia, 60ft (18.5m) in diameter and just under 30ft (9m) high and the towers built by the Prussians at Ulm and Ingolstadt; these tended to become more and more massive. Towers, on the smaller scale we have been here examining, gradually became less common, though the modest La Torreta, or Torre des Fusillons, at Canfranc (*15*) on the Pamplona side of the Somport Pass dates from as late as 1877. Whilst we may be more familiar with the massive stone or brick *caponiers* projecting into the moats at the angles of late nineteenth-century forts both in Britain and on the Continent, there are a few examples of smaller iron *caponiers*. Strasbourg's defences (*16*) dating from the Prussian refortification of the mid-1870s, incorporate some, as do Charlottenlund Fort (*17*), built in 1886-8 as part of Copenhagen's defences, and Fort Hoofdoorp (*18*) on the Amsterdam ring, built in 1904.

Whilst we have been looking at masonry towers in the last few paragraphs, timber was by no means redundant. We left Fort Niagara as it was being given blockhouses which could mount artillery against the native tribes, with little fear of attracting similar retaliation. This was one of the reasons why many of the forts of the American frontier made use of two-storey timber blockhouses in their defences. They were compact, strong, elevated, easily and speedily built from freely available materials, and easy to defend with a small garrison. These blockhouses were usually of two storeys, with the upper over-hanging the lower. Loopholes throughout and murder-holes in the upper storey provided defence both at distance and at close quarters. Such traditional structures were built from the end of the eighteenth century for nearly a hundred years. One example from 1741 stands at Fort King George at Darien (Georgia, USA), another from 10 years later at Fort Halifax (Pennsylvania), and the reconstruction of a third at Fort Harrod (Kentucky) originally from 1776. Plentiful photographs of the American Civil War still show similar blockhouses in use as point defences, particularly on railways and bridges. A typical example is the one defending Aqueduct Bridge in the Washington defences, where blockhouses were used to plug gaps between the larger forts ringing the city. There were variations on the basic design, including a ground-plan shaped like a Greek cross. A more common variant was a rotation of the upper storey through 45 degrees offering a greater overlap of defensive firepower. These structures were considered quite mainstream by the military establishment, with designs published in manuals of military engineering by

15 Canfranc, Pamplona, Spain; the Torre des Fusillons built in 1877 to guard the southern approach to the Somport Pass

16 Strasbourg, Bas-Rhin, France; an iron *caponier* dating from the Prussian refortification of the city in the aftermath of the Franco-Prussian War

17 Copenhagen, Denmark; iron *caponier* at Charlottenlund Fort built 1886–8

18 Amsterdam, Netherlands; an iron and concrete *caponier* designed by Skoda of Pilsen and installed at Fort Hoofdoorp in 1904

architects such as Mahan and put into practice by graduates and former instructors at West Point. Contrary to Hollywood depictions, the forts of the American west in the period following the Civil War tended not to be stockades with a tower at each corner, but an open cluster of military and civilian buildings, with perhaps a single blockhouse to act as a last resort if more than an opportunist hit-and-run attack was attempted. This is illustrated by Fort Hays (Kansas), where the only defensible structure was a substantial, in this unusual case, hexagonal masonry blockhouse. At Fort Larned (Kansas) a similar blockhouse was single-storey. These, however, appear to have been the exceptions, and Forts Reno, Berthold, Lookout and McKeen, for example, were each given a version of the usual timber models. Sometimes, as at Fort Stanton (New Mexico), a blockhouse formed the kernel of layers of defences, in this case outer walls of adobe. Faced by a militant independence movement in Cuba, the Spanish Colonial government constructed a cordon across the island in the 1870s to prevent the rebels of the east from infecting the west. A basic trench line (La Trocha) was reinforced by forts and blockhouses. These blockhouses had five or six loopholes in each face on two storeys. Over the ground-floor entrance was a timber box-machicolation. They appear to have achieved little beyond postponing the inevitable, for Cuba gained its independence in 1898, just as a conflict was getting underway on another continent – a war in which blockhouses were to figure significantly, as we shall shortly see.

THE LATER NINETEENTH CENTURY: THE BRITISH EMPIRE

By the 1870s, the small-scale coastal defences of the Napoleonic wars had been replaced, in Britain by the massive casemated works of the Royal Commission. These came to be remembered as Palmerston's Follies, because of the enormous amounts of money spent on them, quite unnecessarily as it happened, as hindsight would show. Alongside these monumental structures, echoed on Malta, Gibraltar and other major bases, were many British colonial fortifications which were very modest affairs. The campaigns in New Zealand (1846-66) produced mainly earthwork redoubts, many of which contained timber blockhouses which have not survived, although many of their earthworks have. The wars in Zululand, immortalised by the story of the defence of Rorke's Drift, supply some fine examples of extemporised works. Many of these temporary works were simply redoubts constructed of dry-stone walls, supplemented by wire and stake obstacles, walls of provision sacks and tins, and laagers of wagons. The more permanent forts, such as the one built around the mission station at Eshowe, incorporated mainstream features of permanent fortification, but constructed out of ephemeral materials. Thus the *caponiers* and stockaded bastions were built of earth and timber, strengthened with stone. Fort Newdigate was little more than a couple of drystone-walled redoubts linked by a wagon laager. Only at some of the posts established on a more permanent basis to protect lines of communication after hostilities had ceased, was there a real attempt to build durable structures. The ingenuously-named Fort Mistake, for instance, consisted of a stone tower, its entrance screened by a full-height lobed wall, and lavishly furnished with musket-loops at several levels. Its name apparently came from the absence of a convenient water-supply, but the tower was never expected to undergo a long siege. What is fascinating is the fact that one could be forgiven for mistaking this tower for an example of the prehistoric *nuraghi*, which we met at the beginning of this chapter.

We stay in Africa for the final examples from the nineteenth century. During their course, the South African (or Boer) wars changed from a succession of conventional battles, mainly disastrous for the British, through a period of guerrilla warfare, to a campaign of containment, based on the principle of denying territory, support and provisions to the Boer commandos. The key element of this campaign was the blockhouse. Some 441 of these were built in mortared stone and in addition greater numbers, around 8000, were built of corrugated iron on stone bases. There was a standard pattern model designed by Major-General Wood, the chief engineer. This was a three-storey tower, 20ft (6.1m) square, externally entered by a retractable ladder at first-floor height (*19*). The ground and first floors were loopholed, and the open second floor was covered by a pyramid structure of corrugated iron. Set at two opposite corners were overhanging *machicoulis* galleries made of iron sheets, and the gap between the parapet and the roof structure could be closed by canvas curtains. Rainfall was collected via gutters into a water-tank. There were a number of these otherwise Standard Pattern blockhouses built with minor modifications, such as angled loopholes instead of *machicoulis*, fixed staircases, pitched roofs rather than pyramid and concrete construction rather than masonry. There were also groups of masonry blockhouses which were altogether different from those built to the standard pattern. These include V-shaped, hexagonal (*20 & 21*) and circular examples; one with a ground-plan resembling a Scottish Z-plan tower-house; a square design with chamfered corners producing an octagon with loopholes in all eight faces; a square design with an open, octagonal third storey; and a single-storey example with high loopholes reached by a built-in banquette. Dimensions seldom exceed 25ft x 20ft (8m x 6m). Since

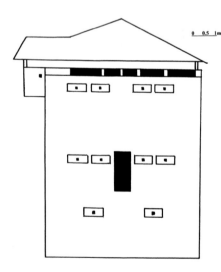

19 South Africa; a British standard pattern 3-storey masonry blockhouse

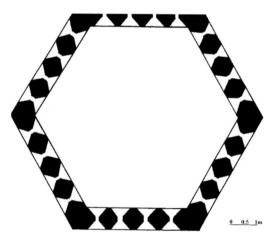

21 Aliwal, South Africa; first-floor plan of the blockhouse

these structures were intended for permanent occupation, the size of garrison has some significance and, despite official silence on the subject, it would appear that anything between 10 and 40 men would be accommodated. One blockhouse has 40 rifle-loops in three tiers. It is likely that around 20 would constitute an average complement. The masonry blockhouses were expensive to build in terms of labour, materials and time, and tended to be placed at important river bridges to protect the railway from attack and to deny freedom of movement to Boer commandos. They cost £800-£1000 and took three months to construct. So, at intervals of anything down to 700 yards, the less-substantial blockhouses, linked by trenches and wire, were built along the railway tracks to form continuous barriers. These blockhouses were constructed out of corrugated iron sheets. The important feature was a cavity wall filled with three inches (8mm) of pebbles or rubble, thus making it bullet-proof. Most of these corrugated iron blockhouses were constructed from a kit of pre-fabricated parts. First a stone base would be built, onto which the corrugated iron sheets, half an inch (12.5mm) thick, would be mounted. Since, initially, the majority of these blockhouses were sited alongside railways, these kits could be dropped off by train with minimal transport effort.

The earliest kits were manufactured by a firm in Portuguese East Africa and a completed blockhouse measured 20ft x 25ft (6m x 8m), with corrugated iron sheets nailed to both sides of wooden posts. The resultant cavity was filled with pebbles and sand. Since so many were needed, Kitchener involved the REs, whose Major Rice came up with a circular design based on concentric rings of corrugated iron sheet, linked by nine or ten steel loopholes. The cavity was, again, filled with shingle. It stood 4ft (1.3m) high, on top of its solid base, and was 13ft 6in (4.1m) in diameter. A flat tin roof was added giving them the nickname of 'pepper-pot'. It is interesting to note that the example of a blockhouse, still being included in the 1914 reprint of the War Office's *Manual of Field Engineering*, has 22 loopholes and one entrance in its eight faces. The blockhouse had a

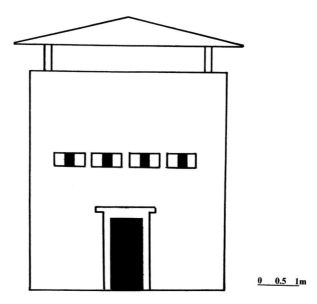

20 Aliwal, South Africa; the hexagonal masonry blockhouse

0   0.5 1m

pitched roof of corrugated iron and was surrounded by fire-trenches, ditches and barbed-wire entanglements, through which an invisible zig-zag pathway gave access. A further accompanying plate shows two mutually-supporting blockhouses within a lozenge-shaped enclosure, the whole ditched and wired, and termed a 'defensible post'. The loopholes in the blockhouses were angled to allow fire into the ditch whose inner face formed a *glacis*. Owing to the splinters caused under rifle-fire, timber was specifically avoided in the Boer War blockhouses, but these textbook blockhouses were made of hollow concentric log-walls filled with crushed stone.

INTO THE TWENTIETH CENTURY: HOME DEFENCE

If field fortifications appear to have moved on very little between the Boer War and the beginning of the First World War, the same cannot be said of fixed defences. Every advance in naval architecture had a concomitant effect on coastal defences. It was the ironclad *Gloire* which had prompted Palmerston's Follies. The evolution of the *Dreadnought* and the torpedo-boat meant that coastal defences were rendered redundant at a stroke. New guns, fire-control systems and the batteries to accommodate them all had to be redesigned. One of the fears was that fast craft would land small parties of what we would now call special forces to disable coastal artillery. Therefore the batteries became self-contained forts, with

22 Rame Peninsular, Cornwall; a projecting, rectangular, concrete *caponier* of 1913–14 at Hawkins Battery, part of the western defences of Plymouth

23 Plymouth, Devon; a 12-sided, detached machine-gun blockhouse at Renney Battery, one of three built in 1914 to defend this 1905 part of the eastern defences of Plymouth

ditches, unclimbable fences, wire entanglements and, in place of the *caponiers* of Victorian forts, machine-gun posts in substantial masonry blockhouses to control access across the ditches and the other approaches to the fort.

The plans of most of the new coastal defence batteries built in the first decade of the twentieth century to mount the Marks IX and X 9.2in (233mm) guns or their high-angle relations, show these blockhouses either built into the perimeter defences or, in a few cases, free-standing outside. This occurred in the Plymouth defences at Raleigh, Hawkins (*22*), Lord Howard's, Lentney and Renney Batteries. One of Renney's three concrete blockhouses remains (*23*), 12-sided with horizontal loopholes for machine-guns, for lights to illuminate the unclimbable fence and for rifles. It has a steel door and some steel shutters survive on loopholes. As well as the prominent embrasures, there appear to be machine-gun ports protected by steel shutters, at a lower level. A blockhouse also survives at Lord Howard's Battery, rectangular with a half-hexagonal end-wall. There are five loops in each long wall and one in each face of the end-wall, all now blocked but discernible. Hawkins' Battery retains the three new-style *caponiers* added in 1913. These are rectangular, of concrete and project from the gorge-wall with three wide horizontal embrasures in each long side and one in the end. Similar provision was made at several of the forts and batteries in the Humber defences, their updating planned just prior to the First World War, but not completed before hostilities had commenced. Godwin Battery had three blockhouses, now disappeared over the eroding cliff-edge, and on the landward side a concrete redoubt, Murray's Post, which survives. This is a semi-sunken square of trenches and machine-gun positions around a central crew-shelter, the whole under a concrete

24 Spurn Head Fort, Humber estuary; a blockhouse built in 1915 on the perimeter wall of the battery complex

canopy and linked to the fort by a trench/tunnel. Both Stallingborough and Sunk Island Batteries had blockhouses built into their perimeter defences. The defences on Spurn Head, rebuilt in 1915 to command the entrance to the Humber estuary, were contained in a fortified perimeter with five blockhouses on the inner side facing the estuary. Two of these were rectangular projections with armoured loopholes enfilading the beach and half-hexagonal end-walls with loops in the slanted faces. One of these blockhouses survives whole (24), the other only at foundation level. The other three blockhouses are built into the perimeter wall at a higher level and have wide horizontal embrasures for machine-guns facing forward and the odd armoured loophole flanking the wall. Rifle-loops were provided for close-defence in the event of the interior of the fort being taken. The Tyne Turrets were surrounded by defensive perimeters which incorporated blockhouses. The northerly Roberts Battery at Hartley retains two blockhouses in the defences of the control and domestic site, now Fort House. One is rectangular with a chamfered corner containing six loopholes and the other is nearer to being square with one loophole. The walls are sufficient only to stop rifle bullets and the rectangular blockhouse enjoys the distinction of being (surely) the only fortified latrine in Britain.

The coastal defence installations in Ulster faced more complex problems. In addition to the universal danger of enemy raids, there was perceived to be a threat from the enemy within as part of the Home Rule campaign and the protestant resistance to any such arrangement. It was felt that there was an urgent need to provide landward defences for the forts at Dunree and Lenan Head (Donegal), and Kilroot Battery in Belfast Lough. At Dunree, the comprehensive defence scheme, planned in 1913 but not completed for another three years, survives intact. The redoubt on top of the hill has two blockhouses built onto it, below this on the north side are two free-standing blockhouses and on the

25 Dunree Fort, Co. Donegal; one of the eight blockhouses built in 1916 to defend this coastal defence battery against attack from land or sea

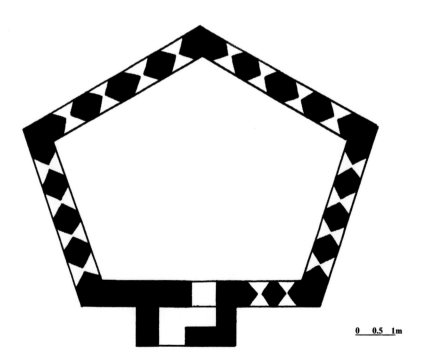

0   0.5   1m

26 Dunree Fort, Co. Donegal; plan of the blockhouse shown in 25

0   0.5   1m

27   Dunree Fort, Co. Donegal; plan of another of the fort's blockhouses

28   Dunree Fort, Co. Donegal; interior view of the iron loopholes in the fort's single octagonal blockhouse

29 Lenan Head Fort, Co. Donegal; a lozenge-shaped blockhouse with 15 loopholes, one of two to this design, defending angles in the dry(ish) moat

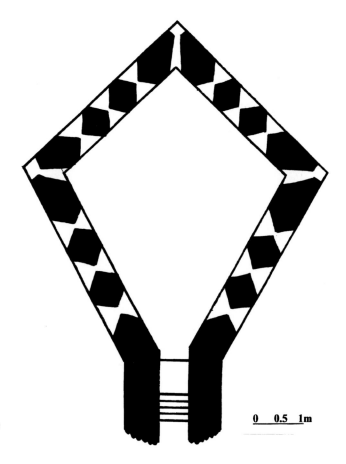

30 Lenan Head Fort, Co. Donegal; plan of blockhouse (*29*)

0   0.5   1m

31 Thionville, Moselle, France; Prussian infantry blockhouse guarding the railway yards; it was probably built along with other Prussian works around 1905

other side are three more, all these to the landward side of the old fort itself. At least two are hexagonal, another is octagonal, one is square with the two forward-facing corners chamfered to provide loops and two more are trapezoidal with chamfered corners making one appear octagonal, and the other hexagonal (*25-28*). They are all sturdily-built of mortared masonry and concrete blocks, and are generously provided with between 11 and 20 loopholes, protected by iron plates. Inside there are no pillars, and the roof is supported on steel beams up to 25ft (8m) in length. The outside of each loophole is stepped to deflect bullets away. Lenan Head has three blockhouses on the landward side, projecting into and enfilading the ditch. One, built onto a straight stretch of wall, is almost square, with two chamfered corners producing 11 loopholes in its five faces. The other two, added where the wall and ditch turns through an angle, are lozenge-shaped with four faces each containing three loopholes, plus three more in the corners (*29 & 30*). They are entered down steps through a passage in the wall. As at Dunree the loopholes have iron plates but are not stepped. They are supplemented by raised musketry walls which may predate the blockhouses.

From further afield there are two interesting examples. Fort San Rocco on Malta was provided with a large fan-shaped defence post on its landward side, and a smaller pentagonal loopholed blockhouse covering the main gate. Both these constructions date from the final phase of work, completed in 1905. In the railway yards, alongside the river at Thionville (Moselle) stands an infantry blockhouse (*31*), around 50ft (15m) square, apparently built by the Prussians during their tenure of Alsace-Lorraine. It has two tiers of seven musketry-loops in each side, and a machine-gun embrasure in each chamfered angle. The whole is built in concrete under a thick, flat, concrete roof with an earth covering.

2

THE DEVELOPMENT OF PILLBOXES IN THE FIRST WORLD WAR

We have seen how a number of defensive structures over long periods of time and across many different parts of the world, shared some of the characteristics we have come to associate with pillboxes, but their real development was accelerated during the course of the First World War. Although there were developments elsewhere, it was particularly on the Western Front that the evolution of the pillbox as we know it occurred. One of the myths of the Great War concerned the predominance of the machine-gun as agent of death. Whilst the lethal results of machine-gun fire on troops advancing in close order out in the open were sufficiently horrifying to give us this impression, it was, nevertheless, constant bombardment by field artillery, mortars and howitzers which actually caused the majority of casualties. Both sides sought to provide some form of protection against the essentially unpredictable effect of shelling and there are large numbers of bunkers on the Western Front whose purpose was primarily that of sheltering troops and *materiel* against the effects of artillery bombardment. Many of these bunkers, especially in the German lines, were buried deep beneath the surface, enabling all those troops who were not actually on guard duty, sniping, or engaged in such nocturnal operations as trench-raids or wiring parties, to sleep safely, regardless of what might be thrown at them. The other advantage of these deep shelters lay in troops' ability to sit out the pre-attack barrages in safety, only coming up to man their machine-guns at the last possible moment. This subsequently forced the Allies into rash attempts to catch their enemy off-guard leading to instances of heightened casualties caused by imprecise creeping barrages, or even lack of any bombardment at all.

Many of these German deep-shelters were quite luxurious homes-from-home. Whole HQ complexes, for instance, were buried underground, echoing the troglodytes' villages of the Middle Ages. It would appear that on the Allied side of the lines, on the other hand, troops were not encouraged to develop such permanent or comfortable accommodation as it might erode their offensive spirit, encourage them to maintain the status quo, and lose any residual enthusiasm they might have felt for storming the enemy's trenches.

The War Office's ambivalence over the whole question of permanence vis-à-vis field defences appears to date back at least to the early years of the twentieth century. We have already seen the limited extent of the defences proposed in the official *Manual of Field Engineering* of 1911. Apart from those fixed defences provided to house coastal defence artillery, little seems to be offered in the more permanent context. Sir George Sydenham Clarke advocated the use of the redoubt defended by what came to be called the Twydall

32 St Mawes Castle, Cornwall; concrete pedestal for a Maxim gun

Profile after the Chatham fort in which it was first used. Defences were now to consist of casemated batteries or barracks buried out of sight or screened by earth traverses and only approached through obstacles such as minefields, *abbatis*, unclimbable (and even electrified) fences, *trous de loups*, wire entanglements and trenches, all commanded by machine-gun positions. The land would fall gently away from the redoubt thus creating a *glacis* with gradients of 1:6 or 1:8, ascending whose slopes attacking troops would be mown down. Sydenham Clarke cites the performance of the Russian works at Port Arthur, attacked by the Japanese in 1905. Here, field-bomb-proof defences of earth and timber, especially when reinforced by iron plates, withstood all but the most accurate shelling; incoming shells tended to glance off sloping concrete faces, and the 4ft 6in (1.4m) of reinforced concrete could withstand bombardment by howitzers up to 11in (28cm). However, rather than being fortress architecture, Clarke's argument seemed to run, these were seen essentially as fieldworks, containing a great deal of very thick concrete admittedly, but also many odd elements of hard landscaping, such as concrete tables for mounting Maxim or Vickers guns. Several of the Falmouth defences retain pedestals for Maxim machine-guns (*32*), and both these and Vickers tables can be seen in the defences of, for instance, the Wardija 6-inch Coast Defence Battery above St Paul's Bay in Malta, where they can be found set in rock-cut infantry trenches, dug in 1915. It must be noted that at least two redundant searchlight emplacements on Malta's Victoria Lines were converted into machine-gun posts during the First World War. This was done by closing the open front with a concrete wall shuttered in corrugated iron sheeting and provided with a horizontal embrasure. These, again, are found in the context of what were essentially fieldworks. Clarke also suggests that a design for a wheeled 1 pounder (450gms) gun in a steel cupola, known as Schumann's Travelling Shield Mounting might have been useful had it contained a machine-gun. Without the wheels, this looks remarkably like the Hobbs Casemate we shall meet in due course.

GERMAN PILLBOXES ON THE WESTERN FRONT

Set against these profiled redoubts with all their outworks, the free-standing defensible strong-point was an entirely different structure, designed to meet quite specific needs. The Germans realised that one of the secrets of successful trench warfare was the ability to channel attacking infantry into paths of the defenders' own choosing, providing that, once there, they could be mown down by machine-guns firing on fixed lines. Whilst previous use of deep shelters had meant that both the crews and their weapons were safe from bombardment, there was no guarantee that their firing positions with their carefully calibrated fields of fire would have remained intact. The answer was therefore to mount the guns with permanent protection and a purpose-built machine-gun emplacement was developed to that end. At first, bunkers were built with machine-gun positions on the roof or alongside and were best described as shelters for machine-gun crews, but by the time of the British attack at Ypres in July 1917, these had been supplemented by reinforced concrete bunkers specifically designed for two machine-guns firing through forward-facing embrasures. These were generally in the size range of around 27ft (8m) across x 20ft (6m) deep. Whether there were machine-gun embrasures or not, the rear wall had two entries separated by a blast-wall or traverse, behind which was a further wall with a single door and rifle-loops covering the entrances. The allied engineers drew plans of these structures as and when they were captured, and very quickly developed their own designs. The REs' field companies attached to the several armies came up with individual designs, as well as with designs for modifying any structures captured intact and capable of being turned. This latter operation was a wholly literal proposition, as in order to use captured strong-points, their new occupants had to block doors which now faced the enemy, and open up new ones on the sheltered side. If there was an intention to mount weapons, then new embrasures had to be cut. Many of the German constructions were inside existing buildings, such as barns, and this often made reuse difficult.

BRITISH PILLBOX DESIGNS

The REs' designs for pillboxes tended to echo the Germans' construction methods. A factory for manufacturing concrete-blocks had been established by the Germans at Werwik in Belgium. Blocks were then used in conjunction with steel reinforcing rods, mortar and a combination of rolled steel joists and iron rails under a cast concrete slab for the roof. In late 1917 the British First Army set up a factory at Aire-sur-la-Lys which would eventually produce 7000 concrete blocks and 700 concrete beams per day. Steel rods, stirrups and expanded metal sheets were used to tie the loose-laid blocks together

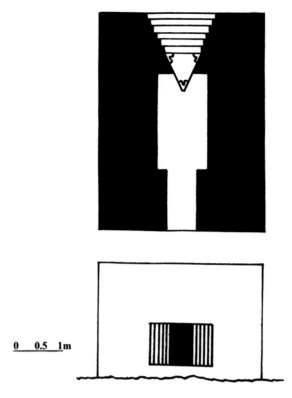

0   0.5   1m

33 British Second Army pillbox
pre-fabricated at the Arques
or Aire-sur-la-Lys works; it
was built in modules of 18in
(45cm) and had a mounting for
a Vickers gun, but very little
interior space

with the roof beams. The walls were pointed inside and out, and a liquid grout poured into special vertical channels to secure the steel bars, as courses of blocks were added. The walls and roof were 45in (1.2m) thick. The British Second Army then set about an improved version, using an established concrete-floor-making factory at Arques. This design used concrete blocks pierced and channelled to take vertical rods for the walls and horizontal rods through the cast roof-beams. In order that informed decisions might be taken as to the relative effectiveness of each design, examples were shipped back to Shoeburyness artillery ranges for testing in August 1918. It was found that a combination of elements from each offered most protection. The optimum design combined the Arques shape with the Aire construction methods. These designs appear very strong, but provided very little interior space, as they measured only 3ft (0.9m) wide and 6ft (1.8m) high inside the thick concrete carapace (*33*). Openings had the potential to weaken the integral structure, so were limited to a single embrasure in the front face and a small door in the back wall.

Even less spacious were the other two common types of pillbox. The Moir pillbox (*34*) was the invention of Sir Ernest Moir of the Ministry of Munitions. It was circular and constructed from curved, interlocking concrete blocks cast at the military port at Richborough in Kent. A concrete dome-shaped roof, inside which was suspended a Vickers 0.303 inch (8mm) machine-gun on a revolving cradle, was mounted on a bullet-proof steel ring mounting. Apart from some regularly-spaced peepholes, the only opening was the embrasure for the gun. The whole pillbox, with an interior diameter of 6ft (1.8m) was designed to be buried to just below the steel ring, with a trench revetted

34 Ypres, Belgium; a British Moir pillbox, a design widely used at home and abroad; the machine-gun was suspended from a rotating mounting in the roof

with a wooden frame behind it to allow access. If necessary, it could be mounted at ground level, when it stood 7ft (2.1m) high, and needed to be given an additional outer skin of concrete and a base. It was tested at Shoeburyness and found to be proof against the average field gun shell, or even a 5.9in (15cm) shell bursting up to 3ft (0.9) away. The Richborough factory produced complete kits for this pillbox to be shipped out to wherever it was needed. About 1500 were produced for overseas use, with another 400 or so for use at home. Many found their way to the Western front, but in 1919 there remained over 700 complete kits at Richborough. A number of RE field companies were trained to erect these pillboxes. Each complete kit contained 48 concrete blocks, four domed roof-sections, a girder, reinforcing rods, the bullet-proof ring, and the Vickers mounting. Just like today's flat-packs, even the requisite tools were included. The whole load of 10896lb (4.8 tonnes) could be carried on four lorries and erected by a team of four sappers and eight labourers, led by a RE corporal with surveying skills. Several Moir pillboxes survive, most notably on the bastions of Ypres town.

The second of these compact mass-produced pillboxes was the Hobbs machine-gun casemate, designed by Major-General J. Talbot Hobbs following his experiences against machine-guns in fortified positions the previous year. The Hobbs casemate was a revolving armour-plated cupola containing a machine-gun, mounted on a steel sheet embedded in a concrete base. Underneath this cupola, a 3ft 9in (1.1m) square chamber had just about enough space for the two-man crew. It was entered through a short tunnel from a living pit, 5ft 9in (1.75m) deep, 6ft 6in (2m) long x 3ft (0.9m) wide, with a drainage sump. Like the Moir, the Hobbs was designed to be buried in the ground (or in concrete) with only 18in (45cm) showing above ground-level. Its major advantage over other pillboxes was that it weighed in at less than a ton, but appeared to have sacrificed none of the others' robustness. Over 250 of these casemates were produced by factories in Glasgow, the majority being emplaced in Australian positions in France and Belgium. It would appear that none has survived, probably because it could so easily be removed for scrap after the War.

However impressive all these different pillboxes may have been in terms of their design, their effectiveness, their use of construction and pre-fabrication technology, or their tactical and strategic deployment, we must remember that most of them, on the Allied side at least, only came on the scene for the final act of the drama. Hobbs designed his casemate only in May 1918. The First and Second Army pillboxes were only tested at Shoeburyness in August 1918, although they had been in production for a few months prior to then, but peak production was reached only in the final month of hostilities. The Moir was being erected in numbers during the summer months of 1918, but production stopped that October.

This is not to say that the REs had been idle. We have already noted how important artillery was both in attack and defence, and one constant challenge on both sides of the line was spotting targets for the guns, especially when most fire was indirect. Large numbers of concrete observation towers, some new builds, others incorporated into standing buildings, were constructed throughout the War. Both sides invented small reinforced observation cells made of concrete and steel, the 'Webb' on the allied side and the 'snail-shell' on the German for instance. Vast numbers of bunkers as troop-shelters, casualty stations or storage for food, fuel or ammunition were built, but, not being defensible, lie outside the scope of this work. We have, however, seen how captured bunkers were often turned to serve their new occupants. Occasionally, a particularly penetrating attack forced defenders to adapt shelters some distance behind the frontline into defensible strong-points and there are instances of 'elephant-shelters' having their doorways partly built up in order to produce a machine-gun embrasure. The elephant-shelter was constructed out of thick iron sheets, bolted together to form short tunnels, a bit like a heavier version of the Nissen hut, or today's poly-tunnel in shape. A thick layer of concrete would then be added over the top to produce a low-profile bunker. In some, towards the end of the War, a loophole for a machine-gun was cut in one end at low level, with the crew sitting almost below ground-level, but under a great deal of protection.

Camouflage was extremely important, particularly for pillboxes in the frontline. If they could remain invisible until the last possible moment then their effect on infantry, oblivious to their danger, would be all the more devastating. Many structures were camouflaged with mud or vegetation, if any survived, and brushwood, when available, had the added advantage of acting as a burster layer against shellfire.

THE HINDENBURG LINE

From Christmas 1914, the Western Front had been a more-or-less fixed series of linear defences. In early 1917, it became apparent to Allied reconnaissance pilots that something was going on in the German lines, particularly between Lille, Arras, Cambrai, St Quentin and Soissons. This was confirmed by escapers and others who had witnessed heightened German activity in these parts. What had happened was that the German forces had built an enormously strong series of in-depth defences, behind which they would shortly fall back. The sacrifice of giving up ground, which had been so costly in terms of lives lost, was deemed to be worthwhile by the gains to be made. These new defences were sited to take advantage of natural high ground, which would greatly benefit their artillery by being able to overlook the enemy positions and thus give them a complete command of the battlefield. Moreover, these defences were between 3.75 to 5 miles (6-8 km) in depth, thus extending the range at which Allied guns had to fire in order to engage their German counterparts. The Germans named these new lines after mythological heroes: the Siegfried Stellung 1 and 2, the Wotan Stellung 1 and 2, the Hermann Stellung 1 and 2, the Hunding Stellung etc., with the Zwischen Stellung between the two main lines. The whole system was better known to the British as the Hindenburg Line. Along with vast fields of barbed wire, booby-traps and mines, trenches and dugouts, there were hundreds of concrete bunkers and machine-gun posts. These latter were built into the several lines, but also grouped in particularly commanding positions so as to dominate large tracts of land. Some were built to tried-and-tested designs, others were quite different. A number were given all-round loopholes, for instance, rather than the traditional, single and forward-facing loophole of many previous models. One of the most significant innovations was the way in which pillboxes had provision for machine-guns to be fired from inside, when, in the past, so many had been merely crew shelters with external firing positions (35).

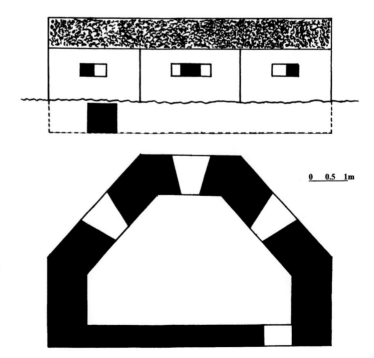

0   0.5   1m

35 German pillbox for three machine-guns, built in 1917 as part of the Hindenburg Line; plan and elevation after Oldham

BRITISH DEFENCE LINES IN FLANDERS

In addition to their forward trench lines, the British, too, built rear defence lines, albeit on a much more modest scale, as a response to the German advances in the last quarter of the War. These were collectively referred to as the GHQ Line. One such constituent line was the West Hazebrouck Line which ran from Hazebrouck south and east toward Armentieres. A number of Moir pillboxes were incorporated in this line, but at Les-Six-Roues is a hexagonal pillbox for two Vickers machine-guns (*36*). It is a sophisticated design which includes a piped compressed air supply which could be converted to mustard gas were the pillbox to be captured and occupied by the enemy. Near Albert at Henencourt is a cluster of similar hexagonal machine-gun pillboxes incorporating a number of different types of mountings for Vickers machine-guns. All these pillboxes are remarkably similar to later models and may well represent early prototypes for some of the designs to emerge in the Second World War. Given the propensity for RE officers to record enemy designs, it is quite possible that these may derive from a German design for a machine-gun pillbox which was hexagonal on a long, straight base, with loopholes in its three forward

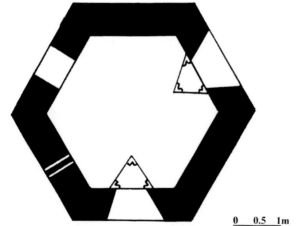

0   0.5   1m

36 Les-six-roues, Nord, France; a British pillbox for two Vickers machine-guns, built in 1918 on the West Hazebrouck (GHQ) Line; note the conduits for pumping gas inside in the event of its capture by the enemy

faces, and measuring 23ft x 15ft (7m x 4.5m). The British example at Les-Six-Roues has embrasures in just two of its corresponding forward faces.

PILLBOXES IN BRITISH HOME DEFENCES

Pillboxes also figured strongly in Britain's home defence schemes. Although any expectations of a German invasion tended to centre on the Royal Navy's bases, there were some attempts to defend against other scenarios. We have seen in the previous chapter how blockhouses were developed to secure many of the new batteries which were being established to defend the ports. Many of these building programmes had been planned and begun in peacetime when time, availability of labour and materials, and the money to pay for them were all under less pressure. Thus those blockhouses we have already looked at were solid constructions, no doubt fit for purpose, but rather extravagant in times of war. What was needed was a simpler design which used fewer materials, needed less input of labour, but still fulfilled the need for fixed defences. We have seen how the individual armies of the BEF met this need by developing designs either based on German models, or created from scratch. A quite separate development appears to have taken place at home. Although many of the Moir pillboxes were allocated to home defence, there would appear to be little evidence of any other overlap. Some designs were simply impractical, such as one particular proposal for a semi-sunken machine-gun post, published by the General Staff in *Notes on Trench Warfare for Infantry Officers* in December 1916. It cleverly recognised the problem of concussion by building in a 2ft (60cm) air space in the roof, basically a double concrete shell, one within the other. Unfortunately, the REs were unable to cast such a structure without linking the two boxes together, which completely defeated the object as shock waves would travel across the linkages. It is also worth noting here that no Moir pillbox has been recorded as a survivor of that home allocation. Whether or not Moir pillboxes were used widely or not at home, there do seem to be at least four other fairly common types of pillbox constructed specifically for home defence, which do not appear to have been used abroad. The four common types of pillbox used at home in the First World War were all fairly simple designs, in order that they could meet the criteria regarding both speed and cheapness of build.

The first recorded use in print of the word 'pillbox', according to the 1989 edition of the Oxford English Dictionary, is recorded in the September 1917 issue of *The Scotsman*. This, in the context of a report from the Western Front, refers to 'the strength of these concreted farm cellars and individual pillboxes' as being 'amazing'. The actual word is reckoned to have been coined with reference to the small, cylindrical container in which Edwardian pharmacists dispensed medicinal pills. This would be more believable if the majority, or a significant proportion, or even the most common type resembled the supposed archetype. Therefore, the first home-based pillbox we will examine is the one design which best fits the universal image. As long ago as Elizabethan times there was a fear that the coast around Weybourne, in north Norfolk, was particularly vulnerable to seaborne invasion, owing to the steeply shelved beaches which could allow ships to come in quite close to disembark troops and stores. This, therefore, was identified as one of the areas of the British Isles where anti-invasion defences were to be constructed in 1914. These defences were initially limited to fieldworks, mainly trenches and gun-positions, but by 1916 increased anxiety about the possibility of a raid in strength caused the erection of more permanent works. The central spine of these defences was a line of circular pillboxes which started on the coast at Stiffkey, ran along past Aylmerton, West Runton and Weybourne, then down the River Ant, past Hanworth, Thorpe Market and Bradfield to North Walsham. Pillboxes survive at all those sites, with several in the North Walsham perimeter and one at Wayford Bridge. In addition there are examples at Bacton and Sea Palling on the Norfolk coast, and then much further down the coast into Suffolk with three near Bawdsey and a pair at Alderton. The basic design (37) is simple. A cylinder of concrete blocks, around 15ft (4.5m) in diameter externally, has a cast concrete roof. Each of the five Suffolk examples has a slightly overhanging roof to produce the lip which one supposes led to the pillbox designation. There is a low entrance closed by a pair of steel doors and up to five loopholes with hinged steel shutters. In some, Aylmerton and

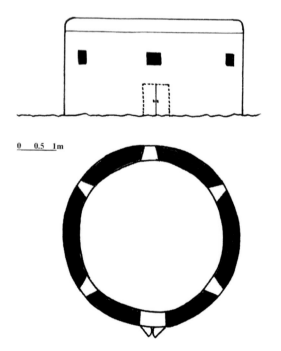

37 Muckleburgh, Norfolk (TG102434); British pillbox designed for home defence, one of 20 or so of this style surviving in East Anglia; note its original steel doors

Hanworth for instance, these loopholes are at different heights. One pillbox at North Walsham is bow-shaped with four loopholes in the curved face, but none in the straight back. At least two have been modified during the Second World War. One at East Runton has been encased in an extra skin of concrete to make it shell-proof and one at Bawdsey has been given an additional hexagonal concrete roof slab. It seems likely that the preferred method was to site them in pairs, usually quite close together. According to a recent survey, some 20 of these pillboxes survive in Norfolk. At least another dozen have gone from Norfolk and there were once many more the whole length of the Suffolk coast, with examples reported from Felixstowe, Lowestoft and Sizewell. At least one, non-standard First World War circular pillbox survives further south. On the rampart of Fort Burgoyne, at Dover, a round pillbox, shuttered in brick, appears to have at least three pre-cast loops.

The second pillbox design widely used in Britain was hexagonal (*38*), and looks very similar to one of the more common designs of the Second World War. This design is a regular hexagon with sides of around 7ft (2.1m). One face held a low entrance closed by a

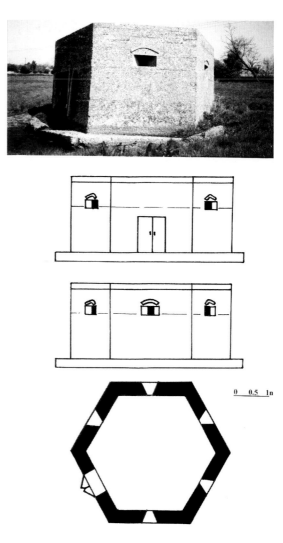

0　0.5　1m

38 Rushmere, Suffolk (TM491870); one of a pair of hexagonal pillboxes sited to defend a river-crossing a little way back from the coast; it retains its steel doors

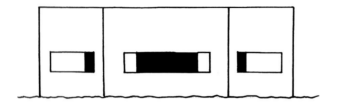

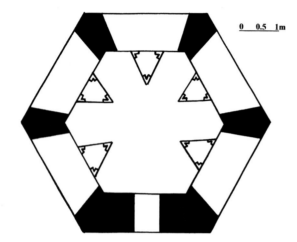

0   0.5   1m

39 British pillbox designed
to mount five Vickers
machine-guns, for coast
defence; reconstructed plan
and elevation

pair of steel doors and there were loopholes in the other five faces. It was built of poured
concrete using timber shuttering. Again, we can see pairs of these pillboxes remaining. The
five surviving examples include one pair outside Great Yarmouth (Norfolk), another pair
at Rushmere (Suffolk) and a singleton at St Olave's boatyard in Norfolk, where an office
has been built on top of it.

   Another design, also hexagonal (*39*), but larger than the previous one, appears in two
locations, on the Lincolnshire coast, and in the defences of the Thames and Medway
estuaries. This design is known only from photographs, as there would appear to be no
standing survivors. It looks to be a regular hexagon with sides of around 10ft (3m) with
wide loopholes in five faces and an entrance in the sixth. Examples stood on the dunes
around the Chapel-St-Leonards, Ingoldmells and Mablethorpe areas, and complemented
the machine-gun posts, of which there is one documented on Zion Hill near Rimac, and
the extensive barbed wire entanglements. In 1916, the Fifth Battalion North Staffordshire
Regiment was on garrison duties in Mablethorpe and, according to a recent memoir,
duties included manning the pillboxes 24 hours a day and rolling out the barbed wire
along the Front every evening. Given that most of the pillboxes built on this part of the
Lincolnshire coast between 1939 and 1941 were to a distinctive local rectangular design,
those hexagonal pillboxes recorded on a County Council map of sites to be demolished
prior to the land being de-requisitioned, most likely represent these First World War
pillboxes. In the stretch of about 7.5 miles (12km) recorded in this document, there are up
to a dozen possible candidates, but none appears to have survived the 1946 demolitions,

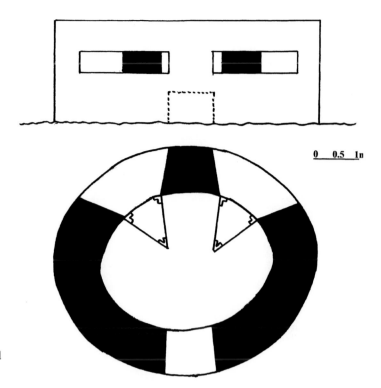

40 British pillbox
for two Vickers guns,
employed in Chatham
defences; reconstructed
plan and elevation

motivated by the need to restore this coast for tourism. Similar to these Lincolnshire ones, and also known only from photographs, examples stood at Sheerness, in front of Centre Bastion Battery, at Fletcher Battery and Warden Point on the Isle of Sheppey, and elsewhere. Photographs held in the Imperial War Museum under the Thames and Medway Garrison title show several views of the front faces of a hexagonal pillbox with very wide embrasures. Taking the scale from a conveniently-located soldier, each face looks to be around 10ft (3m) with the stepped embrasure taking up two-thirds of this span. The pillbox stands around 5ft (1.5m) high. All these examples appear to be constructed from poured concrete in timber shuttering. The figure in one photograph is wearing the shorter, mounted greatcoat which was worn by the Machine-gun Corps, possibly because many of their personnel had been converted from Yeomanry cavalry. This Corps was only constituted in 1916, so that might place these constructions in the second half of the War.

Our fourth pillbox design is about as simple as it could be. It is square with sides of about 7ft (2.1m), a loophole in each of three sides and an entrance in the fourth. Known examples appear to be confined to Kent, with several around Newington and one at Stockbury. Other designs are either apparent one-offs, or confined to a single location. The Chatham Lines, defending the landward approaches to the naval base, barracks and dockyards, contained a number of ovoid concrete pillboxes designed to hold two Vickers machine-guns, mounted on concrete triangular tables and both firing forward (*40*). The pillbox measured some 19ft (6m) across at its widest point and had walls 3ft (0.9m) thick, with an entrance at a point opposite the embrasures. At nearby Chattenden on Hoo, one of three major munitions depots storing shells and explosives for the armed services in

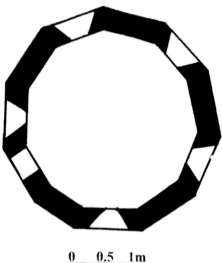

0   0.5   1m

41 Chattenden, Hoo, Kent
(TQ757728); 11-sided concrete
pillbox used to guard the important
ordnance depot and magazines

1913, pillboxes of a most distinctive design were constructed (*41*). A photograph in the
RE library, taken in 1930, shows one of these standing between the nineteenth-century
barracks and the railway. Two further examples still stand on what was once the perimeter
of the magazine complex. This design features 11 faces, five blind, five with letter-box
loopholes, and one with a low doorway. The door is solid concrete and hinged, so that
in the closed position it is perfectly flush with the outer surface of the pillbox. Very high
quality concrete appears to have been used around a steel lining to construct the pillbox
in four stages, with exterior wooden shuttering on a thick plinth and with a cast, domed
roof. The pillbox is about 8ft (2.4m) high, with an interior diameter of around 7ft (2.1m).
Although the pillbox is quite small, the loopholes have a pronounced splay to the exterior
giving a wider field of fire and increased facility for observation. Another local design has
been reported at Redcar in North Yorkshire, built into the promenade which runs along

42 Theddlethorpe-St-Helen, Lincolnshire (TF445958); presumed WWI pillbox with WWII (**6ai**) pillbox built to seaward; there are two loops which enfilade the beach; the rough shuttering is similar to some pillboxes on the Western Front near Ypres

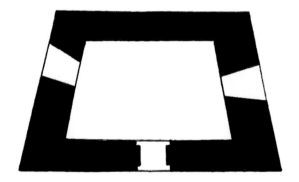

43 Theddlethorpe-St-Helen, Lincolnshire (TF445958); plan of *42*

0   0.5   1m

the sea-wall over the dunes. Here, every 200 yards or so, were chambers about 10ft x 8ft (3m x 2.4m), with three forward-facing loops for Vickers guns. The reinforced concrete was about 12in (30cm) thick and the loops were splayed externally. Access, by 1926, was by circular manhole in the roof, but there may, originally, have been a more comfortable entrance through the dune. One of the machine-gun posts developed by the REs on the Western Front in around 1917, was a square pillbox with two loopholes in each of three sides, the fourth side containing the entrance. A single example of such a design survives on the beach at Bawdsey (Suffolk), buried in the shingle, next to a pillbox from the Second World War. This appears to be one of only a very few examples of any expected cross-over from the sphere of the BEF to that of the home defences. On the Lincolnshire coast there are at least four examples of a design which appears to derive from the Western Front (*42* & *43*). It is trapezoidal with a blank face to seaward, an embrasure in each side wall for a machine-gun to enfilade the beach, and a door in the long rear wall. It is built of

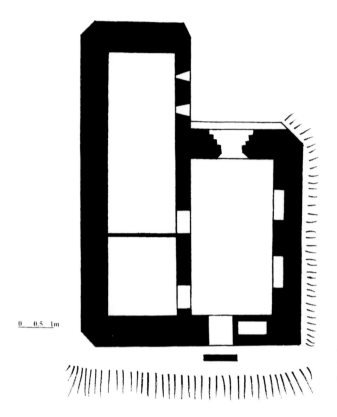

0   0.5   1m

44 German flanking
emplacement for a field-gun
on the Hindenburg Line
(after Mallory & Ottar)

very rough concrete which could almost be taken for an attempt to disguise it as natural rock, were it not for its location in the dunes. This same finish may be seen on pillboxes near Ypres. In two instances a Second World War three-bay pillbox has been built a few feet to seaward, which would suggest that a First World War origin for it is plausible.

One other category of defence work which must not be forgotten, is the field-gun emplacement. The range of designs in German use, particularly in the Hindenburg Line defences, included concrete emplacements for a 77mm (3in) gun, for a field gun (*44*) and for a mortar, this last having provision for firing through a gap in the overhead protection. Photographs show that similar structures were constructed by the British troops, both at home and on the Western Front, but more in the form of fieldworks. Two IWM photographs show examples of these fieldworks. One taken in the Ypres salient shows a 13 or 18 pounder field gun mounted in a sandbagged position held firmly in place by a framework of tree-trunks. Above the gun is a beam on which are piled two courses of railway sleepers to support a roof of sandbags. A similar arrangement in the Chatham defences uses a steel girder to span the mouth of the emplacement. Above this, there is a layer of earth, about 3ft (1m) thick. The girder is supported by verticals of wood, possibly sleepers again. Given the strictures of field artillery mobility and the value of indirect fire from concealed positions, it comes as no real surprise that there is no specific fieldwork for field guns provided in the 1911 Manual. Any future war was, of course, going to be one involving mobility, flexibility and imagination.

3

THE DEVELOPMENT OF PILLBOXES PRIOR TO THE SECOND WORLD WAR

FRANCE AND THE MAGINOT LINE

The experience of the First World War, when long periods of time spent by troops behind fortified lines had been punctuated by calamitous, and usually largely unsuccessful attacks, appeared, somewhat paradoxically, to promote the notion of the heavily-fortified frontier. To be fair, France had always put its faith in such systems, from the time of Vauban in the seventeenth century, through to Sere de Rivieres in the nineteenth. Probably, for the French, the most outstanding memory of the First World War was the disaster of Verdun, where the protracted fighting over this fortress complex produced a million casualties on each side, but once again it was the claimed impregnability of the concrete fortress in which the French were to trust for their future security. The Maginot Line, built primarily to secure the eastern frontier with Germany, was planned from 1922, building commenced in 1928 and troops took up their garrison duties in 1936. Any threat from Italy was met from 1936 by a

45 Beinheim, Bas-Rhin, France; machine-gun pillbox, part of the French Maginot Line defences of the Rhine crossings

strengthening of defences in the Alpine regions, but, crucially, those in the Ardennes were weak and along the Belgian border almost nonexistent. The Commission for the Fortified Regions (CORF) was the body which assumed responsibility for the design of the standardised component structures of the Line. The Maginot Line was essentially a string of heavily-fortified artillery blocks, or *ouvrages*, linked by continuous belts of wire, AT obstacles, potential inundations, minefields and with a screen of blockhouses called *avant-postes*, some of which appeared as houses, the *maisons fortes*. These forward positions were generally built of reinforced concrete, and provided with several machine-gun embrasures to command border crossings. They were expected to achieve little more than provide early warning of an invasion and signal to the enemy that resistance might be expected. The primary defence lay in the mighty *ouvrages* with their steel turrets stuffed with artillery, their underground magazines and barracks linked by tunnels with railway tracks, their extensive belts of obstacles commanded by machine-guns and AT guns in concrete bunkers. There are places, however, along the Rhine for instance, where small free-standing pillboxes (*45*) tasked with defending vulnerable points such as bridges, can be seen. These tend to be in mutually-supporting groupings, but many of the components are quite modest, with discrete steel turrets providing cover for machine-guns.

GERMANY AND THE WEST WALL

By 1936, when Germany re-occupied the Rhineland, plans were advanced for the Westwall, which was to run from Aachen to the Rhine, as Germany's answer to the French defences. Through the next few years work proceeded both here and in the East, where the Oder-Warthe-Bend Line, the Pomeranian Line and the Oder Line all faced Poland. Although it was the intention that both East and West positions were to consist of fortress works, *Panzerwerke* in *Werkgruppen* of similar strength to the Maginot Line *ouvrages*, owing to the natural defences of many of the localities, the majority were relatively small and weak pillboxes. These were constructed to standardised designs, a range of which were provided, housing mortars, AT guns or machine-guns (*46*). Most held from six to a dozen men. The most common bunker on the Westwall was to the B1 standard, i.e. the walls were 1m (3ft 3in), the roof 0.8m (2ft 7in), and most interior walls 0.5m (20in) thick. Although there were dozens of different designs within just this B1 category, they were all pretty similar in having an entrance protected by a canopy, a corridor with chicane and covered by a loophole for a machine-gun, living quarters with bunks and cooking facilities and a combat room in which was located the main armament – a water-cooled machine-gun firing through an embrasure protected, when not in use, by a thick, armoured steel plate. There were also some pillboxes built of logs with concrete fronts. The course of the war meant that many of these defences were never completed as planned. Emergency measures in the east later saw the introduction of many small, circular, concrete, pre-fabricated pillboxes or cloches, Tobruk stands and bunkers mounting Panther tank-turrets with 75mm guns in them, a few of which were also mounted in the West.

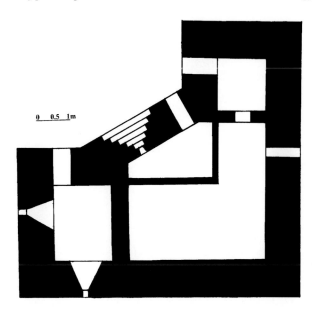

0   0,5   1m

46 German machine-gun
bunker on the West Wall; plan
after Mallory and Ottar

THE DEFENCES OF BELGIUM AND HOLLAND

Despite subsequent assertions to the contrary (mainly by members of the BEF, whose disappointment was based on misconceptions relating to the Dyle Line) Belgium had prepared quite significant fixed defences in the period prior to the German invasion. The defences of Liège, whose most famous fort, albeit for the wrong reasons, was Eben Emael on the Albert Canal, and Namur, were built slightly later than the Maginot Line, but had many similarities. The defences of Antwerp whose earlier forts had not been updated were provided with a number of two-storey machine-gun bunkers (47) to enfilade the canals around the city and to control the sluice-gates which regulated the water in these AT obstacles. Chains of pillboxes of various types were built to link these three main fortresses, but the resumption of neutrality in 1936 caused both a slow-down in the construction of defences and a reduction in the size of the field army which would be needed to support them. The last elements in the Belgian defences were defence lines comprising numbers of mainly small bunkers, such as on the KW Line, from Koningshooikt to Wavre, following the course of the River Dyle, composed of natural obstacles and around 200 pillboxes, or the Gent Bridgehead. The majority of these pillboxes, built in 1938, were given metre-thick concrete roofs and walls, were around 20ft (6m) square and had embrasures for two machine-guns and some grenade-launchers. Most were sited to flank AT obstacles. A network of forward OPs, *postes d'alertes*, was also established there, which had the appearance of normal houses, but were protected by a front wall of concrete. They had ample fenestration giving all-round visibility and some were provided with defensive loopholes. A final extension of the Dyle (KW) Line to Namur was composed purely of AT barriers unsupported by any pillboxes and, in the event, went uncontested.

Holland too looked to update her defences in the lead-up to the Second World War. The traditional barrier of the New Water Line had been greatly encroached on by urban

47   Antwerp, Belgium; two-storey, double machine-gun blockhouse covering a sluice on the AT ditch north-east of Fort Ertbrand

development, so was replaced by the Grebbe Line, 25km (15 miles) further to the east. This Line consisted of a number of old forts with only minimal modernisation, areas prepared for flooding and large numbers of concrete bunkers. These were built to a range of designs, but the most numerous were the Type S, built of 60-90cm (2-3ft) thick concrete, measuring about 3.5m x 6m (11ft 6in x 20ft) and generally equipped with three machine-guns firing to the front (*48* & *49*). It had been intended to furnish many of the machine-gun and AT pillboxes with steel cloches, but much of the order remained unfulfilled at the start of hostilities and only a very few were installed.

SWITZERLAND

Declarations of neutrality had been seen to represent no guarantee of any lack of involvement in the First World War so Switzerland was keen to show that her defences were in order. In addition to updating the nineteenth-century forts covering the main passes into the country, it became necessary to construct whole new defence positions as a response to the fall of France in 1940. Methods of designing permanent fortifications in alpine locations had been pioneered by Swiss engineers to produce immensely strong underground artillery forts, rock-cut galleries for the use of infantry and belts of AT obstacles. Now measures had to be taken quickly to safeguard less inaccessible areas and a standard infantry bunker was designed to hold a 47mm AT gun, separated by an observation cell from a heavy machine-gun. This bunker measured some 12m x 8m (40ft x 31ft) with walls nearly 2m (6ft 6in) thick and a front projection masking the AT embrasure from flanking fire. A cellar, reached by

48 Bourtrange, Groningen, Netherlands; a type S pillbox

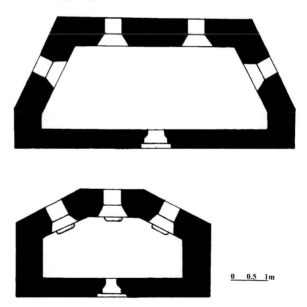

49 Netherlands type
S pillboxes built in the
late-1930s

0   0.5   1m

rungs in the rear-wall, contained a magazine and crew quarters. The ground-level entrance incorporated a chicane covered by a rifle-loop.

SCANDINAVIA

Both Denmark and Sweden put most of their defensive effort into coastal defences sited to control the channels between islands or the approaches to key ports. Both countries also employed pillboxes to secure vulnerable points, but in different ways. All over Denmark can be seen small square pillboxes with four horizontal loopholes mounted on the roofs of shelters (*50*). Sometimes there is a pillbox at each end, usually one in the middle. These can be seen in the intervals between the semi-circle of forts on the land front of Copenhagen, outside the citadel and near bridges and road-junctions in the countryside. Sweden, on the other hand, in the three months leading up to the outbreak of the Second World War, constructed a dense line of pillboxes along the southern coast, known as the Per Albin Line, to defend against any possible German invasion. These were built either for 37mm AT guns, or for machine-guns. They are almost all sited as flanking positions on beaches and many therefore have a shell of local rock laid over their concrete structure for camouflage (*51*). Most have a steel observation cupola on the roof, reached by rungs inside. Large numbers of these pillboxes were built and they are often very close together, but without depth.

RUSSIA AND FINLAND

Russia had enormous problems attempting to defend such vast open spaces. The Stalin Line, commenced in 1930, and still only work in progress by 1939, was well over 1000 miles (1800 km) in length, running from Leningrad to the Black Sea. Although there

50 Vordingborg, Falster, Denmark; standard bunker with pillbox on top

51 Pillbox on Sweden's south coast Per Albin Line; it has the typical machine-gun embrasure enfilading the beach, steel observation cupola and applied rock camouflage

were ambitious underground forts in key locations, many sectors of the defences relied on small comparatively lightly built pillboxes. These were generally built with 1.5m (8ft) of concrete in the front faces, but not much more than a metre to the rear. Many of these pillboxes were simple emplacements for two or three machine-guns, with a few variations. Some had projections to mask flanking fire, whilst others were designed to fire forwards. They were often connected by tunnels reached by vertical shafts in the floor of each pillbox. There were at least 2500 of these pillboxes in the Stalin Line, with a further 1000 in the later Molotov Line along the western border. However, attempts to produce defence in depth meant that they were spread very thinly. Other lines were built subsequently in an atmosphere of desperation and, although many structures were fieldworks of logs and rocks, it is thought that they were often at least as strong as their more permanent predecessors.

After the First World War, the newly-independent state of Finland felt it advisable to defend the Karelian Isthmus against any potential invasion by Russia. The Mannerheim and Salpa Lines were built to provide main and switch lines. With few pre-existing fortifications, the Finns were forced to rely on small bunkers, grouped into resistance points rather than continuous lines of defence. The earliest constructions were mainly weak, constructed of timber, earth and stones, and only later, into the 1930s, were more resilient concrete bunkers built. The majority of these were machine-gun emplacements, although there were some larger bunkers built to hold field guns. A certain amount of modernisation was carried out after 1936, but, compared to other countries' defences we have seen, these were still relatively unsophisticated. The largest artillery bunker, for instance, measured only 7m (23ft) along its longest side. A few bunkers were fitted with cloches, mainly for observation. The later Salpa Line held more concrete bunkers, including some for 45mm AT guns, and more flanking positions for machine-guns. One innovative construction method was to submerge a large rubber ball in a crater, and pour concrete over it, creating a spherical bunker which was then covered in earth and accessed through a trench. These were troop shelters rather than weapons emplacements. Even here, though, many of the bunkers were still made of timber and earth.

CZECHOSLOVAKIA, POLAND, YUGOSLAVIA AND THE BALKANS

So marked were the similarities between the two that the Czechs referred to their northern defences as their own Maginot Line. Almost the entire compass of Czechoslovakia's borders were either given defences or had them projected. The heaviest were along the northern border where 16 *tvrzi* (the Czech equivalent of the French *ouvrages*) were built, with other strong lines to the south, defending Brno and Bratislava. Most of the remaining defences relied on small bunkers, of which there were two main types. The weaker Type 36 pillbox was designed to hold a machine-gun with its crew, but could fire only forwards, and was protected by concrete, only 60cm (2ft) in thickness. The Type 37 pillbox was usually sited to give flanking or oblique fire, had walls and a roof up to 1.2m (4ft) thick and often had armoured doors and embrasures. Many of these had two embrasures giving flanking fire in opposite directions, but those with only a single embrasure were usually sited in pairs to give mutual support.

Although a number of works defending Silesia around Katowice had been completed by 1939, the majority of Poland's fortifications were still under construction when the German invasion came in the autumn of that year. The designs used were similar to those of France and Czechoslovakia, being based on the *schron*, a pair of combat blocks linked by a tunnel. Each fortified position consisted of up to a dozen or more *schrony* with supporting fieldworks. Other free-standing casemates were built to give all-round fire in order to close gaps between the main fortified points. Inevitably there was also a need for small bunkers which might conceal some of the weaknesses caused by the shortfalls in the building programme, particularly on the western borders. These were small machine-gun posts sited to give flanking fire in one or two directions. Most were built to a design of 1939, influenced by the Maginot Line.

Like Czechoslovakia, Yugoslavia was offered help by France in securing her borders. Initially unable for financial and political reasons to benefit fully from French engineering expertise, they did take advice in 1937 and visited the Czech fortifications, actually importing some Czech materials and munitions following the German occupation of the Sudetenland. Whilst the plan was to construct large-scale Maginot-type forts on the borders with Italy, Austria, Hungary, Romania and Bulgaria, neither the budget nor the industrial base was adequate for the whole task. Hence on long stretches of the borders numbers of small-scale pillboxes were built, to be equipped with AT guns and machine-guns. Many of these, in the end, were lightly-armed posts for Frontier Guards with automatic rifles, with only a few stronger bunkers defending the most vulnerable routes of entry and lines of communication. On the western border, however, facing Italy and Austria, was built a continuous defence line, known as the Rupnik Line, after the Slovenian general tasked with building it. Although a number of large combat-blocks were constructed, generally built into the crests of hills, it was the many machine-gun posts upon which the integrity of the Line depended. Those in the front line were rhombus-shaped with embrasures in two, often adjacent, faces. Those in the second line were particularly distinctive in that they were usually on two floors, with one end rising up like the prow of a ship. They had two armoured embrasures for machine-guns or AT rifles, and other loopholes besides for close defence. Many of the semi-circular armoured embrasures had three alternative loops for machine-guns, giving 180 degrees of protected traverse. Some pillboxes were entered through a hatch and then down a ladder, leading to a traverse-wall with a weapons loop and others through a door at ground level, but with the same internal defensive arrangement. Reinforced concrete 60-100cm (2-3ft) thick was used throughout these works.

Both Greece and Romania used small pillboxes in their frontier fortifications, raised in the late-1930s, to house machine-guns and grenade-launchers. Many of the Greek bunkers, particularly on the Metaxas Line facing Yugoslavia and Bulgaria, were built into semi-underground fortified groups. All the countries of the Balkans made as much use as possible of natural barriers, enhanced by extensive belts of AT obstacles.

ITALY

Despite the natural strength of much of Italy's land frontier, rooted as it was in ranges of high mountains, there were still vulnerable passes and gaps to be defended. These were given tailor-made defence works which combined the organisation of the French or Czech systems, with the extempore nature of the Russian or Finnish works. Thus each position, or *opera*, in the Alpine defences was given an individual treatment which produced a whole range of solutions usually involving a cluster of quite small bunkers linked together by tunnel systems containing underground barracks and magazines. The individual bunker or combat block, often well-camouflaged in a cleft in the rocks and covered in rubble camouflage, would contain one or two machine-guns and/or an AT gun, firing on fixed lines. By 1940, when Italy declared war on France, there were over 500 *opere* in service, with over another 1000 under construction. As well as the alpine defences, much of Italy's coastline was fortified against invasion. Large numbers of pillboxes can still be found in Sardinia (52) and in the Bay of Naples for instance.

THE BRITISH EMPIRE

Prior to 1939, Britain's fortification effort had been confined to those bits of the Empire deemed to be vulnerable to attack from the fascist states. This meant, in effect, that Malta and Gibraltar received most attention. On Malta, Fort Campbell was started in 1937, to hold two 6-inch coast defence guns commanding St Paul's Bay. As an acknowledgement of the threat of aerial attack, its defences were less obvious than earlier structures and relied on perimeter walls indistinguishable from the local stone field walls, but incorporating posts with rifle-loops and embrasures for machine-guns, camouflaged with rock skins over their concrete cores, to blend into the landscape. The Abyssinian Crisis of 1935 had prompted a review of Malta's defences and one of the outcomes was plans for a network of pillboxes,

52   Valico Nuraxi de Mesu, Sardinia; interior of pillbox built into rocks

particularly in the west of the island covering possible enemy landing places. Work on this scheme started properly in August 1938 and continued into 1942. The early pillboxes were large, irregularly-shaped, surface structures containing two or three firing chambers for up to four Vickers machine-guns (53). These were mounted on concrete tables backed by benches and fired through concrete embrasures with iron shutters. On the roof there was often an emplacement for a Lyons light and a separate observation position. The whole structure was clad in a skin of local stone. The plan of each individual pillbox was dictated by the situation, so that advantage might be taken of natural features, cover or other particular circumstances. Pillboxes were often painted either to accentuate their appearance as agricultural or domestic buildings, or to blend in to the local terrain. By 1939, however, these idiosyncrasies had been ironed out by the introduction of a range of standardised models, built of reinforced concrete, but only 15in or 18in (37 or 45 cm) thick. The first of these designs was for a rectangular pillbox with a flat roof supported by two pillars, one of which had rungs set into it to give access through a hatch. The pillbox had armoured machine-gun embrasures in three faces and rifle loops in the fourth face and in the chamfered corners. Around the open roof ran a low parapet, looped for prone riflemen. Entry was by an armoured door. The Vickers gun was now on a traversable steel mounting and below each machine-gun embrasure was a thickening of the outer wall. The second design (54) was for a two-storey pillbox with an adjoining, higher stair-turret and OP set in the middle of one face. There were loopholes across all four corners and in the middle of each face, at the higher level, and several on the lower. At least one embrasure, fitted with external wooden shutters, was equipped with a Vickers machine-gun. The height of these structures made them quite obtrusive and as few of them were provided with stone-cladding, they had to be camouflaged, generally as domestic and agricultural buildings. Sometimes the concrete was merely painted to simulate stone, but at other times features such as window-frames were painted on. The third design was simply a development of the second, saving materials and improving communications by placing the OP on the roof. Where little was to be gained by building two storeys, then single-storey pillboxes sufficed. In addition to these four types of pillbox, many

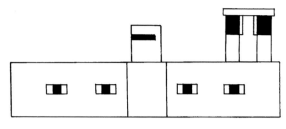

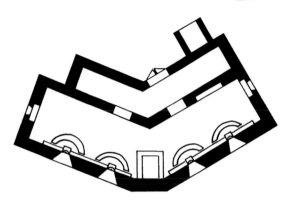

53 Malta; a pillbox for four Vickers machine-guns, Lyons Light and OP; plan and elevation

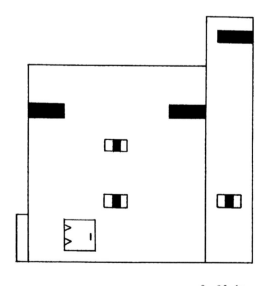

54 Malta; elevation of a two-storey pillbox with stair-turret/OP, for at least two Vickers machine-guns, and four Bren guns

existing buildings, both military and civilian, were converted into strong-points by adding loopholes, or by constructing machine-gun positions on suitable roofs. Included in these conversions were a number of the sixteenth-century Knights' towers such as some of those in St George's Bay, and in Sliema. A number of rectangular, open-fronted positions were also built to house field guns, providing some protection against strafing. An obvious weakness of all these pillboxes was their limitation to mainly forward-facing, rather than flanking, fire, but they were designed to function together in defence lines, so some measure of mutual support and overlapping fields of fire must be assumed.

Elsewhere in the Empire there was also an urgent need to update defences which had not significantly altered from the previous century. Hong Kong's defences had, until around 1938, been generally focused on the coastal approaches. However it was thought necessary to fortify the hills to the north of the Kowloon Peninsular against a landward attack, so the Gin Drinkers' Line was constructed around a central underground citadel, the Shing mun Redoubt, but mainly comprised pillboxes and trenches. Singapore faced very similar problems, and much of the southern coastline of Singapore Island, as well as defence lines behind Changi and running inland either side of Singapore City, were defended by camouflaged machine-gun posts. The situation

55 Gibraltar, King's Bastion; a machine-gun pillbox added to the eighteenth- and nineteeth-century works *c*.1939

at Gibraltar was more straightforward. The Rock itself not only afforded the defenders a birds-eye view of preparations for an assault from La Linea, but also provided the means of burying as much as possible underground. This was all, in reality, an illusion, for had the German Operation Felix been put into effect in 1941, the fortress would surely have fallen. However, the pretence had to be maintained, and pillboxes were added to some of the coastal batteries as at Parson's Lodge, onto the Line Wall as at King's Bastion (55), high up on the Rock, and around the naval dockyard. Others were built facing the approaches from Spain as the Spanish had built a solid line of pillboxes across the isthmus in 1939, just 1200 yards from the British forward positions.

THE US EMPIRE

Uncertainty over the future of colonial possessions affected others besides the British. In Hawaii, for instance, the US military recognised the vulnerability of the island of Oahu with its important naval base at Pearl Harbour, by embarking on a programme of beach defences based on pillboxes. The first 12 were completed in 1934. These appear to have been about 10ft (3m) square, with wide embrasures for 0.3-inch (8mm) machine-guns to enfilade the potential invasion beaches. As early as 1913, the batteries defending the Panama Canal had been backed by hundreds of yards of concrete trenches and concrete stockades, but by the 1930s these had decayed along with many of the older coastal defence guns. Whilst the main effort went into updating the artillery and protecting it against air attack, it was important to protect the new gun emplacements from ground-attack. Consequently, fieldworks were constructed on the hills above the batteries.

4

PILLBOXES IN THE SECOND WORLD WAR

BRITISH PILLBOXES IN FRANCE 1939-40

It is easy to believe that the autumn of 1939 was about to herald a re-run of the First World War. The BEF had been shipped to France and was digging in along the borders of northern France, awaiting a German invasion. This was not a comfortable situation in which the British troops found themselves. One result of Belgian neutrality was that the Maginot Line, to all intents and purposes, stopped at the Belgian frontier. In 1937, the French government had decided to construct defences along this vulnerable sector by extending their AT ditch westwards, but were able only to build interval casemates rather than fully-fledged *ouvrages*, with the available time and resources. These casemates were built of reinforced concrete with steel cupolas and mounted AT artillery and machine-guns, but any heavy artillery would have to be emplaced farther back than was desirable. The French press were encouraged to think that this was a full-strength extension, comparable to the rest of the Line. Belgian strategy was based on a defensive line along the Albert Canal, anchored on the new Fort Eben Emael. In 1939, the truth of the illusory Maginot Line extension was out and the Polish fortifications had been tested in battle. The French Deuxieme Bureau advised from the Polish experience that whilst the concrete emplacements had stood up well to bombardment, their machine-gun ports had often been destroyed by direct fire from tanks. They therefore recommended that more AT guns be mounted in all the fixed defences. However, the lack of urgency engendered during the Phoney War, coupled with appalling weather throughout the winter months, meant that little could be accomplished in terms of stiffening the defences west of the River Meuse at Sedan.

Towards the end of November 1939, the British War Minister, Hore-Belisha had visited the frontlines and had been disappointed by what he saw as a lack of fixed defences. On his own initiative, and against the advice of either the generals in the field or the War Office, he mobilised a dozen Territorial RE Field Companies with a civilian adviser, under the sound-bite name 'Force X', and sent them to France to construct pillboxes. Contrary to Hore-Belisha's impression, much had been done both to construct defences, and to see that they matched a shared view of what was necessary. Montgomery's Third Division had dug AT obstacles around Lille and had laid wire. There had been problems with the rain washing away trenches, but agreement was reached with General Gamelin that the tactics would be based on defended localities, known to the French as 'herissons' (hedgehogs) which even if bypassed by enemy armour would hold up the following

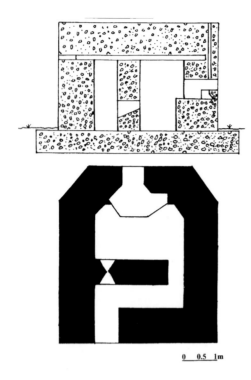

0   0.5   1m

56   British War Office 1936 standard
pillbox for Vickers machine-gun

infantry and supplies, leaving the armour stranded without fuel, ammunition or food.
Decisions relating to the design of concrete defences were adjourned because of the varied
requirements for emplacing the Allies' different weapons. British troops did construct
defence lines composed of concrete pillboxes, but it is unclear where the designs originated.
The War Office's 1936 *Manual of Field Engineering* contains but a solitary suitable design (56)
for a concrete pillbox and as far as fieldwork has revealed, this was not one of the designs
implemented in France. There are, in all, some six relevant designs in the Manual, but one is
too specialised, being built in the ruined shell of a building to exploit the airspace as a shock
absorber, three were essentially fieldworks – machine-gun pits protected by earth traverses
or bags of shingle and rocks over corrugated iron roofs – and the fifth design was a German
one from the First World War, which was similar to the British Second Army design but
used expanded metal in the roof to create an air-pocket. The building work was carried
out by RE regulars as well as the TA companies, and much can still be seen on the ground.

The official history of the BEF describes how, from November 1939, the 12 TA
companies, aided by companies of the Auxiliary Military Pioneer Corps and a special
Excavation Company, worked with 700-800 machines including bulldozers and
concrete-mixers. They constructed 40 miles (64km) of revetted AT ditch, covered by 400
pillboxes. In some places breastworks were built to designs in the 1936 Field Manual,
because the weather precluded the orthodox trenches. In recognition of contemporary
military strategy, these lines were sited to provide defence in depth. The British pillboxes
were apparently built to three main designs, which were most probably issued by the
relevant War Office department, whose Director, in November 1939, was Major-General
Collins. The first of these designs was a rectangular chamber of reinforced concrete

with walls 3ft (0.9m) thick, about 24ft wide x 14ft deep (7.3m x 4.3m). It had two forward-facing embrasures for Vickers machine-guns, capable of traversing on their steel mounts (*57, 58 & 59*). There is evidence that some extemporisation went on, for Jock Hamilton-Baillie, a RE subaltern at the time, introduced his own refinement into at least one of these pillboxes at Cysoing, placing an observation slit between the embrasures, based on the premise that allowing the section corporal to have some idea of what was going on could do no harm. Other examples of this machine-gun post can be found along the N43 Charleville road.

The second design was hexagonal and came as either a regular hexagon (*60 & 61*) with sides of 10ft (3m), or with two longer sides (*62*). The regular version had five loops for Bren guns, whilst the elongated one, somewhat similar to some of the Dutch type S pillboxes, might have three loops in the forward-facing long side and then loops in the short sides as necessary. They were usually grouped in threes to provide mutual support. Groups of these

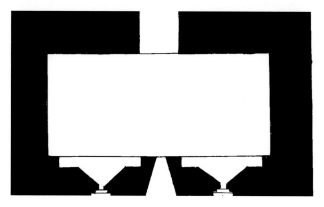

Above 57 Cysoing, Nord, France; BEF pillbox for two Vickers machine-guns, with an observation slit in between the embrasures; built in 1939 by Jock Hamilton-Baillie

Right 58 Cysoing, Nord, France; plan of 57 after Hamilton-Baillie

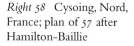

59 Cysoing, Nord, France; interior of *57* showing observation slit and one of the, possibly non-standard, operating cradles for a Vickers gun

60 Cysoing, Nord, France; standard BEF hexagonal, shell-proof pillbox for five lmgs; this example has the domed top

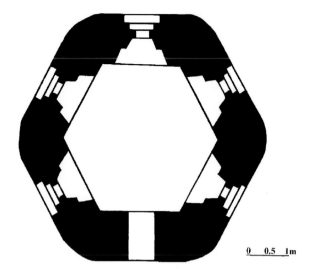

Right 61 Cysoing, Nord, France;
plan of standard BEF shell-proof
pillbox (*60*)

Below 62 Remugies, Nord, France;
BEF hexagonal, shellproof pillbox
with two lengthened sides; this
example has a chamfered top

may be found astride the road from Remugies (France) to Rongy (Belgium) and in the
Bourghelles area south-east of Lille. Both versions were shellproof. There are, however,
clear differences between the two groups. Those near Bourghelles are almost domed, with
rounded corners, whereas those at Remugies have more pronounced angles. This would
suggest merely differences in shuttering techniques or materials, although it could be
argued that the domed design could be intended to make the deflection of incoming fire
more likely. An extant design for these can be dated to May 1940, but could have been in
use since, most probably, the previous year.

The third design (*63*), also for a shell-proof and hexagonal pillbox, had shorter faces
flanking the rear wall, and thus, only three loopholes in the three forward-facing sides.

Rudi Rolf in his German language book on the Atlantic Wall includes a page of comparative plans of 1930s fortifications. He depicts monumental blockhouses from France, Belgium, Russia and Czechoslovakia, but for 'England', he includes the plans for two small hexagonal pillboxes, neither of which was ever built at home, but the smaller of which appears to be the third design used by the BEF, as described above. In addition to these three fairly widespread designs on the ground in northern France, there are AT gun emplacements (*64*) – plain rectangular shell-proof boxes with concrete pedestals for the gun to sit on. The fittings on these pedestals are not unlike those incorporated in the emplacements for 2 pounder AT guns built in Britain in 1940, with slots for the gun's split trail. However, they could also be for a French gun, although none appears to fit the bill, neither the Hotchkiss 25mm nor the Bofors 37mm have the reversible split trail of the British gun. There are also rectangular shell-proof machine-gun emplacements, very similar to one of the British designs in First World War, with a stepped embrasure facing front.

Another pillbox design, slightly wider than the third standard one above, had two embrasures side-by-side. One may have been a smaller version for observation alongside the main one, or, alternatively, there may have been embrasures for both a machine-gun and an AT gun. So this could be Rolf's second mystery design which has side-by-side embrasures in each of two faces. According to German reconnaissance maps of the area around Cysoing, there were two French AT ditches, each provided with interval casemates, and about 2.5km (1.6miles) apart. It is in the area directly behind the forward line that the British-built pillboxes were located.

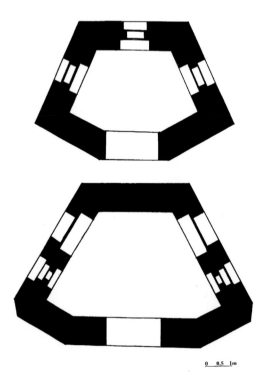

0   0.5   1m

63 BEF pillboxes in northern France, 1939-40; plans after Rolf

64 Bas-Aix, Nord, France; French emplacement for a light AT gun; it has pre-cast sockets for wheels, trail, pivot etc., but the opening in the rear wall does not look large enough to admit an appropriate weapon

BRITISH HOME DEFENCES 1940

After the disastrous (or miraculous) Dunkirk evacuation, a German invasion of Britain was daily expected. The Commander-in-Chief of the Home Forces, General Ironside, had little choice but to initiate a programme to construct networks of fixed anti-invasion defences. In the context of the military orthodoxy of the time, which was all about mobility and flexible responses, this was tantamount to heresy, but he had little alternative. There were few tanks, minimal transport, and barely any artillery or automatic weapons. Much of the BEF's equipment had been destroyed by enemy action or abandoned on the beaches, and until the munitions industry could begin to make good these catastrophic losses, all Ironside could do was to attempt to create delays for an invading force. In effect this meant concrete and lots of it. It is thought that upwards of 18,000 pillboxes were constructed in the nine months after Dunkirk. The majority of these were located in the Coastal Crust or the main inland defence lines which provided AT barriers, behind which what mobile reserves there were could be deployed once the locus of attack was known. The Coastal Crust extended from the far north of Scotland, down the entire east coast, and around the south coast to the West Country, turning round Land's End and running back as far as Bristol. Parts of the South Wales coast, Cardigan Bay, Holyhead, the Wirral and the coast north of Liverpool were fortified, as were most ports.

The main defence line, known as the GHQ Line, ran from Bristol Channel, through the Somerset Levels, along the Kennet and Avon Canal to Reading. A switch line ran north of this along the River Ray and then along the Thames, down through Sulham Valley to rejoin the main line at Reading. From here, it ran eastwards to Farnham, then along the base of the North Downs to Penshurst where it divided, with one line dropping south to Newhaven, and the other running on to Maidstone and up to the Hoo Peninsular above the Medway towns. Having crossed the Thames onto Canvey Island, the Line ran north via Chelmsford and Cambridge to meet the River Welland between Stamford and Spalding. North of here, defences were mainly limited to planned demolitions of bridges, but a notional course was set out as far as Richmond in Yorkshire, with further extensions to Edinburgh and beyond. Supplementary lines were constructed at Command level, examples of such being the Eastern Command Line across East Anglia, the Taunton Stop Line from Bridgwater to Seaton, the Western Command Line from Cardigan to Pembrey protecting Milford Haven and the Scottish Command Line which starts at Loch Tummel, runs along the River Tay and then crosses the Fife peninsular. These all operated at the strategic level. The third element in the system was based on tactical appreciation of the terrain at a more local level. These Corps and Division Lines covered much of Britain plugging the holes and linking up the major lines. In the south of England – the expected focus of any planned invasion – such lines were sited to form a series of interlocking defensible boxes into which enemy forces might be channelled, contained and ultimately destroyed. London had its own defence lines, three of them, with the outer one roughly on the alignment of the London Orbital Motorway, and the innermost anchored on the River Thames.

The lines comprising the three levels of this hierarchy were all based on the principle of the continuous AT barrier, either a river or an artificial waterway or revetted ditch, covered by a mixture of fieldworks and hardened defences. Machine-guns of all types, AT weapons, and field artillery were generally housed in concrete emplacements. These were integrated with trenches, minefields and obstacles of all sorts including flame barrages and mobile forces. As we have seen, in the darkest days of summer 1940, only static defences were feasible. By the autumn, Brooke had taken over from Ironside and had changed the rules. He had seen the problems of relying on fixed defences in France and was keen to avoid replicating this situation in Britain (see Chapter 7). He therefore put a stop on the construction of pillboxes, limited the use of AT obstacles and exploited the productivity of the factories in order to create more mobile forces. At the same time, the growth of a trained Home Guard provided the personnel to hold the static positions, freeing up the regulars as mobile forces. The official policy moved from the linear strategy of Ironside, to an interlocking network of nodal points, in which road, rail and waterway junctions, usually occurring in towns rather than in open countryside, became centres of all-round defence. Many of these locations employed hardened defences as well as fieldworks. The other common location for pillboxes was the isolated resistance point. In autumn 1940 several AA searchlight commands decreed that searchlight-sites should be defensible and that each should include a pillbox as well as fieldworks. In the event of invasion, the site would act as a focus for local Home Guard units and regular units who had become separated from their parent formations. Searchlights soon became much more mobile, and most of the original sites were quickly abandoned, but the pillboxes remained, often to the bewilderment of historians. It is also not uncommon to find odd pillboxes guarding canal-bridges, and road or rail junctions in the middle of nowhere.

THE DIRECTORATE OF FORTIFICATIONS AND WORKS

At the War Office, the DFW was responsible for the design of all military structures, from ablution-blocks to bridges to Z-batteries. Fortifications were included along with everything else and drawings were issued by the DFW in numerical sequence, usually with two final digits recording the year of production. The Army Council regularly issued instruction booklets, for both training and reference, to units in the field. Some were primarily for the REs, but others, more tactically based, were issued to all sections. The *Manual of Field Engineering* was re-issued in its updated form in 1936 and a 64-page pamphlet covering general Field Engineering came out in December 1939 with, almost as an afterthought, an extra page of protection tables glued in. This laid down the minimum amounts of different materials needed to protect against small-arms and AT gun fire. That same month other smaller pamphlets were issued, such as one on the use of Dannert concertina wire. In May 1940 the construction of anti-invasion defences became the priority for the Directorate and, in recognition of this, a dedicated department was established, known as DFW3. This branch produced a suite of design-drawings for hardened defences in its own numbered sequence. This sequence appears to run from 1 to 46, and included nine designs which are known to be for pillboxes. Alongside these there are drawing numbers in the normal DFW sequence which also relate to hardened defences, not only completely new designs, but also modifications to old ones. All these drawings were issued to RE officers in the field, who, in turn, briefed and supervised local contractors and their sub-contractors who built the actual defence works. As well as the official DFW3 effort, private enterprise was at work, for commercial firms also designed defence structures and attempted to sell their ideas to the War Office. Another dimension was added by the RE officers and contractors on the job making their own modifications.

Inevitably, this mixed economy causes many problems of identification in the field. In some instances, the same drawing number appears to have been used for quite different designs. A good example is that of the DFW3 Drawing Number 27, which is usually held to be the design for a large octagonal pillbox with an open central well for an LAA machine-gun, dozens of which ring London to this day. On the Taunton Stop Line however, apparently with   modifications laid out in drawing number TL62, it is the shell-proof Vickers machine-gun emplacement directly descended from that in the 1936 manual. But no amount of local modification could have turned one into the other. Further, on the GHQ Line in Cambridgeshire, drawing number 27A, as recorded by the contractor, appears to relate to the rectangular emplacement for three Bren guns, another entirely different structure. It is clearly unsafe to put too much store in these supposed type numbers, although, in the absence of any other identifier, they are useful as labels. As well as the DFW, several Army Commands, Eastern and Scottish, for instance, and the

Air Ministry were all also issuing numbered drawings to RE officers and contractors. It would appear that the RAF's Works Squadrons (later to be reformed as the Airfield Construction Service) were not concerned with buildings or defences, although their pioneer companies might have provided some labour.

PILLBOXES FOR THE ROYAL NAVY

All the extensive dockyards, ports, magazines and shore establishments administered by the Royal Navy required protection, not necessarily against attack, but for general security. A range of designs for guard-posts was developed for this purpose using established naval designers. Colonel Hazard, better-known for designing hold-fasts, was responsible for some of the pillboxes used by the Royal Marines. GA Maunsell, the civil engineer who instigated the AA forts in the Thames and Mersey estuaries, was the designer of the small, brick and concrete guard-post, still seen at many a naval installation. Other specialist structures used by the navy included EXDO posts for harbour defence and mine-watching posts

PILLBOX CONSTRUCTION

If many of the pillbox designs had military origins, the vast majority of the actual process of construction was a civilian enterprise, with jobs awarded through a system of competitive tendering. In each area, a group contractor was appointed, who would co-ordinate the work, parcelling it out to sub-contractors and attempting to ensure that materials, labour and transport were used effectively and efficiently. The builder was advised and directed by an RE officer, usually from a background of architecture or civil engineering. It was his job to liaise with the troops defending, in order to position structures in tactically sound locations, to contribute to schemes of mutual support, to enjoy wide fields of fire, to benefit from any available concealment and to contrive appropriate camouflage. Typically the group contractor had quite a wide area to cover. The 50 miles or so of the GHQ Line through Cambridgeshire, for instance, was split between Caves of Thorney, and Coulsons of Cambridge, each employing about half-a-dozen sub-contractors. The most problematic sites tended to remain the responsibility of the group contractor, so it was Hugh Cave who laid a railway track across the below-sea-level Bedford Levels in order to get materials to the position at Welches Dam. Both the provision and the transport of materials created difficulties. Timber was in short supply and as a consequence large numbers of pillboxes were permanently shuttered in brick. Mr Green, the civil engineer who supervised the construction of the GHQ Line in Sussex, describes how the proud bricklayers of Crowborough Brickworks built the shuttering in quick time. Similarly, the abundance of Flettons in the Peterborough and Whittlesey brickyards provided Hugh Cave with the raw materials he needed for shuttering. The concrete in-fill was generally applied in two pourings and where timber shuttering has been used, it is often possible to see the line marking the two applications. Cement was also hard to come by and the minutes of the Cambridge Federation of Master Builders are full of references to this problem. In July 1940 the War Office had issued a memorandum entitled 'Economy of Cement in Defence Post', signed by Colonel E.R.B. Buchanan for the DFW, to all Chief Engineers, drawing attention to measures which might be adopted. These included reducing the thickness of floors, or even omitting them altogether, sinking walls below ground-level in order to avoid reinforcing the concrete, using lime rather than cement mortar and, most bewildering of all, using a weaker mix of concrete, i.e. more aggregate to less cement, in 'walls where they are sited so they cannot be exposed to fire'. Different ratios of cement, sand and aggregate were stipulated for different parts of the pillbox dependent on perceived areas of vulnerability. It is doubtful whether the prospective occupants were as confident in their predictions. Out in the field, local initiative was encouraged. Fred Bowman, a senior engineer with John Mowlem & Co, the group contractor for much of the south-east of England, disliked the official War Office design (DFW3/24) for a hexagonal pillbox and decided that for speed of construction, circular shuttering, made of sheets of steel plate would be better. A production line was set up, a gang of steel fixers assembled and work took off. As it happened, there was a thatcher on the workforce and he was able to camouflage some of the more prominent pillboxes, albeit only temporarily on those surrounded by hungry cows.

THE DEFENCE OF AIRFIELDS

We have seen how the life of the pillbox, in terms of its place in the anti-invasion measures, was quite short. The majority were built between May 1940 and spring 1941, and by early 1942, they were out of favour. This was partly because the fear of seaborne invasion was more-or-less over, partly because the tactics of the defenders had changed, and partly because the intensive munitions production of the intervening months had secured greater mobility for the army. It is worth noting that the German army was still standing by in France to carry out the invasion of England until being officially stood down on 13 February 1942, and the inter-Service committee of the Allied Chiefs of Staff, charged with second-guessing the Sealion planners, continued to meet well into 1942. If there was a certain amount of relief from that particular anxiety, there remained, however, the nagging problem of attack from the air. Ever since the airborne assault on Fort Eben Emael, a similar attack on Britain, on a far greater scale, had been half-expected. Amongst a whole range of precautions was the ground defence of airfields. In September 1940, Major-General Taylor, Inspector-General of Fortification at the War Office was invited to formulate a policy for the defence of airfields. This was something about which the Air Ministry had some preliminary thoughts, and it was Air Marshall Portal's contention that airfields should be given defences on the basis of location rather than function. This was a notion which had Taylor's full support, so the prime criterion became proximity to a port. The only category of airfield to enjoy Class 1 status (the highest) without meeting this criterion was the dozen or so Aircraft Storage Units, since it was absolutely essential that the stock of replacement aircraft be safe-guarded. Taylor prescribed a comprehensive package. A Class 1 airfield should have 12-18 pillboxes facing outwards to repel a ground attack, and a further 8-14 facing inwards to defend against one from the air. There should be a trio of the 'disappearing' Pickett-Hamilton forts, plenty of fieldworks, dual-purpose AA guns and armoured vehicles, the latter often homemade. The garrison would be 200-300 regular troops, supplemented by details of RAF personnel and, later on, detachments of Home Guardsmen. The whole defence operation would be co-ordinated from a purpose-built Battle Headquarters (BHQ) equipped with telecommunications and runners (Air Ministry drawing number 11008/41). Later on in the War, it was accepted that the linear defences proposed by Taylor might be better replaced by the concept of the defended locality, but where these were adopted, the pillbox remained a key component, and some of the, now redundant, earlier ones had their operational lives extended as decoy dummy pillboxes.

OTHER HARDENED DEFENCES

Apart from pillboxes, emplacements for field guns or AT guns and BHQs, there are a number of other specialist structures which will concern us here. Both the army and the RAF Regiment designed concrete trenches, L-shaped, V-shaped, W-shaped, as straight lengths, or in hollow squares. These were able to hold up to a dozen or more men and were known as section posts in the army context, or seagull trenches on airfields where a birds-eye-view was more likely. As the Home Guard acquired more weapons and munitions it became necessary to provide secure storage and pairs of explosives and inflammables stores were built in places convenient to their users. The defences of ports invariably included electrically-operated minefields, which were controlled by the Extended Defence Officer from a dedicated, often defensible, building, hence the EXDO post. A range of vulnerable points such as dockyards, ordnance factories, store depots or magazines needed some measure of protection from saboteurs or raids, so various defensible guard-posts were developed for such contexts. Finally, there were the open pits, concrete with built-in expense lockers, which housed either 6 pounder QF Hotchkiss guns, or, much more numerously, spigot mortars. Chapters 5 and 6 will examine this whole range of structures in individual detail, but before that it is instructive to see where else pillboxes were used in the course of the Second World War and what form they took.

GERMAN FORTIFICATIONS ON THE ATLANTIC COAST AND IN ITALY

The most prolific builder of fortifications during the Second World War was Germany. The Atlantic Wall – the Reich's defence against invasion – stretched from Norway, around the coasts of Jutland, past Hamburg and Amsterdam, and along the Belgian and French coasts to the Spanish border at Biarritz. The Channel Islands were heavily fortified, and there were extensions of the defences along the French Mediterranean coast. The building of the Atlantic Wall, which had started off in an ad hoc way with piecemeal developments proceeding independently and carried out by military personnel, was by December 1941 being approached with industrial efficiency and carried out, often using slave labour, by what became known as the Organisation Todt (OT). As in the West Wall, which we have already seen, a standardised collection of designs was used, but on a far greater scale. Despite continuing problems over co-ordination, by September 1942, there was a grand plan for 15,000 bunkers to be manned by 300,000 troops, with the necessary work to have been completed in May 1943. In the two years from mid-1942, the OT used over 13 million cubic metres of concrete and nearly a million and a quarter tonnes of steel. There were almost 250 individual designs of specific structure. These were allocated numbers in sequence which related to the service involved – army, navy or air force – and the date of origin. However, it has been pointed out that much of this numbering is virtually arbitrary and it is dangerous to think in terms of type development over time referenced by these numbers. Some designs from early on were superseded by better ones but later on, speed of build became a more important criterion than solidity and weaker designs were resurrected, modified and given new numbers later in the sequence. Many of these structures, such as the massive casemates for 280 and 380mm (11 and 15in) guns were monumental, but others, like the humble Tobruk shelter were quite tiny. Structures such as the fire-control towers on Jersey and Guernsey, or at Battery Karola on the Ile de Re, were quite sculptural and inspired the Brutalist school of architecture. Concrete thicknesses varied from 1.2m to 2.2m (4ft to 7ft 2in) in army works, whilst the navy preferred everything to be 2m or 3.5m (6ft 6in or 11ft 5in) thick.

Identifying those Atlantic Wall structures which fall into this present overview must, of necessity, involve some measure of arbitrary selection. If we take the largest pillbox of

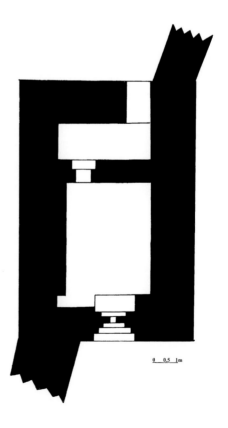

65 German type 676 emplacement for a 47mm AT gun, often integrated into an AT wall in coastal defences

66   Roquaine Bay, Jersey, CI; casemate for 47mm PAK AT gun

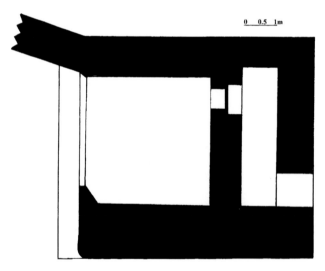

67   German type 667 casemate for a 50mm AT gun enfilading a beach

British origin, the so-called Banstead Fort, as marking an upper size limit, then anything smaller than its 40 x 32ft (12.2 x 9.75m) footprint, combined with the other defining characteristic of defensibility, gives us only 20 types we can really describe as pillboxes. We can add in the several types of Tobruk stand, whether in its simple original state (Type L581 or 58c) or designed as a machine-gun mounting (Ringstand, Type 67), or for mounting a tank-turret (Panzerstellung), or as a mortar emplacement. These generally measured around 20ft x 8-10ft (6m x 3m), although the two latter are larger. Of our 20 qualifying designs, seven are machine-gun bunkers intended for enfilading fire and mainly in the 600 series with the thickest concrete. Two of these were equipped with steel turrets

68 Bleriot Plage, Pas de Calais, France; a German, two-man, pre-fabricated pillbox, possibly added to existing defences prior to D-Day

for light machine-guns. Five are for enfilading 47mm or 50mm AT guns and are, again, from the 600 series (*65* & *66*). The remaining eight, from both the 600 and 700 series, are all designed as artillery casemates: for pedestal mounted guns, for field guns, or for 75mm or 88mm guns in enfilading positions. These standard types were built in large numbers and can be found along the entire length of the Atlantic Wall. Almost 400 Type 612 field-gun casemates, over 200 Type 630 machine-gun bunkers, over 400 Type 667 bunkers (*67*) for 50mm AT guns and over 200 Type 671 machine-gun bunkers were built, towards the end of the war, in 1944, when the defences were given their final strengthening prior to the expected Allied invasion. At this point a variety of new elements were introduced, including a small pre-fabricated pillbox (*68*). A smaller, flat-topped version was used on the Eastern Front and bunkers were built all over the occupied territories to guard railways from sabotage by partisans or commandos.

As well as the enormous effort put into the Atlantic Wall, the German military was responsible for the construction of fortifications of a permanent, or semi-permanent, nature in many other theatres, particularly in Italy (*69*) and on the eastern front. As the Allies advanced up the Italian mainland throughout 1943 and 1944, after the Italian surrender which allowed German troops to fill the resulting vacuum, they were constantly halted by defence lines. These lines are often referred to generically as the Gothic Line, this being one of the best-known. There were, however, at least 25 lines running east-west across the whole, or a part of the peninsular, from the Caesar, the Gustav and the O Lines for instance, between Salerno and Rome, to the Dora, the Anton, the Heinrich and the Green Lines farther north. Fourteen separate lines defended the coastal plain between Ancona and the mouth of the Po, each running from the mountains to the sea,

69 Cagliari, Sardinia, Italy; one of a chain of pillboxes overlooking possible landing beaches

mainly along river valleys. Whilst many of these defences were able to utilise existing Italian pillboxes, German engineers added new concrete machine-gun emplacements and solidly-built fieldworks. They also introduced some innovative ideas which caused problems for the attacking troops, especially when sited in difficult mountainous terrain. One was the use of tank turrets, many from obsolete models, mounted on steel boxes covered in concrete. Whilst many of the guns in these turrets were of small calibre, nearly 50 Panther turrets with 75mm guns were installed. In addition, the OT designed revolving steel hoods to hold machine-guns. The second new addition to the German defensive armoury was the *Abwehrflammenwerfer*, an adaptation of a Russian flamethrower, consisting of small buried fuel tanks feeding nozzles which, ignited remotely, could throw out a jet of flame reaching 50m and lasting for up to 10 seconds. The third invention was the MG Panzernest, an armoured steel capsule sunk into a pit leaving only the upper part exposed. It had a crew of two and was armed with a machine-gun.

German fieldworks were codified in 1943 in a handbook circulated to all German forces. This includes a number of semi-permanent machine-gun bunkers constructed from logs, sandbags laid in bond, rubble and rock infill, and earth covering. One overriding feature of all these designs is the emphasis placed on concealment, achieved by both camouflage and the use of natural materials and also by using simple techniques such as lift-up flaps over embrasures. Many of these installations, like many of their concrete cousins, were intended to give enfilading fire. These fieldworks, along with similar constructions for AT guns or field guns, were used on their own, or to complement those in concrete. The use of tank turrets was also widespread, and many captured French ones, particularly Renault models, may be seen on the Atlantic Wall.

JAPANESE FORTIFICATIONS

Despite having developed a military policy of mobility and a temperamental antipathy to the whole notion of defence, Japan, by 1943, was forced to acknowledge the need to consolidate the borders of its newly-acquired Empire. Great reliance was placed on hardened defences, particularly on the many Pacific islands which were vital as airfields and naval bases, but also vulnerable to attack. There were many similarities between Japanese and German fieldworks, maybe because there were German advisers around at the time that many of the defences were constructed.

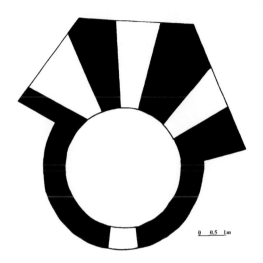

70 Japanese domed bunker for three machine-guns, employed to defend Pacific islands; plan after Denfeld

The prevailing philosophy at first allowed only for the construction of anti-invasion beach defences, but as allied troops got nearer to Japan, fortifications became stronger, more sophisticated and were provided to greater depths. Hardened defences were represented by concrete machine-gun pillboxes (*70*) and casemates for field guns. Many of the pillboxes were sited for enfilade fire (*71*), whilst the casemates were designed for bringing direct fire onto landing-craft. It made sense in terms of availability of construction expertise, camouflage and exploitation of the terrain to construct fieldworks out of coconut logs, coral and other plentiful local materials. Coupled with a widespread use of tunnels, the techniques of building well-hidden weapons positions paid off. The US marines found it extremely difficult to dislodge determined defenders from such positions and suffered crippling casualties each time they tried. One of the more unusual structures (*72*) was a hexagonal, steel pillbox with two machine-gun ports and an opening roof-hatch. It was made of inner and outer skins of quarter-inch (6mm) steel plate, with the resultant 12in (30cm)

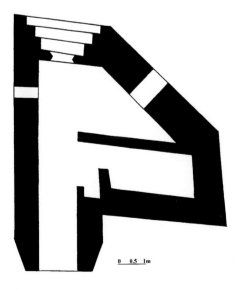

71 Japanese flanking emplacement for 20mm cannon; plan after Denfeld

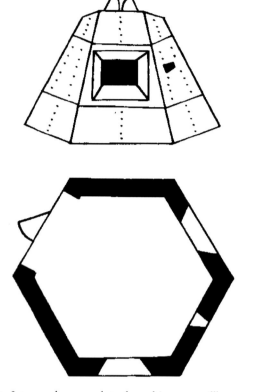

cavity filled with sand. The walls sloped inward at 15 degrees, and sometimes the top was capped with a 12in thick (30cm) layer of concrete. Examples were found on only a few islands, but proved troublesome since they could only be destroyed by shell-fire.

PILLBOXES IN NEUTRAL COUNTRIES

Spain

Somewhat surprisingly, given the parlous state in which she found herself after the crippling Civil War, Spain invested its meagre resources in fortifications during the years of the Second World War. After Operation Dragoon, the allied invasion of the French Mediterranean coast in August 1944, General Franco was

72 Japanese hexagonal steel machine-gun pillbox used in defending beaches on Pacific islands; plan and elevation after Rottman

73 Catalonia, Spain; boomerang-shaped pillbox between St Pere Pescador and l'Armentera on Franco's northern defence line

74 La Linea, Andalucia, Spain; a Spanish pillbox facing toward Gibraltar

concerned that, in view of the support he had given the Axis powers, Spain would be invaded by the Allies. Consequently a line of pillboxes was constructed across the full width of the country just to the south of the Pyrenees (*73*). At the same time, the Balearic Islands were provided with pillboxes to defend potential invasion beaches. Many of these are still visible both on the beaches of Mallorca and Menorca, and to the north of Girona. Many of these pillboxes are circular, in the same style as some of those built earlier across the isthmus at La Linea to seal off access to Gibraltar (*74*). They have domed roofs over wide machine-gun embrasures. Some are incorporated into larger structures and, particularly on the islands, they are given a skin of local rock as camouflage.

Eire

The Republic of Ireland took a number of measures to defend itself against any anticipated German attack aimed at using Eire as a jumping-off point for a seaborne attack on the British mainland, or an attack across the border on Northern Ireland. It would appear that a number of standard pillbox designs were obtained from the War Office DFW3 and used by the Irish military to secure the south-eastern coastal areas in counties Wicklow, Wexford and Waterford. Certainly remains of pillboxes may be seen above Rosslare Harbour (Co. Wexford), but not recognisable as being of British design. A defensive line of pillboxes was established along the south banks of the rivers Blackwater and Boyne, continuing westwards to Carrick-on-Shannon and the Curlew Mountains beyond. Some 40-odd pillboxes have been identified in the Boyne group and many survive (*75*). They are square or trapezoidal, not particularly strong, and provided with two, or sometimes three, generous loopholes. Several have detached protective walls, but not associated with entrances. Although they conform to a very simple design of pillbox, akin to the

75 Beaulieu, Drogheda,
Co. Louth, Eire; pillbox
on the banks of the
River Boyne, built as
part of the Republic's
defences to preserve its
neutrality

76 Monasterevin, Co. Kildare, Eire; pillbox built into the bridge-parapet to defend a crossing of
the River Barrow, on the old road from Dublin to Limerick

DFW3/26, there is nothing that would confirm that design as their origin. Other nodal points, further south, were also defended (*76*). The eighteenth century Magazine Fort in Dublin's Phoenix Park has had concrete pillboxes or raised musketry-walls added to the corner bastions (*77*). Whilst some of this refortification no doubt dates to the troubles of 1916, at least one pillbox appears of much later date. More, it is reported, are to be seen around Cork, most likely in the vicinity of the forts defending the Queenstown Harbour entrance, Forts Camden and Carlisle (since renamed). At Fort Camden a two-storey structure with a wide observation slit and an L-shaped loopholed wall may be seen, and these may represent defences associated with the updating of earlier works in the programme of building to preserve neutrality. Fort Shannon, a new work built in 1942, west of Tarbert Island, to defend the Estuary, mounts two 6-inch (150mm) coast defence guns in concrete emplacements with overhead cover. On the shore, a close-defence pillbox has three lmg mountings on concrete pillars behind its loopholes (*78* & *79*). This pillbox is camouflaged by stone cladding applied to its top half, whilst three others are built into the landward perimeter, which is disguised as a dry-stone field-wall.

77 Magazine Fort, Phoenix Park, Dublin; a hexagonal pillbox added to an eighteenth-century bastion; other bastions have earlier loopholed walls built on them, but this structure appears to date from the time of the Second World War

78 Fort Shannon, Ardmore Point, Co. Kerry, Eire; a pillbox built for the close-defence of this 1942 coastal defence battery

79 Fort Shannon, Ardmore Point, Co. Kerry, Eire; an interior view of *79* showing the pillars with mountings for lmgs

5

PILLBOX TYPOLOGY

INTRODUCTION

This typology is an attempt to categorise as many as possible of the many designs of pillbox, field-gun emplacement and allied structures developed in the British Isles in the Second World War. The present writer's first shot at this (see *Loopholes 3-6 & 8*, 1993-4) was based on known drawing numbers and their variations. Henry Wills' pioneering work in the early 1980s first drew attention to a range of numbered designs issued by the Fortification and Works department of the War Office (DFW3) in 1940. The work of Dr Colin Dobinson has provided a clearer explanation of the status of these official designs, showing that they were simply a suite of drawings from which both RE officers in the field and building contractors could draw, in order to produce effective hardened defences which had been given an official seal of approval. They also made some degree of mass-production possible, either through the pre-fabrication of loopholes, or the serial reuse of wooden shuttering. Moreover, some of these designs came about through the need to accommodate specific weapons. This official output, however, was only part of the story, and many designs in use had no connection to those that the DFW3 promoted. This typology, then, will be based on classification by shape. It takes as its skeleton the taxonomy first put forward by the present writer in Appendix 1 of *Defending Britain* (2004, Tempus), taking the opportunity of this present, more specialised work, to flesh it out more thoroughly, making some necessary modifications. Thus, for instance, we will deal with hexagonal designs, first bullet-proof, i.e. with wall-thickness in the range 12-24in (30-61cm), then shell-proof, of wall-thickness 25-54in (62-137cm), some of which will be from DFW3, whilst others will be from more local sources. The majority of examples included here are all based on the author's fieldwork observation and any references or information from other supplementary sources are included with the relevant entry.

All the known designs are included where either drawings exist or examples have been identified in the field. Attempts have been made to match known designs with standing remains, for instance CRE Eastern Command's three Colchester designs, widely-used on the Eastern Command Line. Such efforts still leave a number of instances where references to design numbers exist but no plans are known. This is true of drawing numbers DFW3/30, 31, 33, 45 and 46, South Eastern Command's 124/41, and Scottish Command's 2717. It may be that no examples of any of these were ever built. Owing to the way in which official drawings were produced and numbered, it is also quite possible that these numbers refer simply to modifications of existing designs, even something as simple as the addition of a blast-wall, or the insertion of an additional loophole. Papers are still being discovered, and maybe, one day, we will know. It could mean that hitherto unascribed examples on the ground will receive an official identity, or it might mean that local modifications can be retrospectively legitimated.

The word *survive* is relative. Examples are described as surviving, based on the fact that they have been visited and photographed by the present writer sometime in the last few years. Given the accelerated assault on brown-field sites by developers, it is inevitable that some at least of these examples will have been demolished in recent years.

Many of the plans included are quite sketchy and are intended to give some notion of scale for comparison purposes, and to show the wide variety of designs constructed. They must not, therefore, be regarded as the measured drawings of architects.

I. BULLET–PROOF PILLBOXES IN THE SHAPE OF REGULAR HEXAGONS

These are often thought of as the archetypal pillbox, since they are often the ones seen in isolated situations guarding road-junctions or long-vanished searchlight sites. The DFW3 drawing number 22 may be the basis for many of the similar designs found, but, as we have already seen, there have been many similar predecessors.

NB: all hexagonal pillboxes will be described numbering the base (usually, but not always, containing the entrance) as 1, and the other five faces clockwise through to 6.

1a. pillbox to drawing number: DFW3/22
A simple, standard design for the protection of a point; also used as a second line behind e.g. GHQ Line, particularly in Eastern Command.

The DFW3/22 has rifle-loops in five faces (2-6), and either one or two pistol-loops in the rear (1) to protect the entrance; sometimes the entrance is sunken, with a rifle-loop above, or it may be protected by a porch, or a full-height, or half-height blast-wall; internally there may be weapon-rests at the loopholes and, usually, there is a Y-shaped or cruciform AR wall. Other variations include: loophole shape, presence of shutters (in wood, steel or asbestos) or doors, presence of AT-rifle loop at low level, external buttresses to height of loophole; enlarged embrasure and table to hold a machine gun. Construction is usually in concrete, shuttered with wood or corrugated iron (removed), or brick (in situ). For camouflage it may be dazzle-painted, have earth heaped on the roof, have concrete sand-castles on the roof, or a wavy roof-line. The pillbox may be sunken, or raised on a raft or platform; many thousands of these were built.

Dimensions:
all sides: 7ft 6in (2m) externally and 6ft (1.8m) internally; wall-thickness 12-15in (30-38cm) height 7ft 6in (2.3m); thickness of roof-slab 12in (30cm)
Examples surviving are widespread, over 1000 were logged by the DoB Project:
TL487047 (RAF North Weald, Essex)

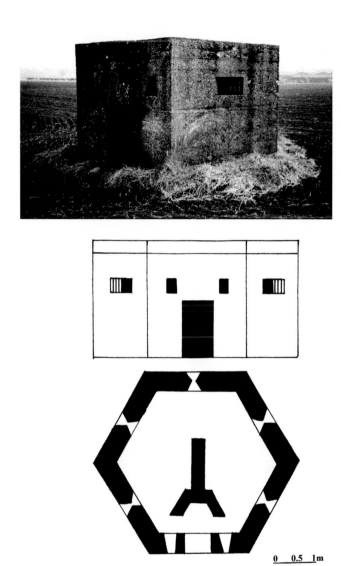

80 Knipton, Leicestershire (SK819300) **1a**; hexagonal, bullet-proof pillbox to drawing number DFW3/22

SK819300 (Knipton, Leics) (*80*)
TM164470 (Ipswich, Suffolk)
TF547742 (Hogsthorpe, Lincs) (*82*)
TL929270 (River Colne, Essex) (*81*)

Refs: fieldwork & DFW3 drawing 19.05.1940

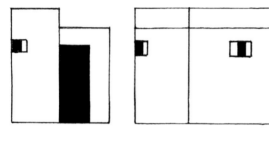

81 River Colne, Essex
(TL929270) **1a**; hexagonal,
bullet-proof pillbox with
integral porch; basically
to drawing number
DFW3/22

1b. pillboxes with upper storeys

There are a number of instances of pillboxes being given a roof-top fighting platform,
probably for a LAA mg; these are often on airfields, but also in other locations; many
characteristics are shared with **1a** but access to the roof provides the alternatives of
external stairs, or vertical rungs set in the wall.

Dimensions: as per **1a** but height is 10ft 6-12in (3.2m-3.7m)

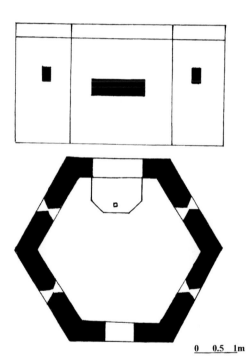

82 Hogsthorpe, Lincolnshire
(TF547742) **1a**; hexagonal,
bullet-proof pillbox
with machine-gun table
& enlarged embrasure,
basically to drawing number
DFW3/22

0   0.5   1m

Examples survive at:
NU238005 (Acklington, Northumberland) *(83)*
TF397424 (Freiston Shore, Lincs)
NZ465157 (Thornaby-on-Tees, N Yorks) *(84)*
SE388716 (Dishforth, North Yorks)
At Canewdon (Essex) and Hawkinge (Kent) there are open emplacements for 20mm AA
cannon superimposed on the roof and walled in brick.

Ref: fieldwork, John Harding, David Burridge

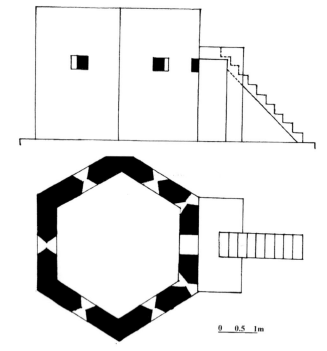

83 Acklington, Northumberland (NU238005) **1b**; hexagonal, bullet-proof pillbox with open upper storey accessed by staircase over porch; basically to drawing number DFW3/22

1c. pillbox with 6 loopholes and sunken entrance

This is found on airfields and represents a bullet-proof version of **3aii**; in the base (1) of some examples the door is to one side with the loophole to the other.

Dimensions: all sides 8ft (2.4m); wall-thickness of 18in (46cm); thickness of roof-slab is 12in (30cm)

Examples survive at:

SK154118 (Lichfield, Staffs) (*85*)

SU542773, 548780 & 547768 (Hampstead Norreys, Berks) (*86*)

TL067311, 073314 & 067318 (Barton-le-Clay, Bedfordshire)

TL912894 & 911893 (East Wretham, Norfolk) pistol-loop beside door

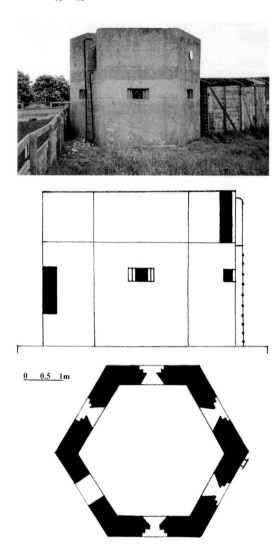

84 Thornaby-on-Tees, North Yorkshire (NZ465157) **1b**; hexagonal, bullet-proof pillbox with open upper storey accessed by external rungs set in wall; basically to drawing number DFW3/22

1d. pillboxes with irregular loophole provision

Whilst a number of pillboxes, notably in Kent and Suffolk are provided with low-level loops for Boys AT rifles, just two known examples survive of a design which places two rifle loopholes, one above the other in opposite or adjacent faces, 3 & 6 or 5 & 6.

Dimensions: as per DFW3/22

Examples survive at:
TL093862 & 091872 (Polebrook, Northants) (*87*)

1e. pillbox with corner loopholes

This pillbox is unique, in that its six loopholes are all placed in the corners rather than the faces; it has an internal corridor round a 12-sided central platform for a LAA mg.

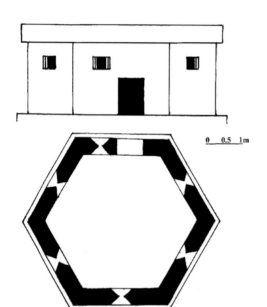

Left 85 Lichfield, Staffordshire (SK154118) **1c**; hexagonal, bullet-proof pillbox with six loopholes and low entrance

Below 86 Hampstead Norreys, Berkshire (SU548780) **1c**; hexagonal, bullet-proof pillbox with low door under central loophole

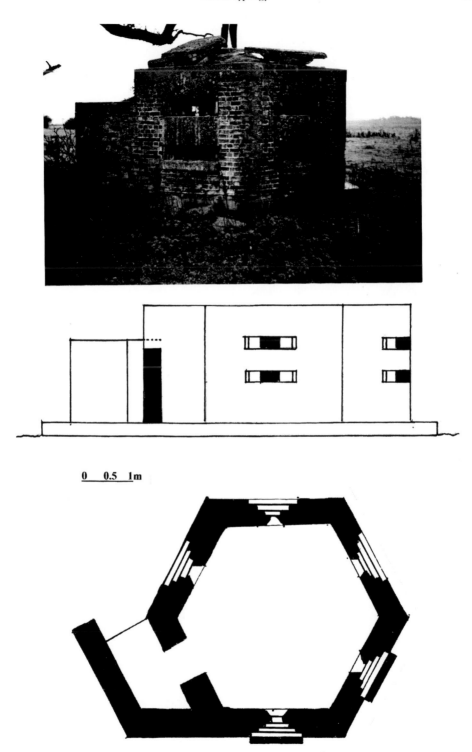

87 Polebrook, Northamptonshire (TL093862) **1d**; hexagonal, bullet-proof pillbox with irregular loophole layout

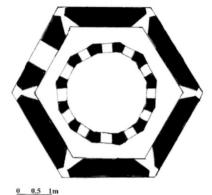

0   0.5   1m

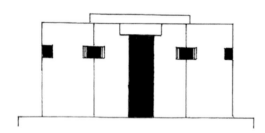

88 Brooklands, Surrey (TQ070630) **1e**; hexagonal, bullet-proof pillbox with six loopholes in the angles and an internal corridor around a central platform for a LAA mounting

Dimensions: all sides 8ft 6in (2.6m); height 8ft (2.4m); wall-thickness 18in (46cm)

Only known example at:
TQ070630 (Brooklands, Surrey) (*88*)

1fi and 1fii. Eastern Command Line pillboxes (?) CRE1094

These are expanded versions of DFW3/22 designed by the CRE at Chelmsford, for use on the Eastern Command Line in Essex and Suffolk. There are also examples of the **1fi** in parts of the GHQ Line East where it is used as a second line of defence. It has six loopholes, sometimes fitted with steel plates, intended for use by Bren lmgs. **1fi** is a conventional pillbox with a Y-shaped AR screen, whilst **1fii** has an internal corridor and central raised platform for a LAA mg; both versions have a half-height porch with a stepped roof and loophole above. Almost all surviving examples are shuttered in wood, leaving clean, concrete surfaces to a high standard of finish; several dozen of each were constructed.

Dimensions: all sides are of 9ft 9in (3m) and wall-thickness of 15in (38cm)

Examples survive at:
1fi TL897285 (Wakes Colne, Essex) (*89*)
TL701135 (Langleys, Essex)
TL905340 (Bures, Essex)
TL901546 (Cockfield, Suffolk), plan (*90*)
1fii TL884599 (Great Welnethan, Suffolk)
TL856650 (Bury St Edmunds, Suffolk)
TL896559 (Oldhall Green, Suffolk) (*91*, *92* and plan *93*);

Refs: fieldwork & WO166/333 via Dobinson

89 Wakes Colne, Essex (TL897285) **1fi**; hexagonal, bullet-proof pillbox with larger dimensions than the DFW3/22, and possibly an example of the CRE Colchester **1094** design

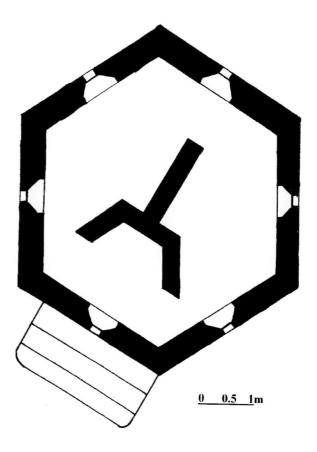

90 Plan of hexagonal pillbox possibly to CRE **1094** design **1fi** (*89*)

0   0.5 1m

91 Oldhall Green, Suffolk (TL896559) **1fii**; hexagonal pillbox with central platform for LAA mounting, possibly to CRE **1094** design

92 Oldhall Green, Suffolk (TL896559) **1fii**; close-up of LAA mount (*91*)

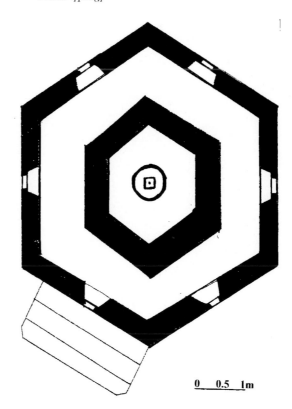

93 Plan of hexagonal pillbox
possibly to CRE 1094 design **1fii**
(*91*)

0 0.5 1m

1g. pillbox

Found only on RAF West Raynham where there were six or seven, of which several
remain; this pillbox is small enough to fit inside the DFW3/22 making the interior
diagonal barely 6ft (1.8m); it has an entrance covered by a full-height blast-wall in one
face and loopholes in faces 2-6. In one example the door has been blocked up, maybe to
produce a dummy or decoy pillbox.

Dimensions: all sides 5ft 6in (1.68m); wall-thickness 18in (61cm); the thickness of the
roof-slab is 21in (53cm); height 6ft 9in (2.1m)

Examples at:
TF837251, 844239 (*94*), 841255, 848251 & 858251

Ref: fieldwork, Simon Purcell and Peter Kent

1h. pillbox with protected entrance

Several examples exist on the Lincolnshire coast of pillboxes based on **1a**, but with
integral porches, some at Gibraltar Point, with low entrances and sloping roofs, others,
near Sutton Bridge, with full-height porches; they have between three and five loopholes,
some with Turnbull mounts.

94 West Raynham, Norfolk (TF844239) **1g**; hexagonal, bullet-proof pillbox with smaller dimensions than DFW3/22

Examples at:

TF486209 & 491208 (Sutton Bridge)

TF556582 & 560578 (Gibraltar Point)

1hi. pillbox based on 1h

Two examples remain of another design of pillbox with protected entrance; it has six loopholes, with an entrance to the end of one face, covered by a dog-legged porch. It appears that an additional thickness of concrete, shuttered in four courses of bricks, has been added to the original roof-slab. There is a 3-leaved, cantilevered AR screen.

Dimensions: all sides 9ft 6in (2.9m); wall-thickness 15in (38cm); thickness of the roof-slab 21in (53cm)

Examples remain at:

SS967717 & 967719 (Llandow, Glamorgan) (95)

1j. skirted bullet-proof pillbox

This pillbox is found only in the coastal defences of Holland Haven between Holland-on-Sea and Frinton in Essex. Essentially it is similar to **1a**, but has a thick skirt wrapped around up to loophole height; access is by a tunnel which runs through this skirt. Some are free-standing and some are perched on top of the sea-wall; the design may derive from **1fi**, as the tunnel entry and the stepping on the roof are similar, as is the finish.

Dimensions: as per DFW3/22, with 15in (38cm) wall thickness and a 4in-thick (1.2m) skirt, with stepped roof

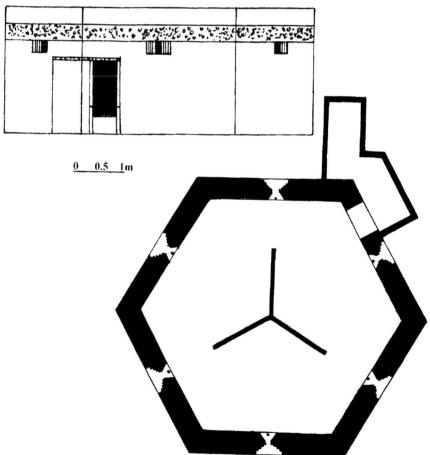

0   0.5   1m

95 Llandow, Glamorgan (SS967717) **1hi**; hexagonal, bullet-proof pillbox with protected entrance

96 Holland Haven, Essex (TM220174) **1j**; hexagonal, bullet-proof pillbox with skirt to loophole height, containing tunnel entry

Examples at:

TM220174 (Holland Haven, Essex) free-standing (*96*)

TM224178 (Holland Haven) on sea-wall

1ji. skirted bullet-proof pillbox

One of the ways of strengthening pillboxes, particularly at RAF establishments, was to thicken the lower walls up to loophole height, inserting an entrance at one corner.

Dimensions as per DFW3/22 plus 30in (76cm) skirt

Examples at:

TL644660, 659657 (*97*) and 662659 (Snailwell, Cambridgeshire)

1jii. skirted bullet-proof pillbox

At least four pillboxes at Bawdsey have been strengthened by building a retaining wall of brick or concrete sandbags about 3ft (90cm) from the base of the wall and about 3ft (90cm) in height, and in-filling with earth, sand, concrete and rubble.

Examples at:

TM335382, 333380, 343386 and 342385 (Bawdsey, Suffolk)

1ki and 1kii pillboxes with open annexe

Two very similar pillboxes are found in quite different locations; **1ki** is used for the defence of three Bedfordshire airfields, it has a square, open enclosure adjoining the entrance face, presumably for a LAA mg, with its entrance protected by a low blast-wall; **1kii** is found as

97 Snailwell, Cambridgeshire (TL659657) **1ji**; hexagonal, bullet-proof pillbox with skirt added to loophole height and tunnel entry

part of the coast defences of the Walton-on-the-Naze area. It has a similar layout, is slightly smaller with a thick, concrete skirt around it, similar to **1j** nearby; from the annexe, steps lead down into the body of the pillbox; there are steel shutters in the loopholes.

Dimensions: **1ki** has sides of 8ft 6in (2.6m); wall-thickness 18in (46cm)
1kii has sides of 7ft (2.1m); wall-thickness 15in (38cm)

Examples:
1ki   TL078464 (Cardington, Beds) (*99* and plan *100*)
        SP942411 & 938414 (Cranfield, Beds)
        TL166381 (Henlow, Beds)
1kii   TM267237 & 267238 (Walton, Essex) (*98*)

Refs: **1kii** fieldwork; **1ki** Fred Nash

1m. pillbox
This is very similar to a DFW3/22 but slightly larger and with a sixth loop over a tunnel entry; two examples guard a HAA site.

Dimensions: all sides 9ft (2.7m); wall-thickness 18in (46cm)

Examples survive at:
TQ532773 & 530774 (Slade Green, Kent) (*101*)

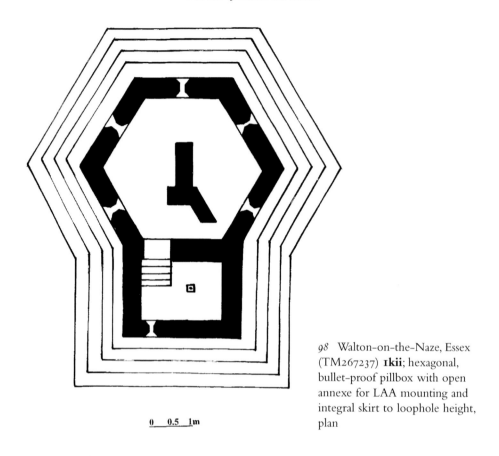

0   0.5   1m

98 Walton-on-the-Naze, Essex
(TM267237) **1kii**; hexagonal,
bullet-proof pillbox with open
annexe for LAA mounting and
integral skirt to loophole height,
plan

99 Cardington, Bedfordshire (TL078464) **1ki**; hexagonal, bullet-proof pillbox with open annexe
for LAA mounting

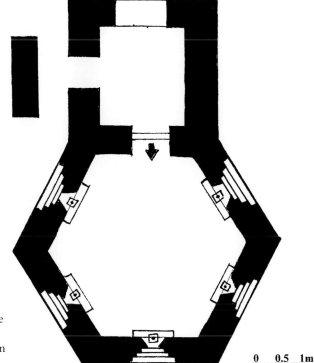

100 Cardington, Bedfordshire (TL078464) **1ki**; hexagonal, bullet-proof pillbox with open annexe for LAA mounting

0   0.5   1m

1n. three-storey pillbox

Basically three DFW3/22 pillboxes piled one on top of the others; doorway in ground-floor; two other storeys each with six loopholes, rising to 22' (6.7m) in height.

Example at SS916794 (Bridgend, Glamorgan) (*102*)

1p. pillbox constructed of concrete sandbags

This example from Orkney is built of about 15 courses of concrete sandbags with six pre-cast loopholes and a concrete roof-slab; it has a very low entrance under a loop.

Dimensions as per **1a**

Example at HY430118 (Kirkwall, Orkney) (*103*)

2 BULLET-PROOF PILLBOXES IN THE SHAPE OF IRREGULAR HEXAGONS

As in the previous section, a DFW3 design, here drawing number DFW3/24, forms the basis for some of the examples in this section, but most have quite individual characteristics.

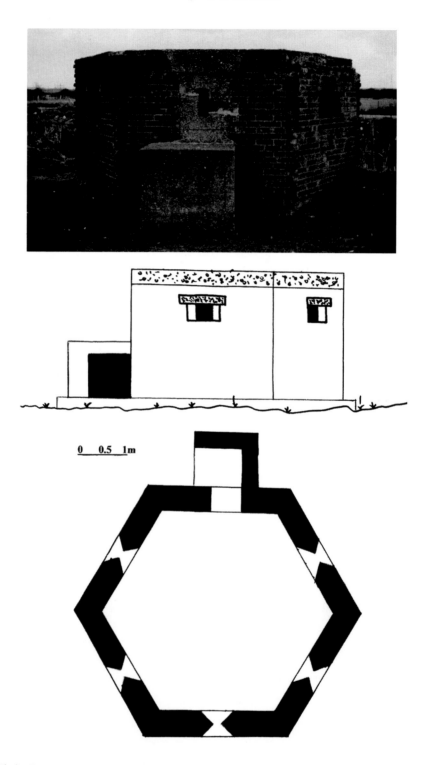

101 Slade Green, Kent (TQ532773) **1m**; hexagonal, bullet-proof pillbox with larger dimensions than the DFW3/22, and a low, covered entry; a pair of them guard this HAA site

102 Bridgend, Glamorgan
(SS916794) **1n**; three hexagonal,
bullet-proof pillboxes, to the
dimensions of the DFW3/22
design, stacked vertically

103 Kirkwall, Orkney mainland (HY430118) **1p**; hexagonal, bullet-proof pillbox constructed
from concrete sandbags

2a. pillbox

This design appears to be based on the DFW3/22, but in a truncated and reduced form; sides 2 and 6 are shortened, and have no loopholes; a longer base has two pistol loops and a low entrance; it is fairly common in Northumberland.

Dimensions: side 1 is 14ft (4.3m); sides 2 and 6 are 3ft 6in (1.07m); sides 3, 4 and 5 are 7ft (2.1m); wall-thickness 15in (38cm)

Examples survive at:
NU089124 (A697 crossing of R. Aln) (*104* & *105*)
NU234253 (High Newton)
NU253199 (Craster
NU179355 (Bamburgh)

2ai. variant of 2a

Here the entrance has been moved to side 6, and an extended AR screen with a loop to cover the entrance has been inserted; no loops in side 1. This particular example is shuttered in corrugated iron sheets.

Dimensions: as per **2a**

Example survives at:
NU064428 (Holy Island Causeway) (*106*)

104 River Aln, Northumberland, crossing of A697, (NU089124) **2a**; hexagonal pillbox with shortened sides and three loopholes

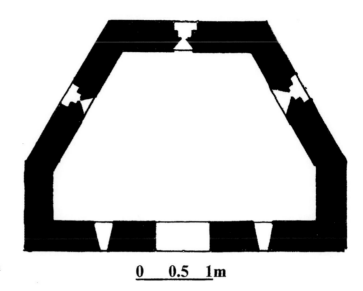

105 River Aln,
Northumberland, plan
of **2a** (*104*)

0   0.5   1m

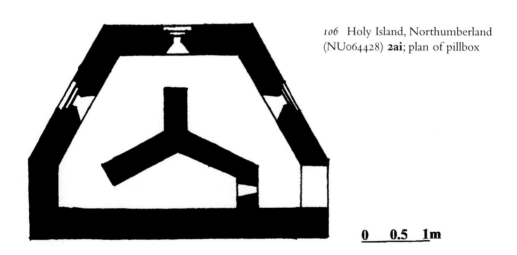

106 Holy Island, Northumberland
(NU064428) **2ai**; plan of pillbox

0   0.5   1m

2aii. variant of 2a

A group of a dozen pillboxes defending the Moray coast have three loopholes each in
their seaward faces. Entrances are either in the rear face, or in either of the rear corners,
sometimes defended by an integral porch, giving four alternative designs.

Dimensions: 5 sides 7ft (2.1m); rear wall 14ft (4.2m); wall-thickness 15in (38cm)

Examples at:
NJ055646, 065645, 044645 etc. (Findhorn Bay, Moray)

2aiii. variant of 2a

This airfield pillbox has three lmg loopholes in forward-facing walls, and a low entrance in the rear wall.

Dimensions: side 1 is 20ft (6m); sides 2 & 6 are 4ft (1.22m); sides 3, 4 & 5 are 12ft (3.6m); wall-thickness 24in (61cm)

Example at:
SJ581108 (Atcham, Shropshire)

Refs: fieldwork, Bernard Lowry

2aiv. variant of 2a

Backing onto a bridge parapet, this pillbox has a loophole in each of three forward-facing sides (3-5), blank faces in sides 2 and 6, an entrance in side 2 and three loopholes in the rear face which overlook the roadway of the bridge.

Dimensions: side 1 is 18ft (5.5m); sides 2 & 6 are 5ft (1.6m); sides 3 & 5 are 7ft 6in (2.3m); side 4 is 8ft 6in (2.6m); wall-thickness 18in (46cm)

Example at:
NT729337 (Kelso, Roxburghshire)

Refs: fieldwork and *Buildings of Scotland: Borders*

2b. pillbox to drawing number DFW3/24

This design was issued in May 1940 and represents the most commonly built of all; it was widely used on the GHQ Line East and on other Command Lines such as the River Dove/Trent Line where 50 remain. There are many individual pillboxes derived from this basic design; a longer rear wall contains the entrance flanked by two pistol loops and the other five sides contain lmg loopholes; there is a Y-shaped AR screen; examples are most often shuttered in wood, but there are many others shuttered in brick which is then left in situ. Simple variations on the basic design include porches, blast-walls, varying heights and combinations of loopholes, camouflage, provision of weapons mountings, shutters.

Dimensions: side 1 is 13ft 6in (4.1m) externally and 10ft (3m) internally; sides 2-6 are 7ft 6in (2.3m) externally and 5ft (1.5m) internally; wall thickness is 15-18in (38-46cm) or 24in (61cm) on some GHQ Line examples; height is 7ft 6in (2.3m)

Examples survive in numbers:
TF231055 (Newborough, Cambs) (*107*)
ST348595 (Weston-super-Mare)
SK185291 (Fauld, Derbyshire)

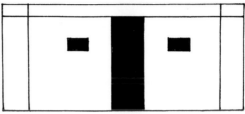

107 Newborough,
Cambridgeshire
(TF218057) **2b**; hexagonal
pillbox to drawing
number DFW3/24;
bullet-proof but with the
thicker than normal walls

0   0.5   1m

2bi. a taller version used at some Royal Ordnance Factories
Dimensions: as per **2b** but up to 11ft (3.3m) high

Examples survive at:
SO332023 (Glascoed, Gwent) (*108*)
TQ373990 (Enfield Lock, Greater London)

Ref: fieldwork and WO166/56 via Dobinson

108 Glascoed, Gwent
(SO332023) **2bi**; taller than
normal version for use at ROFs

109 The Ridgeway, Hertfordshire (TL289035) **2c**; version of DFW3/24 found on Outer London
Line A, with a covered entry and lmg loophole over

110 Euston, Suffolk (TL898782) **2d**; one of several odd pillboxes loosely based on DFW3/24, this one would fit inside its envelope

2c pillbox based on drawing number DFW3/24

This pillbox is identical in every way to **2b** but for the fact that it has a covered entry with a lmg loop over; it was usually shuttered in brick, with the bricks left in situ, marginally increasing the external dimensions, and the wall-thickness. It was used in great numbers on the Outer London Defence Line A.

Examples survive at:
TL289035 (The Ridgeway, Hertfordshire) (*109*)

2d. pillboxes loosely based on drawing DFW3/24

A number of individual pillboxes conform very roughly to **2b** but may differ in minor details such as overall dimensions.

Examples include:
TL919725 (Ixworth, Suffolk) whose external dimensions almost match **2b**'s internal ones
TL898782 (Euston, Suffolk) (*110*) whose internal dimensions match the previous example's external ones

Refs: fieldwork, Peter Kent

111 Pauperhaugh, Northumberland (NZ100994) **2e**; the Northumberland version of the lozenge-shaped pillbox has a mix of lmg- and rifle-loops

2e. lozenge-shaped pillboxes

There are many examples of this shape to be found; they comprise two large groups in Northumberland and in Holderness, in both of which localities they tend to be the norm, and two smaller groups in South Wales and on London's railways.

The Northumberland version (**2e**) has two long sides, and four short ones; the entrance, usually protected by an integral blast-wall, is on one of the long sides; a straight AR wall runs the length of the pillbox; the long walls usually contain three rifle-loops, with a larger mg loop in each short wall, but other combinations are found.

Dimensions: long walls are 12ft (3.7m); short walls are 6ft (1.8m); wall-thickness 12-15in (30-38cm)

NB: at least one larger example (**2eii**) is known with walls 19ft & 9ft (5.8m & 2.7m), one lmg loop and 10 loops for rifles

Examples survive in Northumberland at:
NU257119 (Alnmouth)
NU261145 (Boulmer)
NZ100994 (Pauperhaugh) (*111*)
NU074215 & 075215 (Old Bewick)
NZ412345 (Black Hurworth) (**2eii**) (*112*)

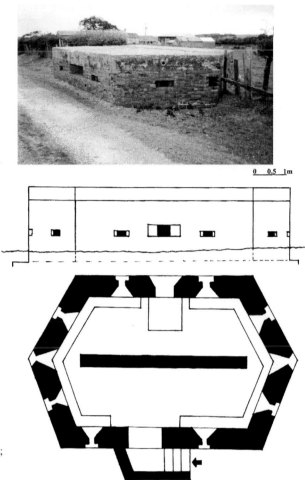

112 Black Hurworth, Northumberland (NZ412345) **2eii**; a larger version of **2e**, with one lmg- and 10 rifle-loops

2ei. lozenge-shaped pillbox

This pillbox is found on the Holderness coast between Spurn Head and Flamborough Head. It is virtually identical to **2e**, but has a more consistent loophole arrangement with four rifle-loops in one long side, two in the other long side with a third in the blast-wall and a lmg loop in each short side; the occasional example mixes loops in the long side.

Examples survive at:
TA168630 (Fraisthorpe E Yorks)
TA404167 (Easington, E Yorks)
TA194511 (Atwick, East Yorkshire) (*113*)

2eiii. lozenge-shaped pillbox

This design is found around London's railway bridges, with one, truncated into a pentagon, on the platform of Putney Station. They are shuttered in brick, with up to six pre-fabricated lmg loops and different combinations of open pits for LAA mgs.

113   Atwick, East Yorkshire (TA194511) **2ei**; the Holderness version of the lozenge-shaped pillbox

Dimensions: all sides are 8ft (2.4m)

Examples survive at:
Kew and Barnes bridges

Ref: fieldwork, Ian Sanders

2eiv. lozenge-shaped pillbox
A design found around Porthcawl in South Wales.

Dimensions: long sides are 11ft (3.35m); short sides are 7ft (2.1m)

Example at:
SS832816 (Pyle, Glamorgan)

2f. machine-gun post, based on lozenge-shaped pillbox
This is found on the Yorkshire coast between Bridlington and Scarborough; it is designed with embrasures in sides 3 and 5, for two Vickers mgs; the two entrances are screened by an E-shaped blast-wall; below each embrasure is a buttress to strengthen the most vulnerable points; it has sometimes been referred to as an 'eared' pillbox owing to the shape of the screen and the protruding entrances.

Dimensions: sides 2, 3, 5, 7, 6 are 8ft (2.4m); side 4 is 6ft (1.8m); the screen wall is 13ft (4m) wall-thickness 15in (38cm)

Examples survive at:
TA254708 (Flamborough Head),
TA171637 (Fraisthorpe, E Yorks) (*114 & 115*)

Refs: fieldwork, David Clarke

114 Fraisthorpe, East Yorkshire (TA171637) **2f**; the 'eared' machine-gun pillbox designed for two Vickers guns

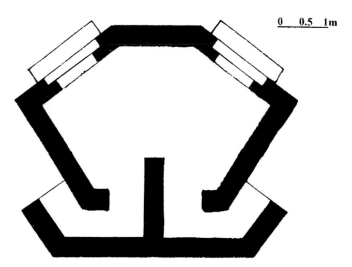

115 Fraisthorpe, East Yorkshire (TA171637) **2f**; plan of (*114*)

2g. pillbox

Unique to Stoke Holy Cross radar site; elongated shape with loopholes in five sides and door in corner, screened by a long rear wall, one example being blank and another having a loop; mounting for a 20mm AA cannon on roof. At least two of these pillboxes stood straddling the security fence.

Dimensions: side 1 is 10ft (3m); sides 2 & 6 are 12ft (3.7m); sides 3, 4, 7, 5 are 5ft (1.5m); wall-thickness 15in (38cm)

Examples at:
TG252025 & 253025 (Stoke Holy Cross, Norfolk) (*116*)

Refs: fieldwork, Peter Kent, Christopher Bird

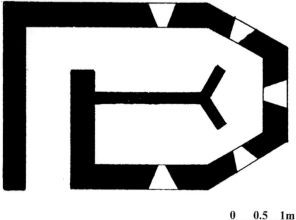

0   0.5 1m

116 Stoke Holy Cross, Norfolk (TG252026) **2g**; one of two in this style guarding a radar site; one has a mounting for a LAA cannon on its roof

2h. pillbox

Another pillbox found only on radar sites; it appears triangular as it has three long sides and three short ones; the long sides each have two loopholes and, in one example, one of the short sides contains an entrance; they were built straddling the security fence; constructed of brick and concrete; one example has a low, open, hexagonal, concrete emplacement on its roof for a LAA mounting.

Dimensions: long sides are 12ft (3.7m); short sides are 4ft 6in (1.4m); wall-thickness (Stenigot) is 15in (38cm), wall-thickness (Ventnor) is 9in (23cm)

Examples:
TF256825 & 255828 (Stenigot, Lincs) (*117*)
SZ566785 (Ventnor, IoW)

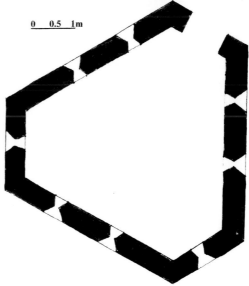

0   0.5   1m

117 Stenigot, Lincolnshire
(TF256825) **2h**; pillbox with
LAA mounting on its roof,
guarding a radar site

2j. pillbox

This pillbox is found only on the Suffolk coast at Walberswick; it is quite small with just three forward-facing loopholes; it presents as a smaller version of **2g**, constructed in wood-shuttered concrete.

Dimensions: side 1 is 8ft 6in (2.6m); sides 2 & 6 are 9ft 3in (2.8m); sides 3, 4 & 5 are 3ft 9in (1.1m); wall-thickness 12in (30cm)

Examples survive at:
TM496744 & 490740 (Walberswick, Suffolk) (*118*)

2k. pillbox

Found only in Barrow-in-Furness, this pillbox has five lmg loopholes in its faces, and

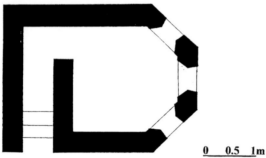

118 Walberswick, Suffolk (TM496744) **2j**; small hexagonal pillbox with three forward-facing loopholes found only in a small area of the coast

four rifle-loops in its angles, along with two more in the rear wall, flanking the doorway, which is protected by a blast-wall; it is constructed of wood-shuttered concrete; there is a Y-shaped AR wall.

Dimensions: side 1 is 16ft (4.9m); other five sides are 6ft 6in (2m)

Example at:
SD180694 (Barrow-in-Furness, Lancs) (*119*)

2m. guard-posts with open rear annexe
These guard-posts appear at ROFs; they consist of hexagonal loopholed chambers with base angles of 90 degrees and open, rear annexes; they are constructed in brick with pre-fabricated loops and a concrete slab roof. Several different types exist with different dimensions.

Examples at:
SJ865336 (Swynnerton, Staffs) (*120*)
SJ391490 (Wrexham, Clwyd) (*121*)

119 Barrow-in-Furness, Lancashire (SD180694) **2k**; an unusual design with five lmg-loops and four rifle-loops in the angles and at a higher level, peculiar to the Barrow defences

0   0.5   1m

2n. two-storey pillbox

Another ROF design; it effectively raises a pillbox with seven loopholes onto a plinth; the upper floor is reached via a ladder through a trapdoor in the upper floor. It is constructed of brick, with pre-fabricated loopholes and a concrete slab roof.

Dimensions: side 1 is 14ft (4.3m); sides 2 & 6 are 10ft (3m); sides 3, 4 & 5 are 8ft (2.4m); wall-thickness 24in (61cm) (*122*)

Example remains at:
SE033447 (Keighley, W. Yorks)

Ref: fieldwork, W. Yorkshire Archaeology Service

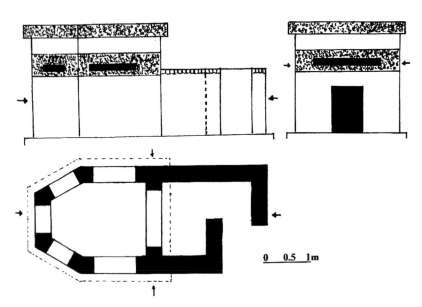

120   Swynnerton, Staffordshire (SJ865336) **2m**; more of a guard-post than a pillbox, at an ROF

2p. two-storey pillbox

Very similar to **2n** this is on the River Ouse defence line in Sussex at Slaugham; access to the upper level is gained via rungs set in the back wall; there is a single loop at ground level covering the doorway.

Example at:
TQ249277

Ref: fieldwork, Martin Mace

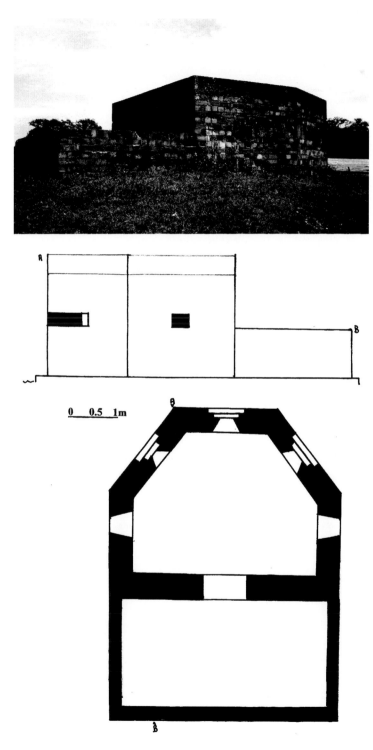

121 Wrexham, Clwyd (SJ391490) **2m**; another ROF guard-post with loops for three lmgs and two for rifles; the annexe may have held a LAA mounting

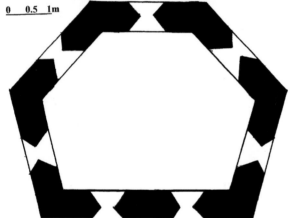

0   0.5   1m

122 Keighley, West
Yorkshire (SE033447)
2n; a two-storey pillbox
with loopholes only at
the upper level, formerly
guarding an ROF

2q. pillbox

Found in Cornwall, this small pillbox has base angles of 90 degrees and is similar to **2m**
with five lmg loopholes; attached is an open walled area, the same height as the pillbox,
with a doorway protected by an integral blast-wall.

Dimensions: side 1 is 12ft (3.7m); sides 2 & 6 are 3ft 6in (1.1m); sides 3, 4 & 5 are 5ft
(1.5m); wall-thickness 24in (61cm)

Example survives at:
cSW352264 (Sennen Cove) (*123*)

2r. machine-gun post

A unique design for three Vickers mgs; it is built into an earth bank, so has two blank
sides; three other faces (4, 5 & 6) have mg embrasures fitted with concrete tables; a dog-leg
entrance is covered by a pistol loop in a traverse.

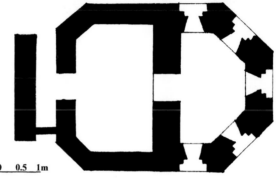

123 Sennen Cove, Cornwall (cSW352264) **2q**; a small hexagonal pillbox with an open annexe and an attached blast-wall

0　0.5　1m

Dimensions: rear wall is 13ft (4m); side 2 is 8ft (2.4m); side 3 is 3ft 9in (1.14m); sides 4, 5 & 6 are 6ft (1.8m)

Example survives at: SO031511 (Builth Wells, Powys) (*124*)

2s. machine-gun post with attached LAA position

Three forward-facing sides have mg embrasures; there are two longer, parallel sides, one of which has a square, open LAA position built on; the rear wall contains an entrance. The whole pillbox is semi-sunken.

124 Builth Wells, Radnorshire (SO031511) **2r**; a pillbox designed for three Vickers machine-guns

Dimensions: side 1 is 12ft (3.7m); sides 2 & 6 are 7ft 6in (2.3m); sides 3 & 5 are 5ft (1.5m); side 4 is 7ft (2.13m); wall-thickness 12in (30cm)

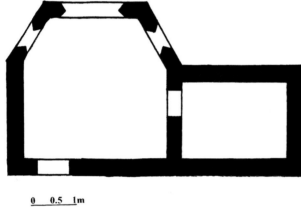

0   0.5   1m

125 Shoreham-on-Sea, East Sussex (TQ203060) **2s**; a sunken pillbox with three wide embrasures for machine-guns, and attached open annexe for LAA gun

Examples at:

TQ203060 & 205057 (Shoreham, West Sussex) (*125*)

3. SHELL-PROOF PILLBOXES IN THE SHAPE OF REGULAR HEXAGONS

Whilst many of the pillboxes were designed to be merely bullet- and splinter-proof, it soon became apparent that hardened defences, especially on defence lines, would need to be able to withstand bombardment from field artillery and dive-bombers. In 1941, both the War Office and the Air Ministry required existing pillboxes to be augmented by the addition of layers of concrete up to 42-55in (1.07-1.4m) thick. The results of this process can be seen, for example, on the airfields of Crail (Fife) or Jurby (IoM), where the original cores stand proud of their new jackets. It would appear that two new designs for shell-proof pillboxes were issued by DFW3 at this time: drawings DFW3/45 and DFW3/46, but these have apparently not survived in the archive, although, of course, examples may survive unrecognised on the ground. The majority of examples in this section and the next are simply bulkier versions of ones we have already seen.

Unbelievably, a directive circulated through the local branches of the Federation of Master Builders encouraged contractors to save on materials, one of the ways suggested was to reduce the thickness of the wall furthest from the enemy. There is an example of the application of this suggestion below (**3ai**). As we saw in **1j** the addition of a skirt up to loophole level was another alternative to a complete thickening. Some examples are given below.

3a. shell-proof pillbox derived from DFW3/22

Here, the internal size is that of the DFW3/22, **1a**, but the walls are thickened; this design was sometimes used on the GHQ Line as an alternative to **4a**; there are five loops for lmgs, a pistol loop beside the door and a Y-shaped AR wall. Construction was in reinforced concrete, shuttered in wood or brick.

Dimensions: all sides 10ft (3m); wall-thickness 42in (1.07m)

Example at:
SU748543 (Murrell Green, Hants) (*126*)

3ai. modification of 3a
This pillbox shows the reduction in the thickness of the rear wall of **3a**.

Dimensions: wall-thickness 12in (30cm); side 1 is 12ft 6in (3.8m); sides 2 & 6 are 7ft (2.1m)

Example survives at:
SP328003 (Tadpole Bridge, Oxon) (*127*)

Refs: fieldwork, Colin Alexander

3aii. modification of 3a
Here there is a simple increase in wall-thickness, and the disappearance of loops in side 1; found on airfields; five loopholes have outward splays and are fitted with slots for monopod lmg mountings.

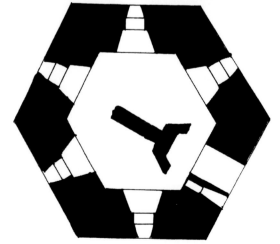

126 Murrell Green, Hampshire (SU748543) **3a**; shell-proof pillbox on the GHQ Line

Dimensions: all sides 10ft (3m); wall-thickness 45in (1.14m)

Example survives at: TG142347 (Matlaske, Norfolk) (*128*) TR334433 (Swingate, Kent) with porch & LAA position on roof (*129*)

Refs: fieldwork, Peter Kent, David Burridge

3aiii. modification of 3a, possibly to drawing 2865

This is another simple enlargement of **1a**; here the loops are splayed to the inside, with built-in ledges for Bren guns; it is found in Scotland on the Cowie Line; constructed of solid granite, with a T-shaped AR wall and most lack loops in side 1.

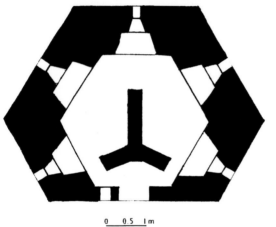

0   0.5   1 m

127 Tadpole Bridge, Oxfordshire (SP328003) **3ai**; shell-proof pillbox with rear wall reduced in thickness

Dimensions: all sides 10ft 3in (3.15m); wall-thickness 42in (1.05m)

Example survives at: NO765874 (Cowie Line, Aberdeen) (*130*)

Ref: Gordon Barclay

3aiv. modification of 3a

A number of enlargements of **3a** are slightly larger than those above by virtue of their thicker walls, from 42in-55in (1.05m-1.4m), increasing overall size accordingly.

3av. modifications of 3a

In a number of locations, partial thickening has been applied by adding a skirt reaching up to the height of the loopholes; this type of strengthening is often found in conjunction with steel plates on the loopholes.

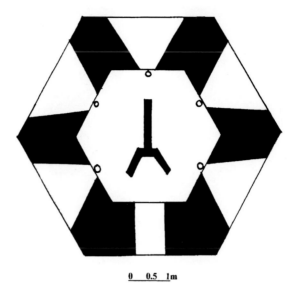

128 Matlaske, Norfolk
(TG142347) **3aii**; shell-proof
pillbox for five lmgs

0   0.5   1m

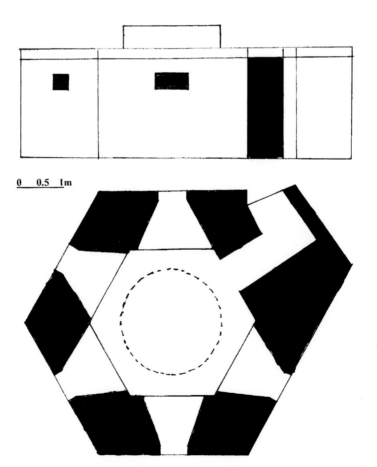

129 Swingate, Dover, Kent (TR334433) **3aii**; shell-proof pillbox with LAA mounting
on roof; plan and elevation after Burridge

0   0.5   1m

130 Cowie Line, Aberdeenshire (NO765874) **3aiii;** shell-proof pillbox for five lmgs; plan after Barclay

Examples survive at:
TQ916874 & 921868 (Rochford, Essex)
TL646659, 661659 & 659658 (Newmarket, Cambs) (97) (see **1j**)

Refs: fieldwork, Alec Beanse

NB: a number of pillboxes at Bawdsey (Suffolk) radar site were given skirts formed by building revetments of brick or concrete sandbags, and the space thus formed was filled with earth and rubble; see **1j**.

3b. Eastern Command pillbox (?) CRE1113
There are large numbers of shell-proof pillboxes of similar design on the Essex coast defences and on the Eastern Command Line; they are likely to represent one of the three local designs issued by CRE Colchester in summer 1940; it is a shell-proof version of **1fi** and **1fii**.

3b has six lmg-loops, one of which is above a sunken entrance porch; there is a diagonal or sometimes T-shaped AR wall from side 1 to 4.

Dimensions: all sides 11ft 6in (3.5m); wall-thickness 42in (1.07m)

3bi is the same as **3b** but has an internal corridor and a raised central platform with a mounting for a LAA mg; see also **16f.**

3bii as **3b** but with prominent roof ventilator, and differing combinations of mg and lmg loopholes.

131 Rochford, Essex (TQ901883) **3b**; shell-proof pillbox, enlargement of **1fi**

3biii as **3b** but only five lmg loops and either a loopholed blast-wall in front of the door, or an integral L-shaped one; it also has a conventional Y-shaped AR wall.

Examples survive at:

3b   TL854437 (Rodbridge Corner, Suffolk)
         TQ901883 (Rochford, Essex) (*131*)
3bi   TL904344 (Bures, Essex) (*132*)
3bii TR007088 (Bradwell, Essex) (*133*)
         TM073154 (Mersea Is. Essex)
3biii TL758727 (Caversham Heath, Suffolk)
         TL787708 (Lackford, Suffolk) (*134*)

Refs: fieldwork, Peter Kent

NB: a pillbox similar to **3bi** but with sides measuring 14ft (4.3m) survives at NJ953088 (Aberdeen).

3c. airfield pillboxes, modifications of 1c

There are a number of different enlargements of the basic type exemplified by those included in the **1c** category; some of these were built with thickening, some had extra layers added; many of those with added layers will have very widely-splayed loopholes; they are to be found on airfields right across the British Isles; most are built of poured concrete into brick shuttering; some, as at Spittlegate (Lincolnshire) are built entirely of brick, with concrete only in the roof-slabs; AR walls are most often solid and Y-shaped, but others, as at Church Lawford, Sywell and Spittlegate, are cantilevered.

Dimensions: basic examples of **3c** have sides of 9ft (2.74m), 10ft 6in (3.2m), 11ft (3.35m), 13ft (3.95m) or 14ft (4.3m); wall-thicknesses range from 3ft 9in to 4ft 9in (1.14m-1.45m)

132 Bures, Essex (TL904344) **3bi**; shell-proof pillbox, enlargement of **1fii**; used on Eastern Command Line

Examples survive on the following airfields:
Cranage (Cheshire)
Debden, Great Sampford, North Weald (*135*)
Stapleford Tawney (Essex)
Binbrook and Spittlegate (Lincs)
Crail (Fife), Forres (Moray)
Jurby (Isle of Man) (*136*)
Hunsdon and Sawbridgeworth (Hertfordshire)
Sywell (Northants), Hucknall (Notts)
Carew Cheriton and Manorbier (Pembrokeshire)
Chetwynd and Shawbury (Shropshire)

Refs: fieldwork, Adrian Armishaw, Alec Beanse

3d airfield pillboxes with central LAA platforms

A few airfield pillboxes shared their layout with **3bi**, but with different dimensions. An internal corridor surrounds a raised platform with a LAA mg mounting; there is a small type at Yatesbury and a larger one at Detling; the Yatesbury model has one mg embrasure

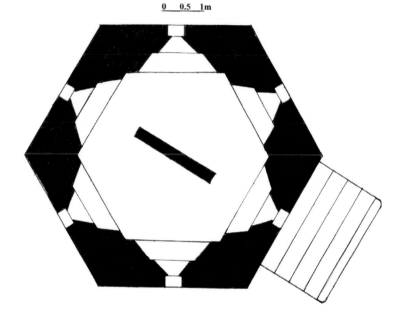

133 Bradwell, Essex (TR007088) **3bii**; shell-proof pillbox, variant of **3b**

134 Lackford, Suffolk (TL787708) **3biii**; shell-proof pillbox, variant of **3b**, but with blast-wall instead of covered entry; used on Eastern Command Line

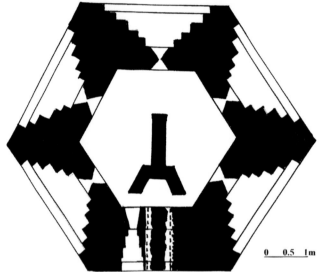

135 North Weald, Essex (TL492500) **3c**; airfield pillbox with thickened walls

136 Jurby, Isle of Man (SC360979) **3c**; airfield pillbox with thickened walls showing original inner core proud of new roof-line

and four rifle-loops, whereas that at Detling, which may be later, is limited to just three lmg loops;

Examples survive at;
SU050712 (Yatesbury, Wiltshire) with sides of 10ft (3m) (*137*)
TQ809589 (Detling, Kent) with sides of 14ft 6in (4.4m) (*138*)

4 SHELL–PROOF PILLBOXES IN THE SHAPE OF IRREGULAR HEXAGONS

Many in this category are derivatives of the design in drawing number DFW3/24; the different Army Commands all appear to have evolved their own version of what quickly became a classic design, present in all the major defence lines; the bottom three examples, in the table below, are all for models with a thin rear wall (**4b**); all other wall-thicknesses are minimum 42in (1.07m). Other variations within this category include: porches and blast-walls, brick or timber shuttering, camouflage and different types of pre-fabricated loopholes.

4a based on the drawing DFW3/24
The table below shows a number of these different versions of enlargements to the drawing DFW3/24.

137 Yatesbury, Wiltshire (SU050712) **3d**; airfield pillbox with central open platform for LAA mounting; smaller version

0   0.5   1m

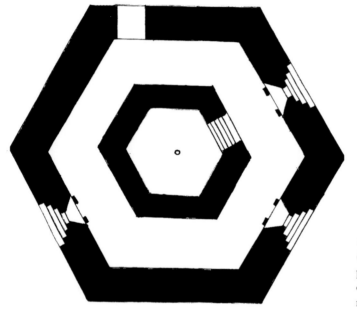

138 Detling, Kent
(TQ809589) **3d**; airfield
pillbox with central
open platform for LAA
mounting, larger version

general location	example	base	sides 2&6	sides 3&5	side 4	references
GHQ Line, Sussex	TQ428149	20ft 9in	11ft 9in	8ft 6in	8ft 6in	Greeves (*139*)
GHQ Line, Fife	NO312103	19ft	15ft	10ft	8ft	
Green Line, Glos.	ST909935	18ft	11ft 3in	9ft 3in	9ft 3in	Green/Plant (*140*)
GHQ Line, Kent	TQ703529	17ft 6in	9ft 9in	9ft	8ft 6in	
GHQ Line, Cambs★★★	TL281957	17ft 6in	11ft 3in	9ft 6in	9ft 6in	Cave papers
GHQ Line, Sussex	TQ511255	17ft 3in	10ft 6in	10ft 6in	10ft 6in	Sholl
E Cmd Line, Norfolk	TF528007	17ft	13ft	9ft	10ft	
Kent Coast	TR090352	21ft	12ft	8ft 6in	8ft 6in	Burridge
Green Line, Glos.	ST889971	16ft 6in	10ft 8in	9ft	9ft	Green/Plant (*141*)
GHQ Line, Cambs	TF277009	16ft 6in	10ft 6in	9ft 6in	8ft	(*142*)
E Cmd Line, Cambs	TL578865	17ft	11ft	9ft 6in	9ft	Kent

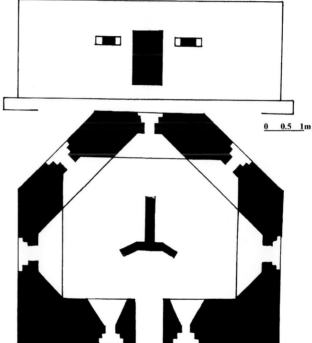

139 Barcombe Cross, East Sussex (TQ428149) **4a**; shell-proof pillbox based on drawing-number DFW3/24 on the Newhaven-Eridge GHQ Line

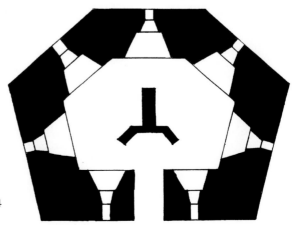

140 Long Newnton, Gloucestershire (ST909935) **4a**; shell-proof pillbox based on drawing-number DFW3/24 on the GHQ Green Line

E Cmd Line, Suffolk	TL624804	16ft	10ft	9ft 6in	8ft 6in	Kent (*143*)
GHQ Line, Essex	TL695162	16ft	10ft	9ft	9ft	
Kent Cmd. Line	TR200550	17ft 6in	10ft	9ft	8ft 6in	Burridge (*144*)
GHQ Line, Berks★★	SU745553	25ft 6in	12ft	8ft 6in		Alexander (*145*)
GHQ Line, Sussex★	TQ424077	19ft	6ft 6in	11ft	9ft 9in	Sholl (*146*)
Norwich defences★	TG201112	16ft	8ft	8ft	8ft	Kent (*147*)
R Ouse Line, Sussex★	TQ206293	18ft	7ft	9ft	9ft	(*148*)

★note these three models have rear walls reduced to 15in (38cm): **4b**

★★note this model consists of only the front half, with a thin rear wall: **4c**

★★★note this model designated in contractor's papers as drawing number 350/40: **4d**

0   0.5   1m

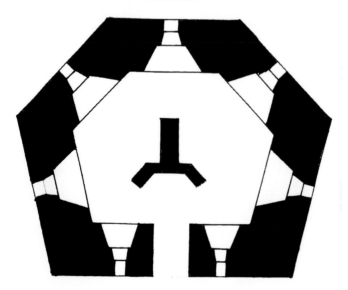

141 Avening, Gloucestershire (ST889971) **4a**; shell-proof pillbox based on drawing-number DFW3/24 on the GHQ Green Line

4ai. raised pillboxes based on DFW3/24

There are several exam-ples on the Taunton Stop Line of pillboxes built up on plinths, as at Creech St Michael, or onto a full -height lower storey as Bridgwater (two).

4aii. partially-thickened pillbox

A pillbox at TR376502 (Walmer, Kent) has had its front walls thickened by the addition of 2ft (61cm) of concrete, contained in brick shuttering.

4aiii. double height pillbox

At ST344171 (Ilton, Somerset) on the Taunton Stop Line is a two-storey pillbox, basically one **4a** stacked on top of another; there are the usual number of loopholes in each level; over the ground-floor door is a protruding steel beam which formerly supported external stairs to the upper door.

4d. pillbox to drawing number 350/40

A shell-proof variation on

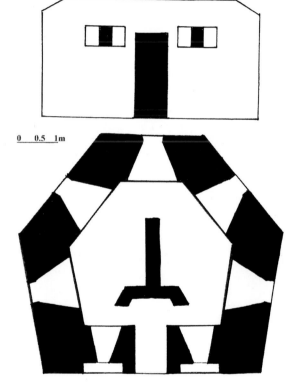

142 Stonebridge Corner, Cambridgeshire (TF279009) **4a**; shell-proof pillbox based on drawing-number DFW3/24 on the GHQ Line

the FW3/24 design, built on the GHQ Line (East) in the Cambridgeshire Fens by Hugh Cave of Thorney and his local sub-contractors; this hexagonal shellproof pillbox has five pre-fabricated loopholes for lmgs and a pistol loop either side of the entrance; it is built on a concrete raft; there are piles of concrete on the roof to break the outline; it fronts the forward AT ditch, here the Whittlesey Dyke; brick outer skin as form-work for poured concrete.

Dimensions: base: 17ft 6in (5.3m); sides 2 & 6 are 11ft 3in (3.4m); sides 3-5 are 9ft 6in (2.9m); wall thickness 42in (1.07m)

143 Prickwillow, Cambridgeshire (TL624804) **4a**; shell-proof pillbox based on drawing-number DFW3/24 on the Eastern Command Line

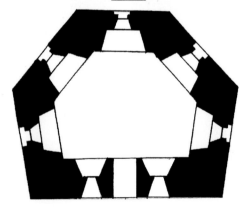

144 Bekesbourne, Kent (TR200550) **4a**; shell-proof pillbox based on drawing-number DFW3/24 on the Southern Command Line

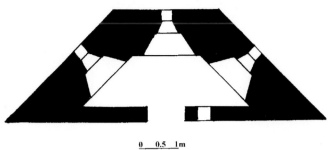

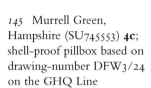

145 Murrell Green, Hampshire (SU745553) **4c**; shell-proof pillbox based on drawing-number DFW3/24 on the GHQ Line

0   0.5   1m

0   0.5   1m

146 Iford, East Sussex (TQ424077) **4b**; shell-proof pillbox based on drawing-number DFW3/24 on the Newhaven–Eridge GHQ Line

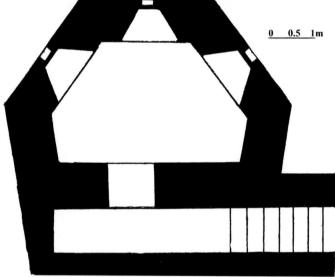

147 Norwich, Norfolk (TG201112) **4b**; shell-proof pillbox based on drawing-number DFW3/24

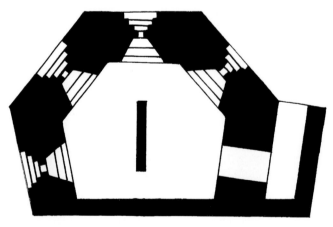

148 Munnings Heath, West Sussex (TQ206293) **4b**; shell-proof pillbox based on drawing-number DFW3/24, on the R.Rother/Arun Command Line

Examples at:

TL281957 (Turning Bridge) (*149*) & 290956, (Kates Farm), Whittlesey

Ref: Contract WO/34664 (5.xi.1940)

4e. pillbox

Unusually for an airfield, this is a shell-proof pillbox based on drawing DFW3/24; there are seven, large, widely-splayed mg embrasures, two of which are in side (1) over a sunken entry; there is a Y-shaped AR wall, and earth is heaped on top of the roof as camouflage.

Dimensions: side 1 is 17ft (5.2m); sides 2 & 6 are 12ft 6in (3.8m); sides 3, 4 & 5 are 10ft (3m); wall-thickness 36in (91cm)

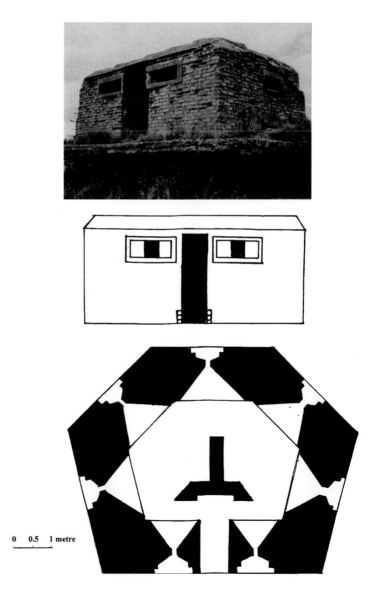

149 Turning Bridge, Cambridgeshire (TL281957) **4d**; shell-proof pillbox to drawing number 350/40, on the GHQ Line East

0   0.5   1 metre

Example at:

TL455465 (Duxford, Cambridgeshire), but that at TL455459 (*150*) has now been demolished

4f. machine-gun post

These mg posts guard the road and railway to the north of the important junction of GHQ lines at Penshurst in Kent; the two north-facing embrasures are fitted with Turnbull mounts; both are shuttered in wood, and finished to a high standard.

Dimensions: side 1 is 27ft (8.2m); sides 2 & 6 are 8ft (2.4m); sides 3 & 5 are 12ft (3.7m); side 4 is 6ft (1.8m); wall-thickness 36in (91cm)

Examples at:

TQ522467 (*151*) & 523467 (Chiddingstone Causeway, Kent)

4g. machine-gun post

This mg post is deployed on the Suffolk coast, sometimes in pairs; it is partly divided into two chambers by a wall which also serves as an AR screen; the two mg embrasures are

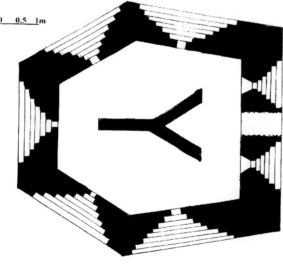

150 Duxford, Cambridgeshire (TL455465) **4e**; airfield pillbox for seven lmgs

provided with tables for Vickers guns; the entrance is shielded by an integral blast-wall.

Dimensions: side 1 is 24ft (7.3m); sides 2 & 6 are 7ft 6in (2.3m); sides 3 & 5 are 11ft (3.4m); side 4 is 10ft (3m); wall-thickness 36in (91cm)

Examples at:
TM528840 (Benacre)
TM456747 a pair, (Blythburgh) (*152*)

5. SHELL-PROOF SQUARE AND RECTANGULAR PILLBOXES

The War Office produced a design for a Vickers mg post which was included in the 1936 *Manual of Field Engineering* (see *56*). This provided the starting-point for a number of similar emplacements for Vickers guns, and also a series of adaptations for Bren lmgs. There were also a few examples of one-off shellproof constructions built on local initiative.

5a.

0   0.5   1m

151   Chiddingstone Causeway, Kent (TQ522467) **4f**; shell-proof mg post with two Turnbull mounts on the GHQ Line

mg

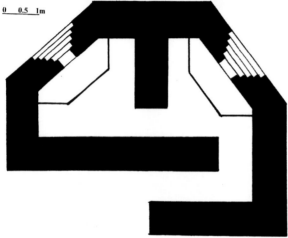

152 Blythburgh, Suffolk
(TM456747) **4g**; shell-proof,
double machine-gun post with
two tables for Vickers guns

post modified 1936 design, sometimes referred to as DFW3/27

This mg post (*153*) is slightly narrower than the 1936 version, has chamfered front corners
and an entrance in the side wall, covered by a blast-wall, rather than a rear entrance with
a traverse; it retains the table for a Vickers gun, behind a deep, stepped embrasure; it can be
found in a number of locations; on the Taunton Stop Line, it is referred to as being built
to drawing number DFW3/27, modified by drawing number TL62; in Scotland, it is also
linked to DFW3/27; it is also found on the GHQ Line in Surrey and Kent, and on the
Norfolk coast; in Surrey and Somerset often deployed in pairs; most are constructed of
poured concrete into timber shuttering, but Surrey examples at Beacon Hill and Ewshott
are shuttered in brick.

Dimensions: 13ft 6in x 14ft 6in (4.1m x 4.4m); wall-thickness 42in (1.07m)

Variations include: plinths, second mg embrasure, sunken entrances, additional loopholes,
AR walls.
Examples at:
ST312220 (Crimson Hill, Somerset)
TQ708528 (Teston Bridge, Kent),
SU796515 (Chequers Bridge, Hampshire (*154*)

153 War Office design
of 1936 for a Vickers
machine-gun post **5a**

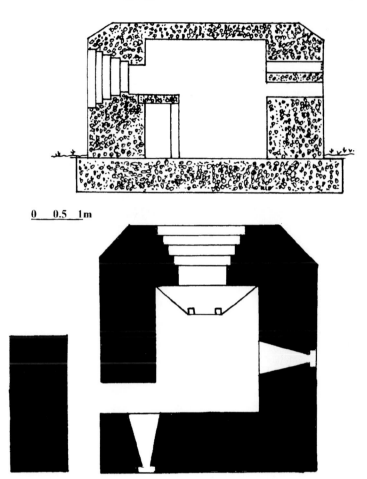

0   0.5   1m

SU824503 (Beacon Hill, Surrey)
ST304277 (Durston, Somerset) with two embrasures but only one table (*155*)

5ai. bullet-proof double mg post

On the north Norfolk coast there are four pairs, and several single examples of mg posts with two chambers, each with one mg embrasure, conjoined at 135 degrees; an entrance is protected by a blast-wall and rifle-loop; though only bullet-proof, with walls 15in (38cm) and 24in (61cm) thick, it is included here as an adaptation.

Examples at:
TF914441 (Wells-next-the-Sea) (*156*)
TF891443 (Holkham)
TG507174 (Hemsby)
Further variations in size and detail on north Norfolk coast at:
TG097438 (Weybourne) & TG345245 (Smallburgh) etc.

5b. lmg pillbox based on 5a

This pillbox is designed for three Bren lmgs; it is common on parts of the GHQ Line, particularly in Essex and Cambridgeshire; the rear wall contains an entrance, protected by a loopholed blast-wall, often integral; the front corners are chamfered. In the Cambridgeshire fens, it is apparently referred to as drawing number DFW3/27a.

Dimensions: 15ft 6in x 14ft (4.7m x 4.3m); wall-thickness 42in (1.07m)

Variations include modifications to blast-wall, loophole combinations, thinner rear wall and overall size:

5bi is as **5b** but measures 15ft 6in x 12ft 6in (4.7m x 3.8m)

5bii is as **5b** but measures 14ft 3in x 14ft (4.3m x 4.2m)

5biii is as **5b** but measures 18ft 6in x 16ft 9in (5.6m x 5.1m) & has two thinner walls

5biv has alternative blast-wall and entrance arrangements

Examples survive at:
TL297878 (Ramsay, Cambridgeshire) **5b** (*157*)
TL520361 (Sparrows End, Essex) roofed mantlet with three loops;

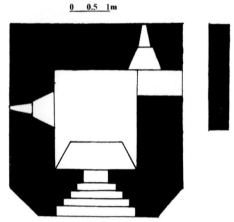

154 Chequers Bridge, Hampshire (SU796515) **5a**; modified version of the 1936 design for a Vickers mg post; photo by Colin Alexander

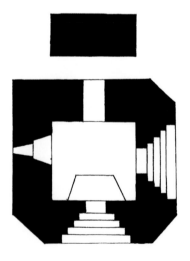

155 Durston, Somerset (ST304277) **5a**; a design for two Vickers guns, with two embrasures, but only one table

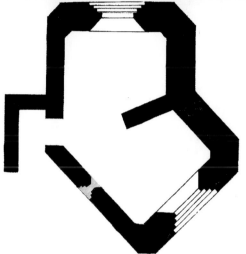

156 Wells-next-the-Sea, Norfolk
(TF914441) **5ai**; a combination of
two mg posts with bullet-proof walls
but derived from **5a**

5b (*158*)
TQ744055 (Chelmsford, Essex) **5bi**
TL308880 (Ramsey, Cambridgeshire) **5bii**
TQ307439 (Horley, Surrey) **5biii**
TL570816 & 570814 (Queen Adelaide, Cambridgeshire), different **5biv**s

Refs: fieldwork, Colin Alexander, Peter Kent

5c. mg post
Found only at Duxford airfield, an emplacement for three mgs, with stepped embrasures
and Turnbull mounts.

Dimensions: 17ft 9in x 15ft 6in (5.4m x 4.7m); wall-thickness is 54in (1.37m)

Examples survive at:
TL459473 & 462474 (*159*)

5d. mg posts
A number of one-off mg posts can be found on the north Norfolk coast and the Teesside

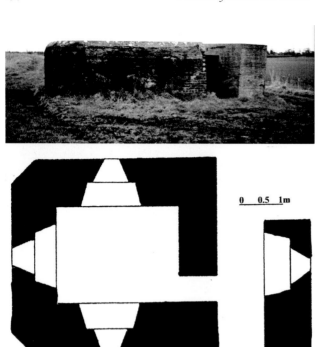

157 Ramsey, Cambridgeshire (TL297878) **5b**; shell-proof pillbox for three Bren guns, with loopholed blast-wall

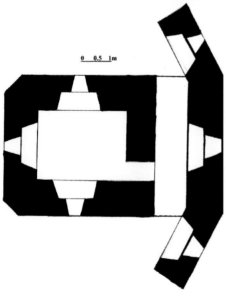

158 Sparrows End, Essex (TL520361) **5b**; shell-proof pillbox for three Bren guns, with extended, part-roofed, loopholed blast-wall

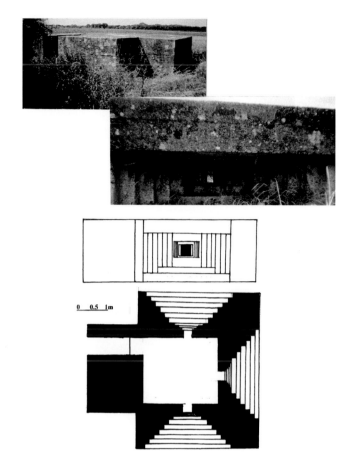

159 Duxford,
Cambridgeshire (TL459473)
5c; massively thick
emplacement for three mgs

and Northumberland coasts; these are generally rectangular or L-shaped, and have one or
two mounts for monopod weapons such as Lewis guns.

Dimensions and examples:
19ft 6in x 12ft 3in (5.9m x 3.7m) at TG119416 (Weybourne Heath, Norfolk) **5d**
18ft x 9ft (5.5m x 2.25m) plus small side annexe 5ft 9in x 6ft 3in (1.75m x 1.9m) **5di** at
TG102438 (Weybourne, Norfolk)
15ft x 10ft (4.6m x 3m) at NZ318881 (Newbiggin, Northumberland) **5dii**
all forward-facing walls usually 42in (1.07m) but rear walls often 15in (38cm)

Refs: fieldwork, Peter Kent, Alan Rudd

5e. mg post
Emplacement for two Vickers guns mounted on a continuous shelf firing through two
open, stepped, forward-facing embrasures; similar to BEF version (see Chapter 4). Found
only on the GHQ Line in Fife; entry in rear wall, down steps.
Dimensions: 25ft 3in x 17ft (7.7m x 5.2m); wall-thickness 51in (1.3m)

Examples survive at: NO302029 & NT306994 (*160*)

5f. mg post

Pillbox with nearly 360 degree field of fire, having low but wide embrasures taking up most of wall perimeter; interior concrete shelf for resting weapons, probably Bren guns; covered porch with steps down to entrance; found in dunes at Camber Sands behind Pevensey Bay and elsewhere in East Sussex; constructed of wood-shuttered poured concrete to high standard, with chamfered roof-line; some have Turnbull mounts.

Dimensions: externally 19ft 6in x 14ft (5.9m x 4.3m); wall-thickness 36in (91cm)

Examples survive at:
TQ574112 (Lower Horsebridge) (*161*)
TQ964184 & 961184 (Camber Sands)
TQ622043 (Pevensey).

Refs: fieldwork, Bill Sholl

5g. mg posts

Very open, vulnerable-looking mg posts at Rye Harbour; six deep, wide embrasures are backed by tables for Vickers guns; there are additional very low loops at the front corners, probably for observation, and a doorway in one rear corner. The embrasures must have been blocked with sandbags.

Dimensions: externally 23ft x 15ft 6in (7m x 4.7m); wall-thickness 30in (76cm)

Examples survive at:
TQ948181 & TQ947180 (Rye Harbour) **5g** (*162*)
TQ933203 & TQ952188 with loops reduced to slits **5gi**
TQ916181 all but one loop with table for Vickers gun, blocked **5gii**

5h. pillbox

Simple pillbox for five lmgs with entrance in one corner;

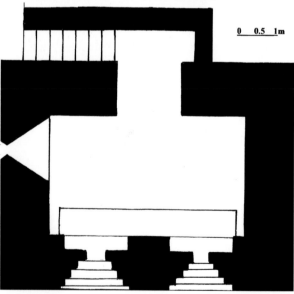

160 Markinch, Fife (NO302029) **5e**; emplacement for two Vickers guns firing to the front, as used on the GHQ Line in Fife

brick shuttering left in situ, as is corrugated-iron shuttering on ceiling, and pre-cast lmg loopholes; unusual to see a shell-proof pillbox of this type.

Dimensions: 23ft x 15ft 6in (7m x 4.7m); wall-thickness 42in (1.07m)

Example at:
SU720038 (Hayling Island, Hampshire) (*163*)

5j. pillbox to drawing number 390 (August 1941)

Design for a pillbox for two Bren guns, issued by Air Ministry for airfield defence, but no example has been identified as yet. Two Turnbull mounts in front long wall, entry in rear; end walls blank; features two bunk-beds and two baths for cooling Bren barrels; three alternative layouts with same provision were issued (*164*).

Dimensions: externally 30ft x 14ft 9in (9m x 4.5m); wall-thickness 42in (1.07m)

Ref: AIR 2/7349 (TNA)

5k. pillbox

Pillboxes with seven assorted, widely-splayed loopholes, one with H-shaped AR wall and the other with a roof-hatch; one has three monopod lmg mounts and the other seven; constructed in poured concrete in brick shuttering.

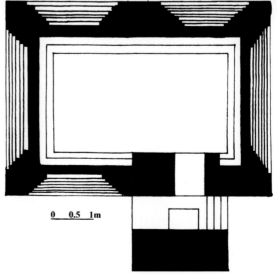

0   0.5   1m

161 Lower Horsebridge, East Sussex (TQ574112) **5f**; pillbox with wide embrasures and continuous weapons shelves, probably for up to five Bren guns

162 Rye Harbour, East Sussex (TQ948181) **5g**; emplacement with open loops and tables for six Vickers guns

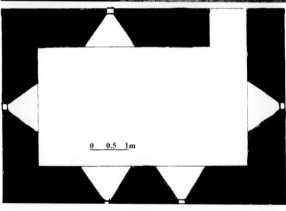

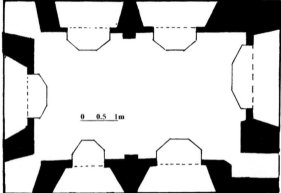

163 Hayling Island, Hampshire (SU720038) **5h**; very plain, shell–proof pillbox for five lmgs

DRG. NO. 390 August 1941

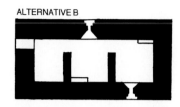

ALTERNATIVE B

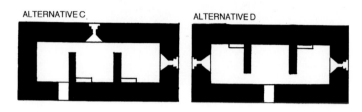

ALTERNATIVE C   ALTERNATIVE D

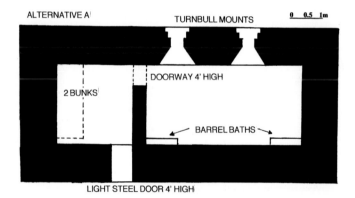

ALTERNATIVE A

TURNBULL MOUNTS

0   0.5   1m

DOORWAY 4' HIGH

2 BUNKS

BARREL BATHS

LIGHT STEEL DOOR 4' HIGH

164 Design to drawing number **390** of August 1941 for a shell-proof pillbox for two lmgs, with three further alternative layouts; no known examples

Dimensions: externally 21ft x 16ft (6.4m x 4.9m); wall-thickness 42in (1.07m)

Examples at:
TG402189 & 275229 (Ludham, Norfolk) (*165* & *166*)

5m. pillbox
Pillbox with three forward-facing embrasures for rifles; constructed of concrete blocks on brick foundations; entry in end wall; other end and rear walls blank.

Dimensions: externally 16ft 6in x 8ft (6.4m x 4.9m); front wall 42in (1.07m) thick, but other three walls only 15in (38cm) thick
Example at:
SU739590 (Hazeley, Hampshire) on GHQ Line; another similar at Boston Haven, Lincolnshire, now buried under sea-bank.

Refs: fieldwork and Colin Alexander

165 Ludham, Norfolk (TG402189) **5k**; airfield pillbox with seven loopholes for lmgs or rifles and solid H-shaped AR wall

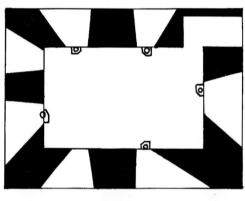

0   0.5   1m

166 Ludham, Norfolk (TG275229, top, & 402189, bottom) **5k**; (**165**); plans of two shell-proof, airfield pillboxes for seven lmgs or rifles

5n. pillbox (Dover Quad shell-proof)

A number of non-standard square pillboxes were built to defend Dover. All are thin-walled except for one at TR314407 which is 16ft (4.9m) square, with walls 48in (1.22m) thick; it has a lmg loop in each of two sides, a pair of widely-splayed loops separated by a mullion in a third side and an entrance in the fourth; see also **6niii**.

Ref: David Burridge

5p. pillbox

This pillbox has an open porch accessed by rungs, and steps down into the chamber, which has three monopod mounts for lmgs in wide, stepped embrasures; there is a double-ended Y-shaped AR wall down the middle; its elevated position gives it enormous vision and fields of fire.

Dimensions: 17ft x 15ft (5.2m x 4.6m) + porch; wall-thickness 30in (76cm)

167 Harpur Hill, Buxton, Derbyshire (SK062690) **5p**; rectangular shell-proof pillbox with three lmg embrasures, and an open annexe

Example:
one of a pair at SK062690 (Buxton, Derbyshire) (*167*)

Refs: fieldwork, Ian Sanders

6. BULLET-PROOF SQUARE AND RECTANGULAR PILLBOXES

This section probably contains most variety in terms of design and layout; these are clearly the easiest shapes to build, if not necessarily the most effective from the military point of view. This category contains just two official designs which were widely built, another which, according to the documentation, was built by the thousands, but hardly survives and one which seems not to have been built at all. In addition, there are a number of groups of designs confined to particular localities, most probably by chance rather than design and these are treated as families.

6a. pillbox to drawing number DFW3/23

This is a quite common design which occurs in a number of locations; it comprises a square, roofed chamber with, usually, three loopholes, which is backed by an open platform with a mounting for a LAA mg. Access to the open platform is by a door or by rungs set in the outer wall; the closed chamber is entered down steps from the open part. Some examples have twin loopholes in the front wall; two examples (at Barrow-in-Furness and at Workhouse Green in Suffolk) are built high up on concrete plinths; several examples in Suffolk stand alone in isolated locations and may have been sited to defend searchlight sites. Construction of poured concrete in timber shuttering is usually of high quality; some examples in South Wales are shuttered in brick.

Dimensions: externally 14ft x 9ft (4.3m x 2.7m); wall-thickness 15in (38cm)

Examples at:
TF327433 (Boston, Lincolnshire) (*168*)
SD304023 (two) at (Hightown, Formby, Lancashire)
TR315408 (St Martins Bty. Dover, Kent) twin loops (*169*)
TL900371 (Workhouse Green, Suffolk) on a plinth
example at SN400047 (Pembrey, Carmarthenshire) has rungs in outer wall, and is brick-shuttered

Refs: fieldwork, War Office plans *c*.May 1940

6ai. variant of DFW3/23

This is found only in Lincolnshire[†] where more than 30 examples survive, the most easterly example sitting plumb on the Norfolk border; it consists of two square, roofed chambers, with an open platform for an LAA mounting in between; the platform is entered through a gap in the front wall, and each chamber is entered down steps from just inside this outer entrance; in some coastal locations rifle-loops are replaced by mg embrasures enfilading the beach.

Dimensions: externally 24ft x 10ft 6in (7.3m x 3.2m); wall-thickness 18in (46cm)
Examples at:
TF475891 (Theddlethorpe-St-Helen)
TF443960 (Warren House) with mg embrasure
TF512842 (Mablethorpe) lintel over door, the whole formerly camouflaged as a house
TF453310 (Holbeach) (*170*)

[†]NB: William Foot reports one at TR259650 (Sarre, Kent)

6aii. variant of 6ai

A handful of examples are found around Saltfleetby and Theddlethorpe, in one near Boston the whole pillbox is roofed to form three chambers, each with a wide mg embrasure; some examples have pistol-loops by the door. One example has a porch, but there are three rifle-loops in each end chamber, with the middle one blank.

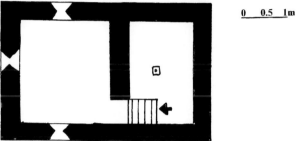

0   0.5   1m

168 Boston,
Lincolnshire (TF329436)
6a; pillbox to drawing
number DFW3/23,
showing open pit for
LAA mounting

169 St Martin's Battery, Dover, Kent (TR315408) **6a**; pillbox to drawing number DFW3/23,
with two loopholes in end wall

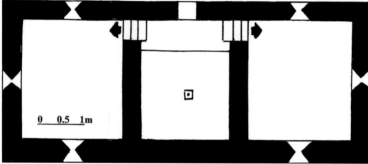

170 Holbeach St Matthew, Lincolnshire (TF453310) **6ai**; local variant of **6a** with two enclosed chambers and central open LAA platform

Examples survive at:

TF452910 (Saltfleetby-All-Saints) mg embrasures (*171*)

TF315529 (Shorts Corner) porch and rifle-loops

6aiii. variant of 6ai

At RAF Newton (Notts) and at RAF Eglinton (Co. Londonderry); here, there are the two chambers, but the open platform between them protrudes front and back.

Example survives at:

SK691413 (Newton, Notts)

6b. family of pillboxes

These are found on Teesside, and appear to share a similar root; their layout is generally uniform but their dimensions differ; they generally consist of two chambers with combinations of rifle and lmg loops, with a cross-wall; the entrance is often dog-legged and covered by a loopholed traverse.

Dimensions: 15ft 6in-19ft x 8ft-9ft (4.7m-5.8m x 2.4m-2.7m); wall-thickness 15in (38cm)

171 Saltfleetby-all-Saints, Lincolnshire (TF452910) **6aii**; a further variant of **6a** with covered central section

Examples at:
NZ492439 (High Throston, Hartlepool) with sliding steel shutters on loops (*172*)
NZ497275 (Greatham) (*173*)
NZ403233 (Thorpe Thewles) NB: two DFW3/23s nearby (*174*)

6c. family of pillboxes

These are found in Northumberland, and appear to share a similar root; their layout is generally uniform, but their dimensions differ; they generally consist of a single chamber with combinations of rifle and lmg loops, with a longitudinal AR wall; the entrance is often dog-legged and covered by a loopholed traverse.

Dimensions: 15ft 3-9in to 10ft-3-9in (4.7m x 3.2m); wall-thickness <15in (30-38cm)
Examples at:
NU219271 (Tughall Mill) (*175*)
NU213285 (Swinhoe)
NU189331 (Sadlershall)
NU051481 (Goswick) with Range quadrant tower built on top (*176 & 177*)
NB: similar style at RAF Culmhead, Somerset at ST206144

Refs for both **6b** and **6c**: fieldwork, Alan Rudd

172 High Throston, Hartlepool, Teesside (NZ492349) **6b**; pillbox with two compartments and a covered entrance in one end

173 Greatham, Teesside (NZ490279) **6b**; pillbox with two compartments and a covered entrance in a side

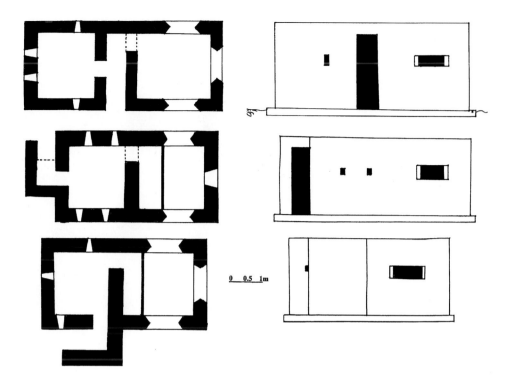

174   Teesside Pillboxes, elevations and plans (top) Eaglescliffe, (middle) High Throston, (bottom) Greatham; after Rudd

6d. family of pillboxes

Three local variations of a widespread non-standard type; this pillbox consists of a square chamber with three lmg loops; each has an enclosed entrance porch, open to the sky and accessed by rungs set in the wall; the three differ in respect of entrance porch, and door orientation. All three are positioned to enfilade the beach.

Dimensions: 11ft or 14ft (3.4m or 4.3m) x 9ft (2.7m); wall-thickness 12-15in (30-38cm)

Examples:
all on Tywyn beach, Gwynedd, at SN586985 (no. 1), SN590977 (no. 2) & SN592969 (no. 3) (*178*)

6e. mg post

This mg post has wide embrasures backed by tables for Vickers guns, in either the front or a side wall; there is a blast-wall covering the entrance and two rifle-loops in other walls; found on the airfield at Weston-super-Mare.

Dimensions: externally 11ft 9in x 9ft (3.6m x 2.7m); wall-thickness 15in (38cm)

Examples at:
ST341604 (*179*), 351608 & 346596 (Weston-super-Mare, Somerset)

175 Tughall Mill, Northumberland (NU219271) **6c**; rectangular pillbox with mix of loops for rifles and lmgs

176 Goswick, Northumberland (NU051481) **6c**; rectangular pillbox with six rifle-loops; a bombing-range quadrant tower has been built on top

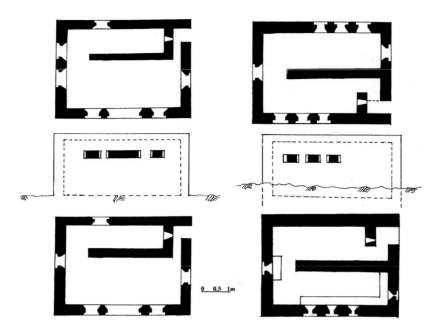

177 Northumberland pillboxes: (top and middle left) Tughall Mill, plan & elevation; (lower left) Swinhoe, plan; (top & middle right) Sadlershall, plan and elevation; (lower right) Goswick, plan; after Rudd

Refs: fieldwork, Paul Francis

6f. mg post

Another mg post, this time with two mg embrasures backed by tables for Vickers guns, sited to enfilade a beach protected by lines of AT blocks; the entrance is covered by a blast-wall and the seaward face is blank. Situated on the Moray coast.

Dimensions: 14ft x 9ft (4.3m x 2.7m); wall-thickness 15in (38cm)

Example at:
NJ330660 (Kingston on Spey, Moray) (*180*)

Ref: fieldwork, Peter Cobb

6g. four compartment defence post to drawing 2843 (Scottish Cmd)

A design for a pillbox for four lmgs, which appears not to have been implemented anywhere; it is divided into four segments by cross-walls (*181*).

Dimensions: 14ft 3in (4.3m) square

Ref: WO 199/2657 via Colin Dobinson

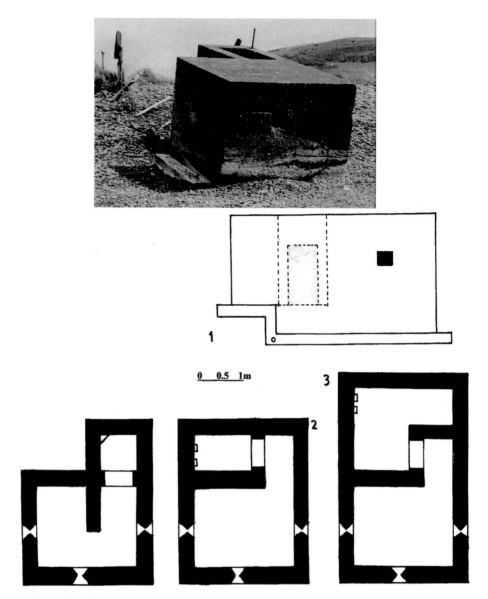

178 Tywyn beach, Gwynedd (SN586985 no.1, 590977 no.2, & 592969 no.3) **6d** three pillboxes with enclosed chambers and open entrance pits accessed by rungs; photo and elevation of no. 1, plans of nos 1, 2 and 3

6h. pillbox

This design, found only on the River Dove defence line in Staffordshire and Derbyshire, is unusual in that it comes in two sizes and has a pentice roof; both designs have four lmg loops and the larger one has a more massive than usual AR wall; some are raised on plinths, and one pair of pillboxes straddles the river.

Dimensions: 13ft 6in x 10ft (4.1m x 3m) and 10ft 6in x 7ft 3in (3.2m x 2.2m); all walls in both sizes of pillbox are 18in (46cm) thick

179
Weston–super–Mare,
Somerset (ST341604
no.1 & 346596 no.2)
6e; two rectangular
mg posts; photo and
plan of no. 1 and plan
of no. 2

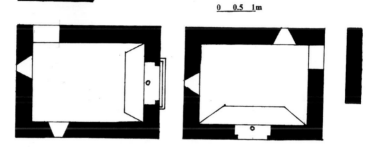

180 Kingston on Spey,
Moray (NJ330660) **6f**;
mg post for two guns
enfilading the beach

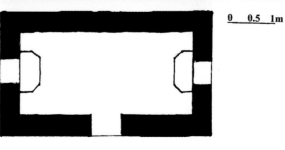

Examples at:
SK243287/8 (Marston-on-Dove, Derbyshire) (*182*)

6j. pillbox built by 558 Field Coy RE

Dozens were built in Suffolk, with only minor differences; there are usually two or three stepped, splayed loops in each of three sides, with one in the side containing the entrance; all have shelves below them; there is no AR wall; the entrance has a low, or full-height L-shaped wall attached in front of it, sometimes chamfered to increase the field of fire of the adjacent loophole; generally shuttered in 2in (5cm) thick concrete blocks, with vertical reinforcing rods through the poured concrete and with pre-cast loopholes; one pillbox is dated 7/8/40 over the door inside and another is signed by the RE unit; many have a loophole in the blast-wall; one at Oxley Marshes has a screen wall projecting from a corner and running parallel to the entrance blast-wall and another has a pistol-loop covering the doorway.

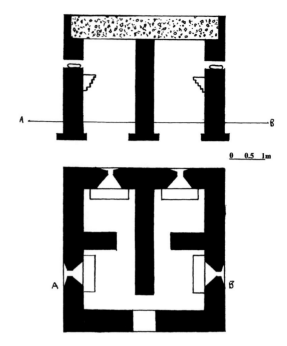

181 Four compartment Defence Post to drawing number 2843, 6g; this is one of the designs produced by the Air Ministry, but apparently never issued

Dimensions: 12ft 6in (3.8m) square; wall-thickness 15in (38cm)

Examples survive at:
TM535837 (Kessingland) (*183*)
TM417594 (Friston)
TM476601 (Thorpeness)
TM551965 (Corton Cliffs)
TM317364 (Felixstowe)
TM470613 (Sizewell) (*183*)

Refs: fieldwork, William Ward, Peter Kent and Alan Lockwood

6k. pillbox to drawing number DFW3/26

This pillbox is the simplest of all the DFW3 designs, consisting of a single chamber with three or, more usually, four loopholes; it has been suggested that it is sometimes referred to in contemporary correspondence as the Stento, so may have been designed

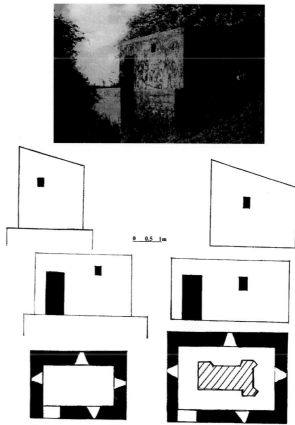

182 Marston-on-Dove, Derbyshire (SK243287) **6h**; this rectangular pillbox, with the unusual sloping roof, came in two sizes by a commercial producer. The

183 Suffolk Pillbox (above) Sizewell (TM470613) photo showing chamfered blast-wall; (below) Kessingland (TM535837) plan showing typical layout

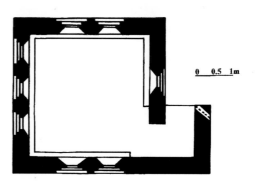

building firm Stent, still in operation in 2007, was responsible for the square pre-fabricated pillbox, which is quite common (see **6t**); at Beachley, under the Severn Bridge, are two examples of a square pillbox which conforms to DFW3/26's dimensions and layout, but is made up of narrow, pre-fabricated slabs of reinforced concrete, bolted together; there are two more, similar pillboxes on the Gloucester and Sharpness Canal which resemble the Beachley ones, but are quite different from the Stent ones, where the pre-fabricated panels form the permanent shuttering for poured concrete; this missing link may illuminate the connection between the three designs, one being a prototype for the other.

Dimensions: 10ft (3m) square; wall-thickness of 18in (46cm)

Surviving examples are, strangely enough, quite hard to find, as there are several which are smaller, or else are provided with fewer loopholes than the standard. The example at TG388304 (Happisburgh, Norfolk) appears to be as good an example of the standard design as can be found:
TF317323 (Fosdyke, Lincs) three loops, 8ft (2.4m) side (*184*)
ST547903 & 549903 (Beachley, Gwent) standard, but pre-cast slabs (*185*)
SO746085 & 757095 (Gloucester Canal, Gloucestershire) as Beachley
SU163174 & 163175 (Breamore, Hampshire) possibly standard
SY544855, 570848 & 575846 (Chesil Beach, Dorset) three loops
TL706896, 702886, 702887 & 704879 (Feltwell, Norfolk) (*186*) with Turnbulls and

0   0.5   1m

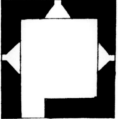

184 Fosdyke, Lincolnshire (TF317323) **6k**; square pillbox, generally to drawing number DFW3/26, but with no loophole in rear wall similarly two at TL737945 (Methwold, Norfolk) SM990351 (Llanychaer Bridge, Pembs) integral, loopholed L-shaped blast-wall, and two loops in one wall.

6ki TQ655074, 654074& 655075 (Wartling, E Sussex) 9ft (2.7m) sides, each with two or three loopholes with monopod mounts for Lewis guns; two have open, circular annexes for LAA mounts, the third has an L-shaped blast-wall (*187*)

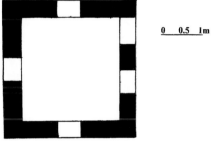

6m pillboxes
A very loosely-related clutch of pillboxes from the Shropshire/ Staffordshire area, with dimensions within a

185 Beachley Point, Gloucestershire (ST547903) **6k**; square pillbox built to the DFW3/26 specification, but out of pre-fabricated concrete panels bolted together

186 Feltwell, Norfolk (TL706896) **6k**; airfield pillbox built to the design in drawing number DFW3/26

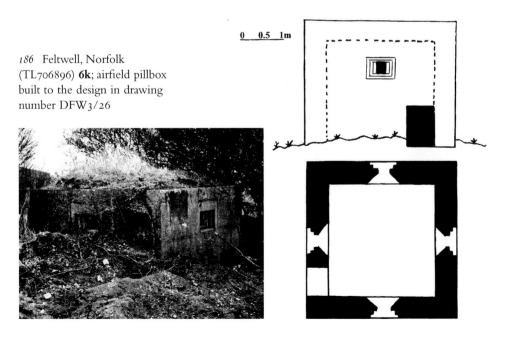

wide range, some had fake gabled roofs for camouflage, all have different combinations of lmg and rifle-loops, most appear to be one-offs.

Dimensions within the range 11ft 6in to 24ft (3.5m-7.3m) x 8ft to 18ft (2.4m-5.5m); wall-thicknesses 15in to 24in (38cm-61cm)

Examples include:
SJ599189 (*188*), 598180 & 604187 (High Ercall, Shrops)
SJ373271 (three) at(Rednal, Shrops)
SK210022 (Fazeley, Staffs) (*189*)
SJ956579 (Harpers Gate, Staffs) (*190*)
SK019203 (Wolseley Bridge, Staffs)
SK153131 (Lichfield, Staffs)

Refs: fieldwork, Roger Thomas, Bernard Lowry

6n. open-topped pillboxes
There are two groups of such structures, one centred on the coast north of Liverpool, and the other in Cheshire around Woodford; they are square and have walls up to chest height, with a pillar at each corner, which supports an overhanging slab roof; there are some variations on this too.

0   0.5   1m

187 Wartling, East Sussex (TQ655074 no.1, TQ654074 no.2 & TQ655075 no.3) **6ki**; three pillboxes guarding a radar site; each is square with either a circular open LAA pit, or a porch. Photo and plan of no.1 and plans of nos 2 and 3

188 High Ercall, Shropshire (SJ599189) **6m**; rectangular pillbox disguised as a barn

189 Fazeley, Staffordshire (SK210022) **6m**; rectangular pillbox with five loopholes, beside the Coventry Canal, here forming a defence line

190 Harpers Gate, Staffordshire (SJ956579) **6m**; rectangular pillbox with fake gable-ends to support a roof as camouflage

Dimensions: externally 8ft x 8ft (2.4m x 2.4m); walls 4ft (1.22m) high & 15in (38cm) thick

Examples survive at:
SD314067 (*191*) & 316080 (Formby, Lancashire)
SJ915817 & SJ900807 (Woodford, Cheshire)

Variations include:
6ni SJ915822 (Woodford, Cheshire) measures 13ft x 10ft (4 x 3m) (*192*)
6nii SJ892832 (Woodford, Cheshire) as **6ni** but one curved corner (*193*)

6niii often referred to as Dover Quads

A group of around 20 pillboxes in Dover have overhanging slab roofs, most commonly 17ft (5.2m) square over chambers with very open and wide embrasures; some are smaller, and different in shape; wall thickness ranges from 12in (30cm) to 48in (1.2m); see also **5n** and **7d**

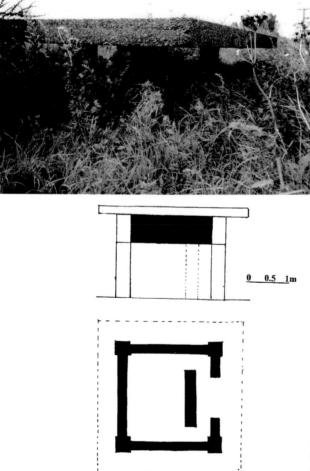

0   0.5   1m

191 Formby, Lancashire (SD314067) **6n**; open pillbox with roof supported on pillars

Examples include:

TR306406 (Dover, Kent) (*194*)

Refs: fieldwork, David Burridge

6p. pillbox with rooftop LAA position

There are two examples of this pillbox defending the perimeter of a radar site at Bempton; the loopholes are set high in the walls, with one in the middle of each side, and one in each of three corners; the entrance is raised; the LAA position, in one corner of the roof platform is accessed by an external ladder, fixed to the side wall; the holdfast for the LAA weapon stands on a low platform surrounded by an L-shaped brick wall. An aerial photograph of August 1941 shows both pillboxes and circular pits for LAA lmgs.

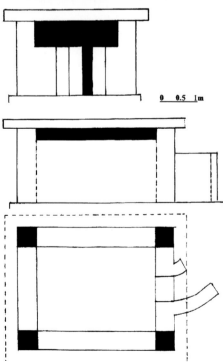

192 Woodford, Cheshire (SJ915822) **6ni**; open pillbox with supported roof and curved half-height screen to entrance; photo, elevations and plan

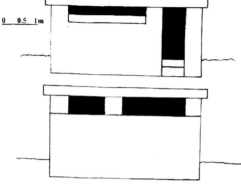

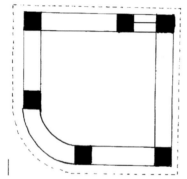

Right 193 Woodford, Cheshire
(SJ892832) **6nii**; open pillbox, similar to
192, but with one curved angle

Below 194 Dover, Kent (TR306406)
6niii; square pillbox, often referred to as a
'Dover Quad', with over-hanging canopy

Dimensions: 13 (4m) square under 16ft (4.9m) square overhanging concrete roof-slab; wall-thickness of 12in (30cm)

Examples at TA191735 & 192735 (Bempton, N. Yorks) (*195*)

6q. pillbox

This group of pillboxes defending Bramcote airfield is unusual in that, like **6p** they have corner loopholes; construction is of poured concrete into brick shuttering, and the loopholes appear to have been cast on site; there is a loophole in the middle of each side, and one at each corner; one pillbox has two loops in one long side, **6qi**; the entrance is at one corner reached down two or three steps.

Dimensions: externally 11ft x 9in (3.6 x 2.7m); wall-thickness 15in (38cm)

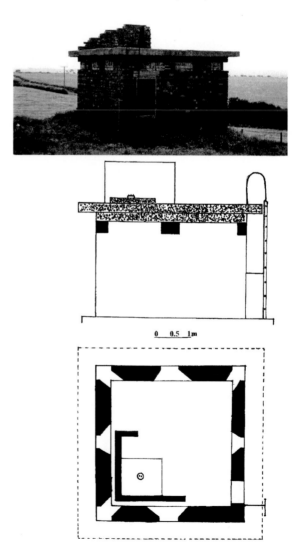

0   0.5   1m

195 Bempton, East Yorkshire (TA191735) **6p**; square pillbox with loopholes in the sides and some angles, and a rooftop LAA position reached by an external ladder

Examples at:

SP405874 (*196*), 417875, 417878 & 405869 (**6qi**) (Bramcote, Warwickshire)

6r. paired pillboxes

Here are pairs of rectangular pillboxes joined together under a single roof-slab; each pillbox is split into two compartments by a cross-wall, each having two loopholes; a passage runs the length of the structure between the two sections; a single version is close by; these are at Brackenborough Hall, the HQ for anti-invasion forces in 1940-1.

Dimensions: externally each unit is 28ft x 12in (8.5m x 3.7m); wall-thickness 24in (61cm); the double one sits under a roof-slab measuring 28ft (8.5m) square.

Example is at:

TF330906 (Brackenborough, Lincolnshire) (*197*)

6ri. paired pillboxes at Royal Ordnance Factories

There are a number of such pairings but here they are of unequal length, and have individual roof-slabs; the two units are linked by roofed porches; there is a pre-cast loophole in each outward-facing side and, where one unit is shorter than the other, one covering the porch.

Dimensions: units are 18ft x 9ft (5.5m x 2.7m) or 12ft x 9ft (3.7m x 2.7m)

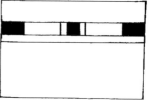

0   0.5   1m

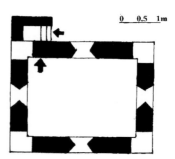

196 Bramcote, Warwickshire (SP405874) **6q**; group of pillboxes, all different, but sharing some characteristics such as corner loopholes

197 Brackenborough Hall, Lincolnshire (TF330906) **6r**; two rectangular pillboxes joined under a single roof with central corridor; each module has four loopholes and a cross-wall; an additional, single module is close by

Examples at:
Wrexham ROF: SJ381483 (*198*), 382484 & 389494

6s. Ruck pillbox

This was a development of the Stanton shelter which was made out of ogival sheets of concrete, bolted together at the roof; it was designed by James Ruck, a Civil Defence adviser, and was produced by Hydroprest Concrete of Scunthorpe; it consisted of a pre-fabricated framework of three or four concrete ribs with gaps between, covered with concrete paving slabs, mounted on walls made of earth-filled, hollow concrete blocks; loopholes were either cut in the sides if the sheets were solid, or formed by leaving out a slab between ribs; there were also sometimes loopholes in the roof; it sat in a trench and the lower walls were earthed up; unless it was on a bank of some sort it had little command of the ground, and was not popular for this reason; nevertheless an order for 6000 was made by Northern Command by September 1940; see also **6ee** (below).

Dimensions: 12ft x 6ft (3.7m x 1.8m); wall-thickness 3in (7.5cm) of concrete rib, 2in (5cm) of concrete slab, plus 18-40in (46-102cm) of earth
Despite the large numbers built, there appear to be very few survivors:
TF400337 (Holbeach St Matthew, Lincolnshire) loops in roof, pre-cast loops in side and in end wall
TF391410 (Freiston Shore, Lincolnshire) fragmentary remains of two
SK478378 (Stapleford, Notts) solid walls as in Stanton with cut loopholes (*199*)
TA141764 (Reighton Gap, N Yorkshire)
TF565595 (Gibraltar Point, Lincolnshire) four ribs and slabs (*200*)

Refs: fieldwork, William Foot, Colin Dobinson

198 Wrexham, Clwyd (SJ381483) **6ri**; two rectangular pillboxes of unequal length, linked by a common porch; one of several similar combinations on this ROF site

6t. Stent pre-fabricated pillbox

This design is found throughout England; it often conforms to the dimensions of DFW3/26, but is constructed of hollow concrete sections, bolted together and filled with rubble and/or poured concrete; there is a pre-cast loophole in the centre of each of three walls, and an off-centre loophole and doorway in the fourth; one example has a table for a Vickers gun incorporated; papers related to the defence of Eckington Bridge in Worcestershire appear to have highlighted the name Stent for this type of pillbox; Stent Pre-cast Concrete Ltd manufactured railway sleepers through the 1930s and 1940s for military use, and is now part of Balfour Beatty as the Stent Piling Co; see also **6k**; it was used on the GHQ Line, Hampshire, and the Oxford Canal.

199 Stapleford, Nottinghamshire (SK478378) **6s**; example of a Ruck pillbox constructed of solid concrete panels with loopholes cut in the side

200 Gibraltar Point, Lincolnshire (TF565595) **6s**; another RUCK pillbox, this time constructed with an outer skin of paving slabs, in which gaps could be left for loopholes

Dimensions: 10ft (3m) or 11ft (3.35m) square; double of 19ft 6in x 10ft 9in (5.9 x 3.7m); wall-thickness 20in (51cm)

Examples at:
TA106799 (Filey Brigg, North Yorkshire) double version
SK628152 & 623154 (Ratcliffe on Soar, Leicestershire)
SZ412823 (Brighstone, Isle of Wight) with Vickers table (*201*)
SU816688 (Wokingham, Berkshire)

Refs: fieldwork, George Dawes, William Ward, Mick Wilks

6u. L-shaped mg post

This is a square pillbox with one corner cut out; a table for a Lewis gun is located behind the front embrasure; a rifle-loop and entrance are in the rear wall; other walls blank; the mounting for the Lewis gun was removed to Fort Nelson (1975 UKFC).

Dimensions: 14ft (4.4m) square minus 5ft x 4ft (1.5m x 1.2m) corner; wall-thickness 24in (61cm); 15in (38cm) roof-slab

Examples at:
SZ833944 (*202*) & 833946 (Selsey, West Sussex)

Refs: fieldwork, Peter Cobb

201 Brighstone, Isle of Wight (SZ413823) **6t**; Stent pre-fabricated pillbox, this particular example is fitted with a table mount for a Vickers machine-gun

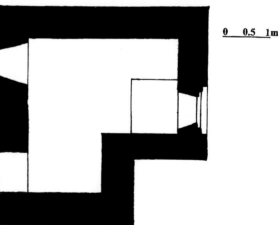

202 Selsey, West Sussex (SZ833944) **6u**; L-shaped pillbox originally equipped with a Lewis gun mounted on a concrete table

6ui. L-shaped pillbox

Roughly rectangular main chamber with three loops in each of three walls, consisting of horizontal pre-cast lmg loop flanked by two vertical, brick rifle-loops; fourth wall has full-height jamb containing three assorted loops with entrance under one of them. High Street radar site at Darsham, Suffolk is defended by six of these pillboxes; four straddle the perimeter fence of the main site and these have rooftop defence positions constructed of sheets of armour plate.

Dimensions: 11ft 6in x 12ft (3.5m x 3.7m) plus jamb 5ft x 7ft (1.5m x 2.1m); wall-thickness 15in (38cm); 12in (30cm) roof-slab

Examples:
TM407716 (*203*), 407717, 406717, 406716, 413717 & 409719

6v. pillbox sometimes described as 'infantry blockhouse'

Found on Lincolnshire coast (nine or ten examples) and on Teesside, this could be seen as a small section-post (see *14*); three loopholes in each long side, loophole and doorway in each end; the distinguishing feature is open mortar/LAA pit attached to low, L-shaped blast-wall outside each door.

Dimensions: 18ft 6in x 9ft 6in (5.6m x 2.9m); wall-thickness 15in (38cm)

Examples at:
NZ562264 (Teesmouth) (*204*)
TF449322 (Holbeach St Matthew, Lincolnshire)

Ref: fieldwork, Sam Thompson

6w. Royal Marine pillbox

Designed for use by RM in Portsmouth; one square example

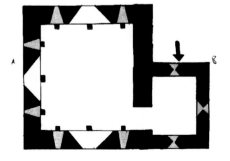

203 High Street, Darsham, Suffolk (TM406716) **6ui**; L-shaped pillbox with entrance under loophole in extension

with four loops in each of three walls, entrance in the fourth and cruciform AR wall; another, rectangular (**6wi**) with six loops in one long side, four in one end and entrance protected by half-height blast-wall and four loops in other end; the fourth side has three loops and what appears to be an observation slit supported by an RSJ. Square pillbox constructed of concrete blocks with pre-cast, stepped loops; **6wi** constructed of stone blocks.

Dimensions: **6w** is 13ft 6in (4.1m) square; wall-thickness 18in (46cm), **6wi** is 19ft x 13ft (5.8m x 4m)

Examples at:
6w   SU594020 (Fort Brockhurst, Gosport, Hants) (*205*)
6wi SZ675989 (Eastney, Hants)

Refs: fieldwork, Peter Cobb, William Ward

6x. Royal Naval pillbox
This consists of a roughly square chamber with a loophole in each side, one of which has an entry below and an open, rectangular annexe for an LAA mounting; it is found on naval installations; constructed mainly of brick with pre-cast loops.

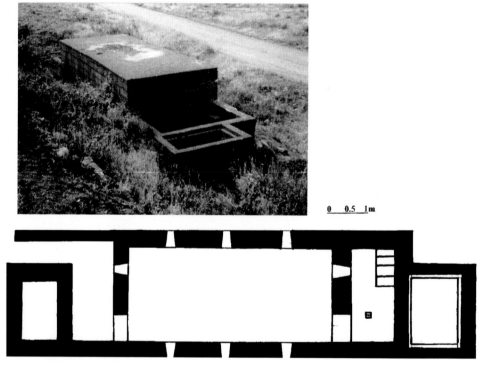

0   0.5   1m

204 Teesmouth, Teesside (NZ562264) **6v**; rectangular pillbox sometimes referred to as 'infantry blockhouse'; the central chamber has eight loopholes and there are open pits at either end for LAA guns or small mortars; photo and composite plan showing end arrangements at Teesmouth & Boston Haven

Dimensions: chamber 9ft x 9ft 6in (2.7m x 2.9m); annexe 19ft x 7ft (5.8m x 2.1m)

Example at:
SU615013 (Priddy's Hard, Gosport, Hants) (*206*)

6y. guard-post

Small chamber with three or four loopholes depending on whether blast-wall is integral or not, or full-height or half-height; used by Royal Navy and ROFs.

Dimensions: 6ft x 7ft (1.8m x 2.1m)

6y low entry in half-height, integral roofed blast-wall, or free-standing half-height blast-wall
6yi full-height porch
6yii 10ft (3m) square, with open upper storey reached by ladder, for LAA mounting
6yiii *c.*8ft (2.4m) square, made of reinforced concrete panels bolted together; one slot in each side and rear door; pyramid roof
6yiv as **6yii** square with open upper storey with LAA mounting, but shell-proof with walls 42in (1.1m) thick

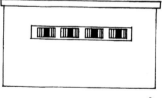

0   0.5   1m

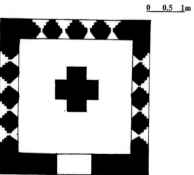

205 Fort Brockhurst, Gosport, Hampshire (SU594020) **6w**; pillbox with 12 loopholes, designed for use by Royal Marines

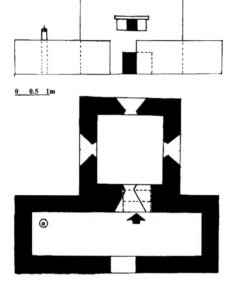

206 Priddys Hard, Hampshire (SU615013) **6x**; square naval pillbox with four loopholes, under one of which is a low entrance, and open annexe for LAA mounting

Examples at:

6y SW884712 (two) at (St Merryn, Cornwall)

6y NO624092 & 623092 (Crail, Fife) (*207*), **6y** SJ391491 (Wrexham, Clwyd) (*208*)

6yi SU616013 (Priddy's Hard, Hants) integral; full-height porch with loophole (*209*)

6yii ST201259 & 206256 (Norton Fitzwarren, Somerset)

6yiii SY952921 (Holten Heath, Dorset)

6yiv SO839739 (Summerfield, Worcestershire)

6z. mine-watchers' post

This is designed for coast-watchers to spot mines out at sea, so vision is maximised by provision of two wide openings taking up most of the front face; occasionally there is a loophole inserted between these; in the rear wall is loophole and an entrance.

Dimensions: externally 8ft 6in x 8ft (2.6m x 2.4m); wall-thickness 18in (46cm)

Examples at:

SU616014 (Priddy's Hard, Hampshire) (*210*) and most naval bases

6aa. open pillbox known as Worcester Fortlet

This open pillbox with battlemented walls is found only in the Worcester area.

Dimensions: 15ft 6in x 8ft 6in (4.7m x 2.6m); wall-thickness 12in (30cm)

Examples at:

SO870580 & 861579 (Perdiswell, Worcestershire) (*211*)

Ref: Mick Wilks

207 Crail, Fife (NO624092) **6y**; naval guard-post with half-height blast-wall, low entry and four loopholes, on top of building at this Royal Naval Air Station

208 Wrexham, Clwyd (SJ391491) **y**; guard-post with roofed, half-height blast-porch, at an ROF

6bb. guard-post

Used at ROFs it is square with a diagonally-set loopholed porch; it is sunken, accessed down six steps, but sited on top of a hill; it has five loopholes; similar in conception to an example at Sinfin, Derby (SK343321).

Dimensions: 9ft (2.7m) square; wall-thickness 15in (38cm)

Example at:
NT585294 (St Boswells, Borders) (*212*)

6cc. pillbox

Here a pillbox is built into the parapet of a road bridge over a railway in order to command both carriageways; loopholes are sited to cover all approaches.

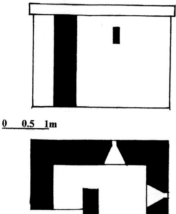

0   0.5   1m

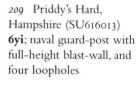

209   Priddy's Hard, Hampshire (SU616013) **6yi**; naval guard-post with full-height blast-wall, and four loopholes

0   0.5   1m

Bottom left 210 Naval minewatchers' post **6z**

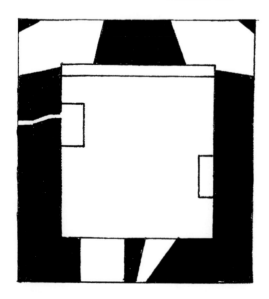

Dimensions: 12ft x 15ft (3.7m x 4.6m); wall-thickness 24in (61cm)

Example at:
SZ194496 (Hinton Admiral, Dorset) (*213*)

6dd. rectangular bullet-proof pillbox

Two examples of this simple rectangular pillbox with two loops in one long side, one in each end and a fifth over a sunken entry protected by a half-height, L-shaped blast-wall, stand on Bagshot Heath.

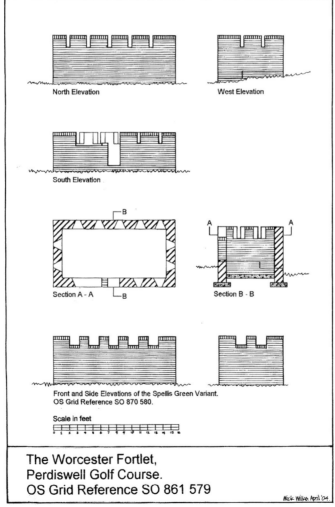

211 Perdiswell, Worcestershire (SO861579) **6aa**; open-topped pillbox with battlements known as the Worcester Fortlet; photo, elevations and plans by Mick Wilks

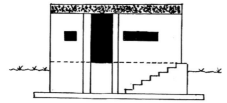

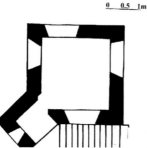

0   0.5   1m

212   St Boswells, Borders (NT585294) **6bb**; guard-post at MAP shell-filling factory

0   0.5   1m

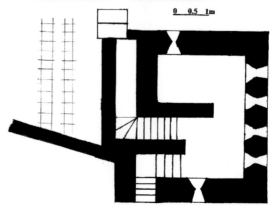

213   Hinton Admiral, Dorset (SZ194496) **6cc**; pillbox built into railway-bridge parapet

Dimensions: 14ft (4.3m) x 9ft (2.7m); wall-thickness 15in (38cm)

Examples at:
SU890632 (*214*) & 889631 (Bagshot Heath, Surrey)

Refs: fieldwork, Tim Denton

6ee. square observation post

About half-a-dozen of these remain on the Lincolnshire coast associated with Ruck pillboxes/Stanton shelters (see *6s/200*). The OP has a wide horizontal slit in each of its four sides and sits above a tunnel entered through the Ruck/Stanton, which, given its construction of loose, concrete slabs, in most examples is very ruinous, making it impossible to do much more than infer the former presence of loopholes.

Dimensions: 6ft-7ft (1.8-2.1m) square with wall-thickness of 12in (30cm)

Examples (of OPs) at:
TA352031 (Tetney Haven)
TA381019 (Horseshoe Point)
TF482895 (Theddlethorpe-St-Helen) (*215*)
TF570642 (Skegness)
TF565595 (Gibraltar Point)

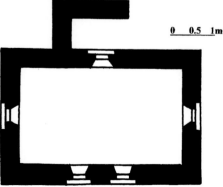

0   0.5   1m

214 Bagshot Heath, Surrey (SU890632) **6dd**; one of a pair of rectangular pillboxes with five loopholes and half-height blast-wall

7. IRREGULAR FOUR-SIDED PILLBOXES

This is a small category of one-off examples; shuttering normally demanded regular shapes and little seemed to be gained from a tactical perspective by creating odd trapezoidal ones.

7a. shell-proof pillbox

This pillbox has two lmg loops on each of three sides and an entrance protected by a blast-wall in the fourth; on one side the loops are extended through holes cut in a wall running alongside the pillbox.

Dimensions: 3 sides of 12ft 6in (3.8m); rear wall 16ft (4.9m); walls 42in (1.07m) thick

Example at:
SU862465 (Moor Park, Surrey) on GHQ Line (*216*)

Ref: Colin Alexander

7b. bullet-proof pillbox

Here we have, in essence, a half-hexagon with two loops in each of three forward-facing sides, by a road; the rear wall, with entrance, is tied into the bank by two short spur-walls; the whole is constructed of granite, with 'framed' loopholes;

215 Theddlethorpe-St-Helen, Lincolnshire (TF482895) **6ee**; square observation-post, accessed through tunnel from adjacent Ruck pillbox; see **6s**

Dimensions: three faces of 12ft (3.7m) and rear wall of 24ft (7.3m); wall-thickness 15in (38cm)

Example at NJ528063 (near Alford, Aberdeenshire) (*217*)

7c. bullet-proof pillbox

A pillbox with two long sides, and two shorter, together containing five stepped, loops, one of which, with the entrance, is in the rear wall.

Dimensions: front wall is 12ft 6in (3.8m), two sides are 8ft 3in (2.5m) and rear wall is 20ft 9in (6.3m); wall-thickness 15in (38cm)

Example at TM269829 (Mendham, Suffolk)

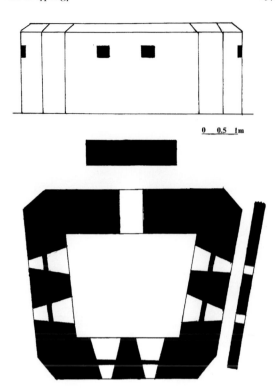

0   0.5   1m

216 Moor Park, Surrey (SU862465) **7a**; shell-proof pillbox on the GHQ Line; two loopholes fire through a field-wall

7d. variation of 6niii

This pillbox has diagonally-set corner pillars creating six wide embrasures, plus a pistol-loop and an entrance, all under a rectangular roof-slab; one of the Dover Quad family;

Dimensions: front face is 9ft (2.7m); two sides of 11ft 6in (3.5m); rear face 15ft 9in (4.8m); roof-slab 22ft x 17ft (6.7m x 5.2m); wall-thickness 24in (61cm)
Example at:
TR 306406 (Dover, Kent) (*218*)

Ref: fieldwork, David Burridge

8. PENTAGONAL PILLBOXES

These are relatively rare, presumably as they will have presented problems with the provision of shuttering and because little extra tactical advantage was to be gained by this shape; the majority of five-sided designs appear on airfields; most are one-offs.

8a. shell-proof pillbox to drawing number 391, August 1941

This is an Air Ministry design which was not, apparently, widely used, as fieldwork has revealed examples in only one location. The drawing gives two alternative layouts which

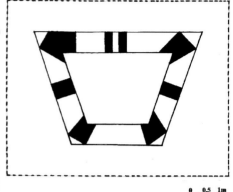

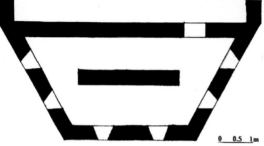

218 Dover, Kent (TR306406) **7d**; one of
the 'Dover Quad' family, see **6niii**; it has
seven very wide loopholes under a generous
overhanging roof; plan after Burridge

217 Alford, Aberdeenshire (NJ528063) **7b**; bullet-proof,
granite pillbox with six loopholes built into a roadside bank

both include the same elements: two loopholes fitted with Turnbull mounts, two bunks,
a low steel door, two baths for Bren-gun barrels and a three-way AR wall.

Dimensions: sides 16ft (4.9m); wall-thickness 42in (1.07m)

Example at:
TA134477 (Catfoss, E Yorks) (*219*), another (damaged) at TA133490
Ref: fieldwork and FSG report on Holderness

8b. shell-proof mg post

This post for two mgs has table mountings behind wide, stepped embrasures; it has an
entry in the rear wall, protected by a blast-wall, and is divided into two chambers by a
cross-wall acting as an AR screen; the concrete tables are mounted on brick pillars and
had tripod weapon mountings; the two front corners are chamfered; constructed of
poured concrete in permanent brick shuttering, except for the embrasures which were
shuttered in timber; a strong-point is formed by two of these mg posts, two pillboxes and
an ammunition store in one corner of the airfield.

Dimensions: front walls 14ft (4.3m); sides 10ft (3m); rear wall 16ft (4.9m); wall-thickness
45in (1.14m)

Examples at:

TL911894 & 911893 (East Wretham, Norfolk) (*220*)

Refs: fieldwork, Peter Kent

8bi. bullet-proof mg posts

Similar structures to **8b** at TL884754 (Honington, Suffolk) (*221*) where there are three loopholes with tables and Turnbull mounts, plus two rifle-loops and a protected entrance; at nearby TL887768 (Fakenham Heath, Suffolk) there are two loops backed by tables and two rifle-loops; wall-thicknesses are 18in (46cm) and 24in (61cm) respectively, but the Fakenham Heath post has a thinner rear wall.

Refs: fieldwork, Simon Purcell

8c. shell-proof lmg pillbox

This pillbox on the GHQ Line has four lmg-loops and a blast-wall with two rifle-loops covering the entrance in the thinner rear wall.

Dimensions: front faces 9ft (2.7m); side faces 7ft (2.1m); rear wall 18ft (5.5m) as is parallel blast-wall; wall-thickness 48in (1.22m), but rear walls 18in (46cm)

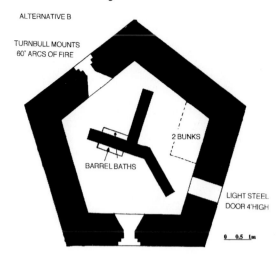

DRG. NO. 391   August 1941

ALTERNATIVE B

TURNBULL MOUNTS 60° ARCS OF FIRE

2 BUNKS

BARREL BATHS

LIGHT STEEL DOOR 4'HIGH

0   0.5   1m

219 Catfoss, East Yorkshire (TA134477) **8a**; shell-proof pillbox to drawing number **391**, possibly one of only two examples built

0   0.5   1m

220 East Wretham, Norfolk (TL911893/4) **8b**; shell-proof machine-gun post, one of two in a strong-point with two other pillboxes; photo and plan after Kent

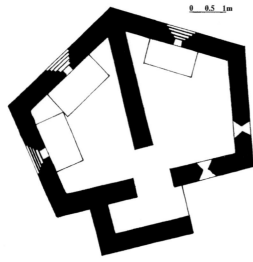

221 Honington, Suffolk (TL884754) **8bi**; bullet-proof machine-gun post, with table-mounts and Turnbull mounts

Example at:
TQ523260 (Buxted, East Sussex) (*222*)

Refs: fieldwork, Bill Sholl

8d. bullet-proof pillbox
This pillbox has four loopholes with Turnbull mounts; it has an odd, curved, rear wall with two entrances; a Y-shaped AR wall connects to an ammunition recess.

Dimensions: four walls 10ft (3m); curved base wall 8ft (2.4m); wall-thickness 24in (61cm)

Examples at:
SU102623, 103624 & 104623 (Alton Barnes, Wiltshire) (*223*)

8e. bullet-proof pillbox
Two pillboxes with three or four rifle-loops and entry in side wall; these are part of the airfield defences, but also defend a bridge on the canal defence line.

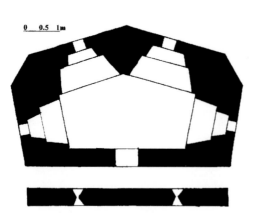

222 Buxted, East Sussex (TQ523260) **8c**; shell-proof pillbox for four lmgs, on the Newhaven-Eridge spur of the GHQ Line

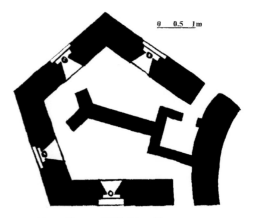

223 Alton Barnes, Wiltshire (SU102623, 103624 & 104623) **8d**; unusual design with four Turnbull mounts, a curved rear wall with two entrances

Dimensions: front faces are 6ft 6in (2m); side faces are 8ft (2.4m); rear wall is 11.3in (3.4m); wall-thickness 15in (38cm)

Examples at:
SK145137 & 146137 (Lichfield, Staffs)

Refs: fieldwork, Lindsey Archaeological Services

8f. bullet-proof machine-gun post

This is an individual design for a cross between a pillbox and a concrete trench; three faces of the structure are open under a canopied roof supported on two brick pillars and provided with a continuous shelf for mounting mgs; behind is a screen wall and sunken entrance; it appears on two Yorkshire airfields.

Dimensions: it is roughly 15ft (4.6m) minus a corner; wall-thickness is 15in (38cm)

Examples at:
SE601646 (East Moor) (*224*)
SE388706 (Dishforth)

Refs: fieldwork, John Harding

8g. bullet-proof mg post

The apex contains an embrasure with a solid brick table for a Vickers gun; there are rifle-loops in each side wall and an entry in the rear.
Dimensions: four walls 5ft 6in (1.68m); rear wall 8ft (2.4m); wall-thickness 15in (38cm); roof-slab 24in (61cm) thick

Examples at:
TG143275 & 141276 (Oulton Street, Norfolk) (*225*)

Refs: fieldwork, Peter Kent

NB: other five-sided pill-boxes of irregular shape are at: TG269221 (Coltishall, Norfolk), TL103023 (Leaves-den, Herts), TG381311 (Hap-pisburgh, Norfolk)

9. OCTAGONAL PILLBOXES

Although many casual observers appear to think of all pillboxes as octagonal, very few in reality are. This category includes two designs found in numbers, several designs found in particular localities and a few one-offs. It is possible that, where single examples are found on airfields, they functioned as Battle HQs (see **13**).

9a. shell-proof pillbox to drawing DFW3/27

We have already encountered the problems caused by the apparent duplication of drawing numbers (see **5a**); this large pillbox is a regular octagon with lmg loops in seven sides, and an entrance protected by a two-way, loopholed porch in the eighth; an internal corridor encircles an open central platform, usually, but not always, with a LAA lmg mount; double steel doors provide access from the corridor to the platform; large numbers of these

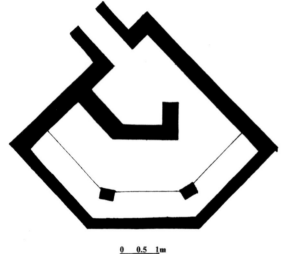

0　0.5　1m

224 East Moor, North Yorkshire (SE601646) **8f**; three faces form an open concrete trench, with overhead cover and defended entrance

225 Oulton Street, Norfolk (TG142276) **8g**; mg post with massive overhead protection

pillboxes were built on the Outer London Line A, where around 30 remain; they are generally shuttered in timber, producing a high-quality finish.

Dimensions: sides 11ft 6in (3.5m); wall-thickness 30in (76cm)

Examples at:
TQ079941 & 079940 (Rickmansworth, Herts)
TL335045 & 339045 (Cheshunt, Herts)
TL339045 (Broxbourne, Herts) (*226* & *228*)

9ai. bullet-proof pillbox adapted from 9a

This is slightly smaller than **9a**, has an enclosed porch and sometimes has an external locker; some examples have steps built into the central platform; it is found in Scotland at airfields (Drem, Kinloss, Lossie-mouth, Macmerry, Montrose etc.) and radar sites such as Drone Hill.

Dimensions: sides 10ft (3m); wall-thickness 18in (46cm)

Examples survive at:
NJ056624 (Kinloss, Moray)
NT848670, 849665, 847666, 846664 etc. (Drone Hill, Berwickshire) (*229*)
NT505810 (Drem, Lothian)
NH628668 (Evanton, Highland)

Refs: fieldwork, Bill Bartlam, Ian Brown

226 Broxbourne, Hertfordshire (TL339045) **9a**; shell-proof, octagonal pillbox to drawing number DFW3/27, on the Outer London Line A; the two-way, loopholed porch and the coping of the LAA platform are visible

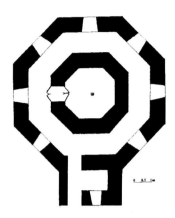

227 Parvills Farm, Essex (TL427037) **9a**; detail of an octagonal pillbox built to drawing number DFW3/27, showing the platform for observation or LAA mounting and the double steel doors providing access to the internal corridor

9aii.228 Plan of octagonal pillbox to drawing number DFW3/27, with alternative porch arrangement

bullet-proof pillbox adapted from 9a

Dimensions: sides 7ft (2.1m); wall-thickness 18in (46cm)

Example at:
SP182119 (Windrush, Glos)

NB: hold-fast on roof not on platform

9aiii. bullet-proof pillbox adapted from 9a

One face curved and no central platform, two AR walls; six lmg-loops and a seventh loop with solid, semi-circular table for Vickers gun (see **8g**).

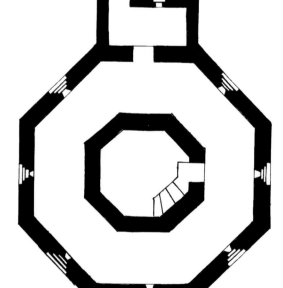

229 Drone Hill, Berwickshire (NT848670) **9ai**; bullet-proof version of **9a**, used mainly on Scottish airfields and radar sites

0   0.5   1m

Dimensions: sides 7ft 3in (1.9m); wall-thickness 18in (46cm)

Example at:
TG151278 (Oulton Street, Norfolk) (*230*)

9aiv. bullet-proof pillbox adapted from 9a
Eight straight sides and loophole over low entrance; dimensions as **9aiii**.

Example at:
TG228130 (Horsham St Faith, Norfolk)

9b. bullet-proof sea-wall pillbox
This is either an octagonal pillbox with two long sides, or two hexagonal pillboxes sharing a common rear-wall, sometimes at different heights; it was designed to straddle a sea-defence bank and has been described as a sardine-tin shape; the double version has one entrance on the side, protected by a blast-wall, and a long, cruciform AR wall; the twin version has entrances on opposite sides; loopholes total 10, in whichever formulation, some with mg tables.

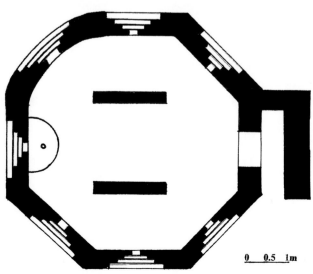

230 Oulton Street, Norfolk (TG151278) **9aiii**; version of **9a**, but smaller and with no open centre; one machine-gun table, six other loops

0   0.5   1m

Dimensions (double): two long sides of 18ft 6in (5.6m); six sides of 6ft (1.8m); wall-thickness 15in (38cm)

Examples on Essex coast at:
TM014152, 015514, 031087 & 032079 and at TQ696748 (Cliffe Fort, Kent)
There is a split-level version at TM028164 (*231*)

9c. shell-proof pillbox
Another elongated octagon with two long sides, and a protected entrance; nine loops with Turnbull mounts; two short AR walls divide into three unequal compartments.

Dimensions: two long sides of 21ft (6.4m); six sides of 10ft (3m); wall-thickness 42in (1.07m)

Example at:
SK150121 (Lichfield, Staffs)

Refs: fieldwork, Lindsey
Archaeological Services

9d. shell-proof pillbox
Essentially square pillbox with four chamfered corners wide enough to accommodate a lmg-loop; one long side has an entrance at each end protected by a *pentice*; it would appear that these were built after the Air Ministry directive limiting the number of loopholes, like the nine examples at Tollerton, only between two and five of the eight faces are loopholed; only some have AR walls and all have Turnbull mounts; some have external brick lockers.

Dimensions: four long sides of 20ft 6in (6.2m); four short sides of 7ft (2.1m); wall-thickness 30in (76cm)

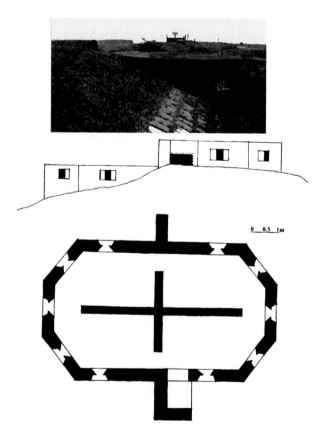

231 Fingringhoe, Mersea Island, Essex (TM028164) **9b**; double-ended, split-level pillbox built into flood-bank; split-level elevation

Examples at:

SK618358 (*232*) etc. (Tollerton)

SK673406 (Newton)

Refs: fieldwork, D. & M. Sibley

9e. shell-proof pillbox

This irregular pillbox has sides of varying length; each of the two longest sides has two loopholes and, apart from the one with the entrance, the other five sides have one loop each. Additionally, three sides have low-level loops, probably for Boys AT rifles.

Dimensions: sides, clockwise from the entrance: 4ft 6in (1.4m), 16ft (4.9m), 8ft (2.4m), 8ft (2.4m), 8ft (2.4m), 14ft (4.3m), 8ft (2.4m) & 12ft (3.7m); wall-thickness 36in (91cm)

Example at:

TR370554 (Deal, Kent)

Ref: fieldwork, David Burridge

9f. shell-proof pillbox

This pillbox has nine loops with Turnbull mounts; it is divided in half by a cross-wall; the loops are stepped and very wide.

Dimensions: two long walls of 16ft (4.9m) and 14ft (4.3m); six short sides of 8ft (2.4m), one of which contains an entrance; wall-thickness 39in (1m)

Example at:

TL573344 (Debden, Essex) (*233*)

9g. bullet-proof pillbox

Essentially a rectangular pillbox with chamfered corners providing 12 assorted loops in the eight faces; one long side contains the sunken entrance, protected

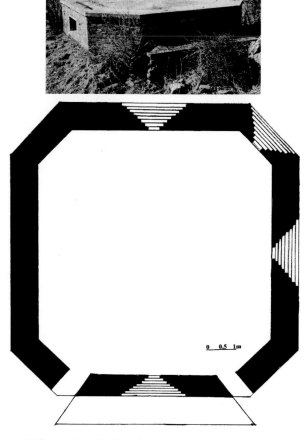

232 Tollerton, Nottinghamshire (SK618358) **9d**; airfield pillbox with limited number of loopholes in eight available faces

by a low wall; there is a longitudinal AR wall.

Dimensions: two long sides of 12ft 9in (3.9m), two end walls of 7ft (2.1m) and four corner walls of 3ft 6in (1.1m); wall-thickness 15in (38cm)

Example at:
SJ414855 (Allerton, Liverpool) (*234*)

9h. bullet-proof pillbox

Another square with three chamfered corners and an entrance with blast-wall on the fourth corner; there are two double loopholes in each of the three seaward-facing sides and a further loophole in each chamfered corner, making nine in all; there is a Y-shaped AR wall.

Dimensions: three sides of 11ft (3.35m), three of 5ft (1.5m) and one of 14ft (4.3m); wall-thickness 15in (38cm)

Example at:
NJ977176   (Balmedie, Aber-deenshire)

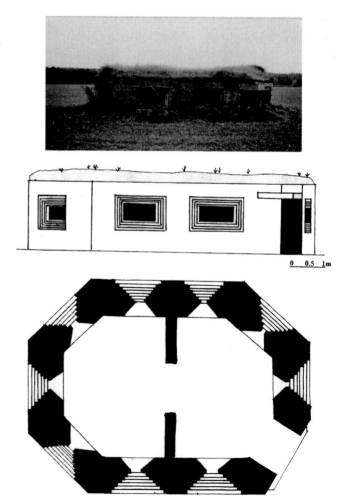

233 Debden, Essex (TL573344) **9f**; shell-proof pillbox with eight loopholes with Turnbull mounts and a corner entrance

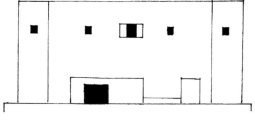

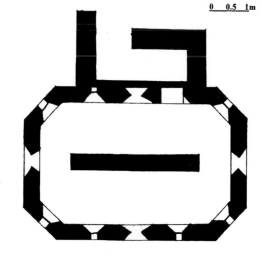

9j. bullet-proof pillbox

Three long sides with three loopholes in each, four short sides each with one loophole, and large loopholed porch on eighth side; straight AR wall bisects chamber.

Dimensions: overall 13ft x 9ft (4 x 2.7m); porch is 5ft 6in x 4ft (1.7 x 1.2m); wall-thickness 15in (38cm)

Example at:
NH783454 (Kenmore, Perth and Kinross)

9k. bullet-proof pillbox with LAA position attached

Built into a bank, this pillbox has four longer sides and four shorter; one of the longer ones contains an entrance, approached up six steps built against a blast-wall; two longer sides have loopholes, as do the four shorter ones; the fourth longer side gives access to an attached, open square LAA position with hold-fast for, probably, a 20mm cannon.

Dimensions: long sides 7ft 6in (2.3m); short sides 5ft (1.5m); wall-thickness 12in (30cm)

Example at:

234 Allerton, Liverpool (SJ414855) **9g**; pillbox with four lmg-loops, and eight for rifles, one of which is over the entrance; photo, elevation and plan

TQ207054 (Shoreham-on-Sea, West Sussex) (*235*)

9m. bullet-proof pillbox

This is apparently the only one of its type in existence and, strangely, is on the GHQ Line, where hardened defences were so standardised; it is a regular octagon with eight loopholes and a low entrance under one of them; each loophole is equipped with a curved shelf, and there is a solid square central pillar which both supports the roof, and acts as an AR screen. This pillbox sits between two Vickers emplacements (**5a**) and may be covering an area of otherwise dead ground.

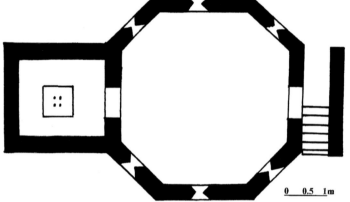

235
Shoreham-on-Sea,
West Sussex
(TQ207054)
9k; bullet-proof
octagonal pillbox
with attached
annexe for LAA
cannon; it is built
into the flood-bank
of the River Adur,
on the eastern edge
of the airfield

Dimensions: eight sides of 6ft (1.8m); wall-thickness 24in (61cm)

Example at:
SU789515 (Chequers Bridge, Hampshire) (*236*)

Refs: fieldwork, Colin Alexander

10. GUN-HOUSES FOR ANTI-TANK AND FIELD GUNS

This category includes emplacements designed for particular weapons, principally the 2 pounder AT gun, but also the 6 pounder Hotchkiss QF gun, as well as structures which could accommodate the variety of odd weapons which constituted the national armoury in 1940. This range included museum pieces, obsolete and superannuated weapons, trophies, test and practice pieces, and recycled guns. Despite the generals' exhortations to maintain mobility, a large number of concrete emplacements were built on designated defence lines and at isolated vulnerable points; construction was poured concrete into either brick or timber shuttering.

10a. shell-proof gun-house to drawing number DFW3/28a (Twin)

This combines two **28a** gun-houses giving an emplacement which allows a 2 pounder AT gun to be fired through either of two adjacent embrasures, thus increasing the field of fire from around 70 degrees to around 140 degrees; there are wells for the gun's pivot in the centre of the floor and sockets for the forward-facing trail legs under each embrasure; there are lmg-loops alongside each embrasure, separated by an AR wall, as well as in the other two sides; a wide entrance in one rear face, allowing for the introduction of the gun, would have been sandbagged to provide some protection to the crew; this was used on the GHQ Line in Wiltshire but mainly in the Sulham Valley on the Red Line west of Reading.

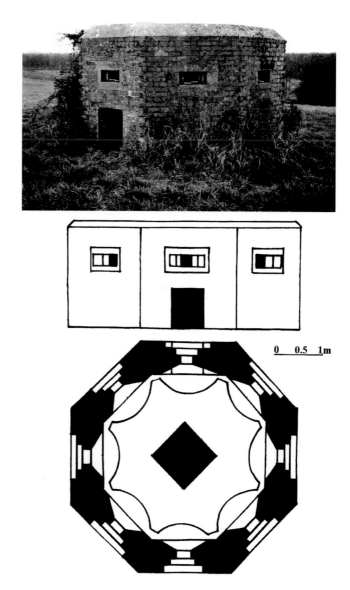

0   0.5   1m

236 Chequers Bridge, Hampshire (SU789515) **9m**; small octagonal pillbox with eight stepped loopholes and semi-circular shelves; *photo by Colin Alexander*

Dimensions: 26ft 3in x 27ft (7.9m x 8.1m); wall-thickness 42in (1.07m)

Examples at:
SU643742 (*237*), 351683, 194627 & 638744

Refs: fieldwork, Colin Alexander

10b. shell-proof gun-house to drawing number DFW3/28a

This is the standard emplacement for the 2 pounder AT gun; it has all the features of **10a**, but for only one gun; this is a much more common structure and was used throughout Britain, particularly on defence lines; variations include rear blast-walls and assorted loophole configurations.

Dimensions: 27ft x 19ft (8.2m x 5.8m); wall-thickness 42in (1.07m)

Examples at:
TF507003 (*238*)
SU575665 & 599672
TL470592

Refs: fieldwork, Colin Alexander

10bi. shell-proof gun-house to drawing number DFW3/28a

Identical to **10b** except for narrowed embrasure with pedestal mount for 6 pounder Hotchkiss QF gun; this mounting consists of a holdfast with 9 (occasionally 12) bolts, on a concrete block (*239*); variations include loophole configuration, conversion to spigot mortar mounting, positioning of entrance, porches, shape etc; used widely (*240*).

Dimensions: as **10b**

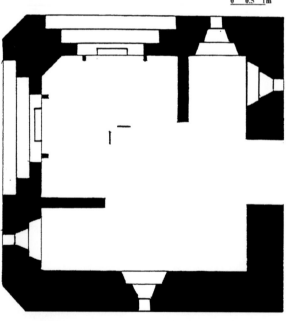

237 Sulham, Berkshire (SU643742) **10a**; the twin version of the gun-house for 2 pounder AT guns based on drawing number DFW3/28a; a single gun was mounted, but could fire through either embrasure; plan after Alexander

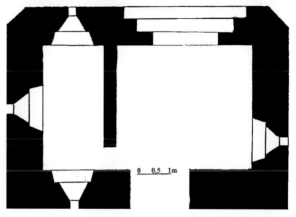

238 Three Holes, Norfolk (TF507003) **10b**; the gun-house for 2 pounder AT guns based on drawing number DFW3/28a, with Bren chamber alongside

Examples at:
TF344583 & 351583
TL520368
TQ308283

Refs: fieldwork, John Guy, Colin Alexander

10bii. shell-proof gun-house to drawing CRE1116

This design appears to be identical to **10bi**, but was developed by the RE office of Eastern Command at Colchester; it was used extensively on both the GHQ Line (East) and the Eastern Command Line; variations of shape and loophole configuration.

Dimensions: as **10b**

Examples at:
TL772725, TL520368 & TL603266

239 Littleport, Cambridgeshire (TL573869) **10bi**; narrow embrasure and pedestal for 6 pounder Hotchkiss QF-equipped gun-houses (**10bi**, **10bii**, **10ci** etc)

Refs: fieldwork, Colin Dobinson

10biii. adaptation of shell-proof gun-house DFW3/28a

Possibly owing to a shortage of suitable weapons, a number of gun-houses, designed for either 2 or 6 pounder guns, were converted to infantry pillboxes by blocking up the main embrasure and substituting rifle- or lmg-loops; in one case (at SU638753, Pangbourne, Berkshire) this change took place during the original build, whilst its partner never got beyond its concrete raft.

Dimensions: as **10b**

Examples:
TL900492, 904545 (Suffolk)
TL876834 (Norfolk)
NH608913 (Highland)

Refs: fieldwork, Colin Alexander

10c. shell-proof gun-house to drawing number DFW3/28

This is **10b** without the lmg chamber; it is a single chamber for a 2 pounder AT gun with the relevant features; there are usually lmg-loops in the side walls; variations include location of entrance; used particularly on GHQ and Eastern Command Lines.

Dimensions: 20ft x 19ft (6.1m x 5.8m); wall-thickness 42in (1.07m)

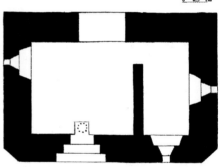

240 Gun-house for 6 pounder Hotchkiss QF guns based on drawing number DFW3/28a, showing the pedestal and narrowed embrasure; after Alexander

Examples at:
TF498002 (*241*), TL393879 & TL544337
Refs: fieldwork, Colin Alexander

10ci. shell-proof gun-house to drawing number DFW3/28

This is like **10c** but for a 6 pounder gun, so has the relevant features; variations of entry, loophole layout etc; used widely on GHQ and Eastern Command Lines.

Dimensions: as **10c**

Examples at:
TQ174512 (*242*), 339441, 524443 & 295448 (Surrey)

241 Three Holes, Norfolk (TF498002) **10c**; gun-house for 2 pounder AT guns based on drawing number DFW3/28, without the Bren chamber alongside

NB: there are a number of one-off adaptations of both the 2 and 6 pounder versions which go beyond the normal modifications noted above; examples can be found at: TQ785255 (Bodiam, E Sussex) loopholed screen-wall to porch, 5 lmg-loops and one pointed end, in modified **10bi**

TL897285 (Wakes Colne, Essex) screen-wall to porch, extra loopholes in three corners, in modified **10ci**

TF662366 (Heacham, Norfolk) *(243)* separate, smaller-than-normal lmg chamber with own entrance, in modified **10b**

TQ771246 (River Rother, E Sussex) *(244)* screen-wall to porch, extended rear chamber for two lmgs, in modified **10ci**

10cii. adaptation of 10c

A one-off adaptation of a gun-house into a lmg pillbox with four loopholes.

Dimensions: as **10c**

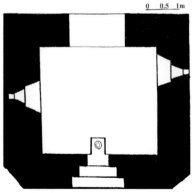

242 Box Hill, Surrey (TQ174512) **10ci**; gun-house for 6 pounder Hotchkiss QF guns based on drawing number DFW3/28

243 Heacham, Norfolk (TF662366) modified **10b**; gun-house for 2 pounder AT gun based on drawing number DFW3/28a, but with completely separate Bren chamber alongside; each chamber is entered through its own door

Example at:
TQ490230 (Buxted, East Sussex)

10d. shell-proof gun-house to drawing number TL55

Designed locally for the Taunton Stop Line (hence TL) where 15 were completed; it is an open-fronted emplacement with a semi-circular, rectangular, or half-hexagonal roofed back half and a half-hexagonal, or semi-circular canopied pit at the front with a cast-iron pedestal mounting with 18 bolts for a Hotchkiss gun; at least one example (SY290983) has a central pier supporting the canopy but bisecting the field of fire.

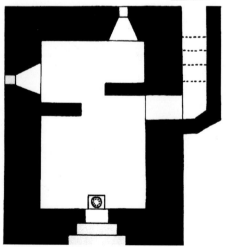

244 River Rother, East Sussex (TQ771246) modified **10ci**; gun-house for 6 pounder Hotchkiss QF gun based on drawing number DFW3/28, but with extended rear section to accommodate two lmgs

Dimensions: varies from example to example, but would be contained in an envelope around 25ft (7.6m) square

Examples at:
SY261924 (*245*)
ST317216 (Curry Mallet)
ST308224 (Wrantage)

NB: single, isolated, circular example at TM552954 (Corton, Suffolk)

Refs: fieldwork, Patrick Rushmere

10di. emplacement for 6 pounder Hotchkiss QF gun

This is essentially an open, hexagonal pit with overhead concrete canopy mounted on a rear wall and two concrete pillars near the front; the mounting is a circular, concrete pedestal with nine bolts; found on the Avon and Severn Stop Lines in Worcestershire; the gun has a total traverse of 251 degrees.

Dimensions: sides of 10ft (3m); wall-thickness of low walls 3ft 9in (1.14m) and of rear wall 13in (33cm)

Examples at:
SO825634 (Holt Fleet) (*246*)
SO952449 (Pershore)
SO807713 (Stourport)

Ref: Mick Wilks

245 Colyford, Devon (SY261924) **10d**; gun-house for 6 pounder Hotchkiss QF guns based on drawing number TL55, on the Taunton Stop Line and numbered S A/T 603 in the local sequence

246 Holt Fleet, Worcestershire (SO825634) **10di**; gun-house for 6 pounder Hotchkiss QF gun, used on the Severn and Avon stop lines

10dii. emplacement for 6 pounder Hotchkiss QF gun

As **10di** but no protective cover, only camouflage; used on GHQ Line Red.

Dimensions: sides of hexagonal pit 8ft (2.4m); wall-thickness 30in (76cm)

Examples at:
SU443971 (Frilford, Oxon) (*247*)
SU593852 (Cholsey, Oxon)

NB: single example built of concrete sandbags at TM551955 (Corton, Suffolk); there are examples in Kent of isolated 6 pounder pedestals with no other discernible structure; presumably they were contained in fieldworks; example at Snowdown.

Refs: fieldwork, Colin Alexander, David Burridge

10e. shell-proof field-gun shelter

Field guns were deployed both for coastal defence and as components of defence lines; a number of shelters were provided such as this one, allegedly for 25 pounder guns in Sussex, where over 20 were built, at least half of which remain; it consists of a half-hexagonal, roofed shelter, with a wide stepped loop, and a completely open back; the height of the embrasure would appear to be insufficient for the 25 pounder to operate at the elevation of which it is capable, so maybe it was for a 75mm gun. Well-built in poured concrete into timber shuttering.

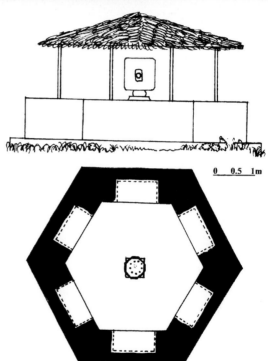

247 Frilford, Oxfordshire (SU443971) **10dii**; gun-pit for 6 pounder Hotchkiss QF gun on the GHQ Line

Dimensions: front 13ft (4m); two sides of 15ft 6in (4.7m) and 25ft 7.6m) across the back; wall-thickness 45in (1.14m); roof-slab 12in (30cm)

Examples:
TQ003042 (Arundel Junction)
TQ 040188 (Pulborough)
TQ195087 (Coombes) (*248*)

Refs: fieldwork, Martin Mace, Ron Martin

10ei. shell-proof shelter for 4.5in howitzer

Several troops of 4.5in howitzers were deployed around the Lowestoft area in 1940, and were apparently provided with hexagonal shelters, open at the front for the guns to be run out prior to firing; nothing now remains at the locations recorded (*249*).

Dimensions: 31ft (9.45m) wide and 16ft (4.9m) deep; wall-thickness *c*.36in (91cm)

Ref: fieldwork, Robert Jarvis

10eii. shelter for LAA gun(?)

A number of examples have been noted in Kent and Dorset of small concrete shelters which are capable of holding a wheeled LAA gun prior to firing.

Dimensions (approx): 10ft (3m) wide and 20ft (6m) deep; wall-thickness 12in (30cm); roof-slab 6in (15cm) thick

Examples at:
TR085604 & 223510 (Dunkirk & Aylesham, Kent)
SY70-73- (Portland)

Refs: fieldwork, Peter Cobb, John Guy

10f shell-proof gun-house for field gun

Particularly on the stretch between Farnham and Tilford, the GHQ Line in Surrey was strengthened by the construction of emplacements for (most probably) the old 13 and 18

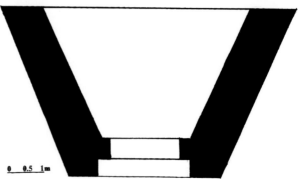

248 Coombes, West Sussex (TQ194087) **10e**; open-backed shelter for field-gun, used along the rivers Adur and Arun

249 Lowestoft, Suffolk **10ei**; shelter for 4.5in Howitzer deployed by a battery of field artillery on coast defence duties in 1940–1; after Jarvis

pounders with which the First and Second Reserve Field Regiments (RA) supporting the Fifth Canadian Infantry Brigade were equipped; all are different, but generally have a wide stepped embrasure under a thick concrete roof; the side walls may have lmg-loops and there is usually a wide entrance at the rear for introducing the gun; one at Waverley Abbey has a crenellated and loopholed wall behind it; another at (SU931439) has mouldings in the floor for a split trail.

Dimensions: generally in the range 30ft (9.1m) wide; 22ft (6.7m) deep; wall-thickness 48in (1.22m)

Examples at:
SU921441 (Somerset Bridge) (*250*)
SU860472 (High Mill House)
SU867462 (Moor Park)
SU871455 (Waverley Abbey)
SU874435 (Tilford)
SU927443 and SU938437 (Peperharrow)

Refs: fieldwork, Colin Alexander

10fi. shell-proof gun-house for field gun

This example at Dover is horse-shoe-shaped and

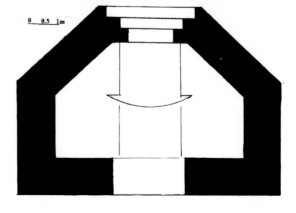

250 Somerset Bridge, Surrey (SU921441) **10f**; gun-house for field-gun, one of several of different shapes on the GHQ Line in the locality

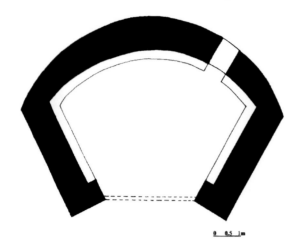

0 0.5 1m

251 Dover, Kent (TR318430) **10fi**;
horse-shoe-shaped field-gun shelter

open-fronted so that the gun may be both introduced and fired; a steel girder supports
the roof above this opening; there is an entrance for personnel at the back.

Dimensions: 30ft (9.1m) wide and 23ft (7m) deep; wall-thickness 39in (1m)

Example at:
TR318430 (Dover, Kent) (*251*)

Refs: fieldwork, David Burridge

10fii. bullet-proof gun-house for field gun

This gun-house covers a bridge on the River Dove Line; it is hexagonal but has been
disguised as a rectangular farm-building by the addition of a pitched roof supported at
the front on concrete posts; the rear entrance is reached down steps and protected by a
blast-wall, so whatever gun was intended to be housed here would have been introduced
through the embrasure.

Dimensions: open front 9ft (2.7m) wide; two faces 8ft (2.4m) wide; two sides 11ft (3.4m);
back wall 22ft (6.7m); wall-thickness 24in (61cm)

Example at:
SK120424 (Ellastone, Derbyshire) (*252 & 253*)
another possible at Woodford airfield, Cheshire

Refs: fieldwork, Henry Meir

10g. bullet-proof gun-house for 75mm gun

Found at various places on the south coast, this structure consists of a rectangular
gun-chamber, with crew-room to one side and magazine to the other, all under a
concrete canopy; at the front dwarf walls delineate the firing position and the gun would
have been lifted down into it. There are some obvious differences between examples.

252 Ellastone, Derbyshire (SK120424) **10fii**; disguised gun-house for field-gun guarding a crossing of the River Dove

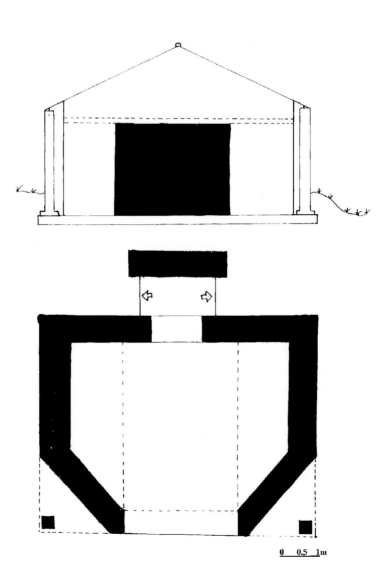

253 Elevation and plan of *252*

0   0.5   1m

Dimensions: central chamber 10ft x 13ft (3m x 4m); two side chambers each 8ft (2.4m) square; wall-thickness 15-18in (38cm-46cm)

Examples at:
SU667040 (Hilsea, Hants) *(254)*
SY542858 (Chesil Beach, Dorset)

Refs: fieldwork, Peter Cobb

10h. shell-proof gun-house for 2 pounder AT gun

This design is specifically for the 2 pounder gun as it has the appropriate fittings; it has a large, open-fronted chamber under a canopied roof, with lmg-loops in the side walls; attached at the back is an open platform with an LAA mounting; located on the River Wyre Line; Freethy refers to five gun emplacements on the sea-wall at Pilling, suggesting that they were designed for 4.7in (120mm) naval guns, but his sketch is very similar to the Inskip example which is clearly for a much smaller gun.

Dimensions: main chamber is 19ft x 17ft (5.8m x 5.2m); rear platform 10ft x 19ft (3m x 5.8m); wall-thickness 42in (1.07m) and 15in (38cm) at the back

Example at:
SD477378 (Inskip, Lancashire) *(255)*

Refs: fieldwork, Ron Freethy, Alan Rudd

10j. bullet-proof gun-house for field gun

This open-fronted struc-ture has two rifle-loops in each side and another loop and an entrance in the back; it is built of brick with a concrete slab roof, concrete pillars framing the open-front and concrete loopholes; it is located on the River Wyre Line.

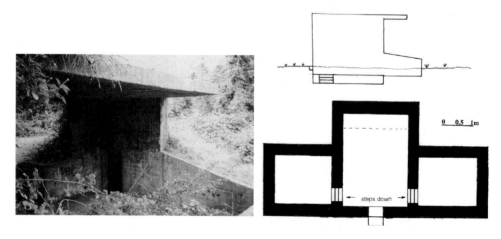

254 Hilsea Lines, Hampshire (SU667040) **10g**; gun-house for 75mm field-gun defending the approaches to Portsmouth; it has a magazine to one side and a crew-room to the other

Dimensions: 12ft x 13ft (3.7m x 4m); wall-thickness 18in (46cm)

Example at: SD485475 (Garstang, Lancashire) (*256*)

Refs: fieldwork, Alan Rudd

10k. shell-proof gun-house

Very plain rectangular chamber with splayed embrasure in front wall and open back; in one side wall is an alcove, half-hexagonal externally, but rectangular internally; there are no features which might suggest any particular weapon was to be mounted here; there is a possible OP next door to it.

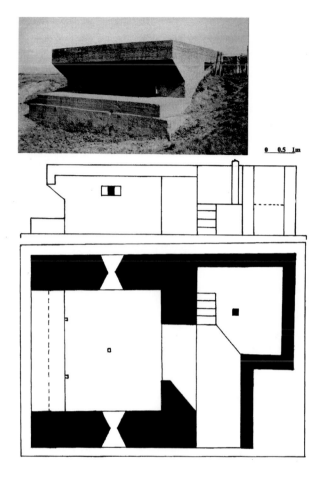

255 Inskip, Lancashire (SD477378) **10h**; gun-house with fittings for 2 pounder AT gun, with an open deck with LAA mounting behind

Dimensions: 18ft x 21ft (5.5m x 6.4m); wall-thickness 54in (1.37m)

Example at: TG098433 (Weybourne, Norfolk) (*257*)

Refs: fieldwork, Christopher Bird

10m. shell-proof gun-house for 6 pdr. Hotchkiss QF gun

In the Shalford sector of the GHQ Line in Surrey, the contractors, Mowlems, developed a way of constructing shell-proof lmg pillboxes by using curved sheets of corrugated iron, producing a D-shaped pillbox with a straight rear wall (see **11a**); the accompanying gun-house was completely circular; it has an embrasure with concrete pedestal for the gun, a lmg-loop and entrance.

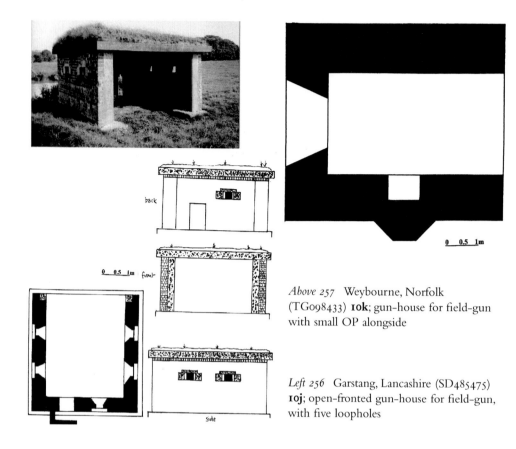

Above 257 Weybourne, Norfolk (TG098433) **10k**; gun-house for field-gun with small OP alongside

Left 256 Garstang, Lancashire (SD485475) **10j**; open-fronted gun-house for field-gun, with five loopholes

Dimensions: 18ft (5.5m) in diameter; wall-thickness 42in (1.07m)

Example at:
TQ012475 (East Shalford, Surrey) (*258*)

Refs: fieldwork, Colin Alexander, William Ward

10n. bullet-proof gun-house for 6 pounder Hotchkiss QF gun

Nineteen of these rectangular gun-houses were built on the Northumberland coast to house Hotchkiss guns; they are rectangular, with a concrete pedestal behind the embrasure; one of the two survivors has a rear entrance down a short flight of stairs protected by a sloping concrete roof; one of the six at Druridge Bay, all now destroyed, had a dummy position alongside with a telegraph pole protruding from it; of two survivors, one was shuttered in corrugated iron, whilst the other used timber.

Dimensions: approx 12ft x 16ft (3.7m x 4.9m); wall-thickness 18in (46cm)
Examples at:
NU178355 (Bamburgh)
NZ314895 (Lynemouth) (*259*)

There is a very similar gun-house at NJ558660 (Sandend, Aberdeenshire) and a picture in Foster shows one at North Gare on the Tees, identified as being designed for a 4in gun.

Refs: fieldwork, Alan Rudd

10p. gun-house for field gun

A single example at Newhaven Fort is entered down a ramp with a right-angle turn into the chamber; an embrasure, almost as wide as the chamber, enfilades the cliff; there is a small recess on each side of the chamber.

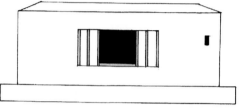

Dimensions: 24ft (7.3m) long chamber x 10ft (3m) wide, narrowing to 7ft (2.1m) at the embrasure

0   0.5   1m

Example at:
TQ450002 (Newhaven, East Sussex)

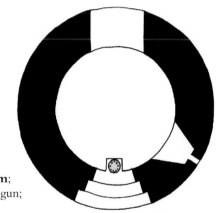

Right 258 East Shalford, Surrey (TQ012475) **10m**; circular gun-house for 6 pounder Hotchkiss QF gun; built by Mowlem on the GHQ Line

259 Lynemouth, Northumberland (NZ314895) **10n**; gun-house for 6 pounder Hotchkiss QF gun, one of only two left on the Northumberland coast

10q. shell-proof gun-house for (?) 3.7in howitzer

Probably the largest inland gun-emplacement built in Britain, this may have been intended for the 3.7in howitzer, a number of which are known to have been allocated to the sector of the Outer London Line A, where six of these gun-houses, recently dubbed the Banstead Fort, were built; it has a large, stepped embrasure in one face, lmg-loops in another six, with a wide entrance in the back under a canopy and protected by a thin blast-wall, above which was what may have been an open LAA position; it may be a distant relative of the DFW3/28a; it is known only from photographs, which have been the basis for this attempt at reconstruction (*260*)

Dimensions: approx. 34ft (10.36m) wide and 32ft (9.75m) deep; wall thickness of main chamber was 42in (1.07) and of the rear wall 12in (30cm)

No examples remain; formerly at TQ249604, 248598 & 275583 (Banstead, Surrey)

Ref: Mike Shackel

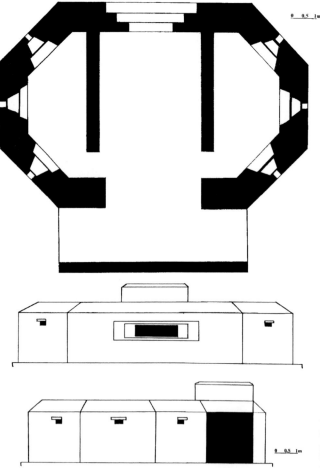

260 Banstead, Surrey **10q**; reconstruction of gun-house, possibly designed for the 3.7in Howitzer

11. CIRCULAR AND ROUNDED PILLBOXES

There is a wide range of diversity in this category as examples range from the sewer-pipe simplicity of the Norcon (**11g**), to Mowlem's innovative engineering (**11a**), or from the quaint medievalism of the Holyhead castles (**11c**) to the sophisticated technological experimentation of the mushroom (**11n**).

11a. shell-proof lmg pillbox adapted from drawing number DFW3/24

This, strangely, is based on the hexagonal DFW3/24, but the contractors on the spot decided to experiment with curved corrugated-iron shuttering to produce a D-shaped pillbox with five lmg-loops in the curved part and two rifle-loops flanking an entrance in the straight rear wall; around a dozen were built in Shalford; see also **10m**.

Dimensions: diameter 19ft (5.8m) with straight rear wall of 14ft (4.3m); wall-thickness 42in (1.07m)

Examples at:
TQ025476 (*261*), 029477
& 015475 (East Shalford,
Surrey)

Refs: fieldwork,
Frederick Bowman of
Mowlem quoted in
Colin Alexander

0   0.5   1m

261 St Martha's Hill,
Surrey (TQ025476) **11a**;
shell-proof pillbox built to
drawing number DFW3/24
specifications but with
curved shuttering instead of
hexagonal

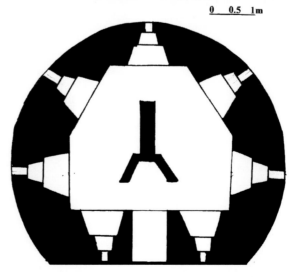

11b. bullet-proof pillbox

This D-shaped pillbox has four mg loops backed by a continuous shelf; it is entered down steps through the straight rear wall.

Dimensions: diameter 15ft (4.6m); rear wall 15ft (4.6m); wall-thickness 15in (38cm)

Examples at:
TR324435 (Duke of York's School, Dover, Kent)

Refs: fieldwork, David Burridge

11c. disguised pillbox

The island of Holyhead off Anglesey was identified as being vulnerable to an invasion through Ireland and was defended by some very individual pillboxes disguised as medieval towers; they are stone-built with different configurations of loopholes, some low down for mgs; a course of stones on end around the rim of each pillbox gives a battlemented effect; see also **19a**; about a dozen were built, at least one with an annexe and most had blast-walls covering the entrance.

Dimensions:
diameter 16ft (4.9m);
wall-thickness 24in
(61cm)

Examples at:
SH251823 (*262*),
252793, 261805 &
252796 (Holyhead,
Anglesey)

Refs: fieldwork, John
Harding

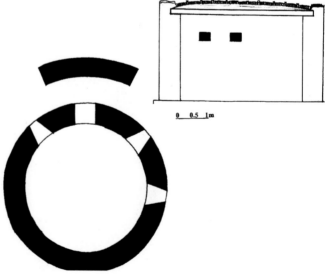

0   0.5   1m

262 Holyhead, Anglesey
(SH251823) **11c**; circular
pillbox built in local
stone and disguised as
medieval tower

11d. bullet-proof pillbox

This circular pillbox has a very thick roof-slab supported on four pillars giving 360 degree vision.

Dimensions: diameter 10ft (3m); wall-thickness 15in (38cm); roof-slab 24in (61cm) thick

Example at:
ST504873 (River Severn, Gloucestershire)

Refs: fieldwork, Medwyn Parry

11e. bullet-proof pillbox

This is a circular pillbox with six loopholes at one level, and five of a different design alternating at a higher level; it is entered by a curved half-height tunnel extending a third of the circumference of the pillbox.

Dimensions: diameter 10ft 9in (3.3m); wall-thickness 15in (38cm)

Example at:
TF858247 (West Raynham) (*263*)

11ei. bullet-proof pillbox similar to 11e

Lower than **11e**, with only one line of loopholes and smaller entrance.

Example at:
SO353058 (Bettws Newydd, Gwent)

263 West Raynham, Norfolk (TF858247) **11e**; circular pillbox with loopholes at two levels and tunnel entrance

11f. bullet-proof pillbox to drawing number DFW3/25 (Armco)

Produced, and probably designed, by Engineering & Metals Ltd of Millbank, London, who produced corrugated-iron sheets at their Letchworth factory under the trade name of Armco (there is still a specialist stainless steel company called 'Armco' based in Baldock) these were provided with pre-cut loopholes as the basis of a shuttering kit for the construction of these pillboxes in the field; there are a number of examples where the shuttering has been left in place as the manufacturers intended, but it would appear that many kits were reused; usually there are three loopholes, but more (or less) could be provided to suit the site; the entrance was low, or, in wet areas, raised as a hatch; some were built without one layer of shuttering, giving a lower profile, but requiring their occupants to fire from a sitting position; the two examples on the GHQ Line at Bramshill have two courses of brick edging the roof-slab.

Dimensions: diameter 8ft (2.4m); wall-thickness 12in (30cm)

Examples at:
TV519989 & 521978 (Cuckmere Haven) (264)
NO724568 (two) at (Montrose, Angus)
SU741612 & 742600 (Bramshill, Hampshire)

Refs: fieldwork, Colin Dobinson

264 Cuckmere Haven, East Sussex (TV519989) **11f**; pillbox built to drawing number DFW3/25 by Armco of Letchworth; the imprint of the corrugated-iron shuttering is clearly visible

11g. bullet-proof pillbox to drawing number CP/6/40/11 (Norcon)

This pillbox probably contravenes the Trades Description Act as tests showed it unable to resist consecutive bursts of fire; nevertheless it was widely used; it consisted of an upright length of sewer-pipe buried in the ground up to loophole-level; the loops, usually four or five, were simply holes cut in the side; its open top increased its vulnerability, so some examples were given flat or domed roofs, the one at Finstown had an access hatch in it; see also **18a**; these are designed as free-standing structures, but at Southrop two have been incorporated into the two forward angles of a rectangular pillbox and teamed with a single **11j**, to form a strong-point on the edge of the airfield.

Dimensions: diameter 6ft (1.8m); wall-thickness 4in (10cm); height 4ft (1.2m)

Examples:
HY361140 (Finstown Broch, Orkney)
SP362097 (two) at (Witney, Oxon)
ND423937 (Hoxa, Orkney) (*265*)
TF768368 (Docking, Norfolk) roofed examples, (*266*)
composite at SP175035 (Southrop, Glos) (*267*)

Refs: fieldwork, Colin Dobinson

11gi. variation on Norcon pillbox

Here a 6ft (1.8m) diameter base widens to 10ft foot (3m) with wide embrasures.

Examples at:
SP766597 (Northampton Power Station/River Nene, Northants) (*268*)

Refs: fieldwork, Adrian Armishaw

265 Hoxa, Orkney (ND423927) **11g**; pillbox built to drawing number CP/6/40/11 by **Norcon**, basically a loopholed sewer-pipe

266   Docking Hall, Norfolk (TF768368) **11g**; one of two, roofed examples of the Norcon (*265*)

267   Southrop, Gloucestershire (SP175035) **11g**; a pair of Norcon-derived pillboxes combined with a rectangular pillbox into a strong-point

268 Northampton Power Station, (SP766597) **11gi**; one of a pair of Norcon adaptations on the bank of the River Nene

11h. bullet-proof pillbox to drawing number PD541 (Croft)

Similar to **11g** this pillbox was built for Scottish Command by the Croft Granite, Brick & Concrete Company of Leicester; sketches suggest it was designed to be sunk in a pit, to be clad in concrete sandbags, or to be buried in earth over a flat roof; any entrance would be sunken and approached along a revetted trench.

Dimensions: diameter 6ft 8in (2m); wall-thickness 4in (10cm) plus earth etc.

No identified examples but several concrete sandbag structures in Northumberland, two at NZ235769 (Seaton Sluice) and three at NU202137, 203136 & 207129 (Alnwick) meet some of the criteria for this design.

11j. bullet-proof pillbox

This design is similar to **11g** and **11h**, but is made of pre-fabricated concrete panels bolted together on site, on a prepared concrete base; there are three lifting-rings on the roof, whose central open hatch, equipped with a traversing ring for a lmg, is closed by a removable cupola; the full-height doorway has a steel frame to carry a hinged steel door; there are six loopholes.

Dimensions: diameter 9ft (2.7m); wall-thickness 9in (23cm)

Examples at:
SP330139 (Akeman Street, Oxon) (*269*)
SP175035 (Southrop, Glos)

269 Akeman Street, Oxfordshire (SP330139) **11j**; one of two pillboxes at this airfield constructed from pre-fabricated concrete panels

Refs: fieldwork, Adrian Armishaw, Allen Mutti

11k. two-storey bullet-proof pillbox

Two-storey pillbox with loopholes on both levels and sunken entrance; there are pre-cast, stepped loops at the upper level; substantial AR screen at lower level acts as support for upper storey; smaller loops (T-shaped at Westhampnett) in lower level.

Dimensions: diameter *c.*20ft (6m); wall-thickness 15in (38cm); height *c.*15ft (4.6m)

Examples:
SU876077 & SU872070 (Westhampnett, West Sussex)
TQ771243 (River Rother, west of Bodiam) (*270*)

Refs: fieldwork, Martin Mace, Peter Longstaff-Tyrrell

11m. bullet-proof pillbox

Sunken chamber with deep slab roof mounted on six pillars giving all-round vision; entered by steps down into rectangular porch; a step runs around the internal circumference; several on Ouston airfield.

Dimensions: diameter 10ft (3m); wall-thickness 12in (30cm); roof-slab *c.*27in (68cm)

Examples at:
NZ077687 & 077688 (Ouston, Northumberland) (*271*)

Refs: fieldwork, Alan Rudd

270 River Rother, East Sussex (TQ771243) **11k**; two-storey pillbox with 10 loopholes and low entrance, guarding a bridge on this defence line

271 Ouston, Northumberland (NZ077687) **11m**; circular pillbox with all-round observation, with entrance making a key-kole-shaped structure

272 Kingscliffe, Northamptonshire (TL027972) **11n**; circular mushroom-shaped pillbox built by F.C. Construction for the Air Ministry; one of a pair linked to the adjacent (and just visible in the background) Battle Headquarters

11n. F.C. Construction pillbox

This structure is described on official Air Ministry plans as *the Mushroom, the Oakington* and *the Fairlop,* and is associated with drawing numbers TG14, 9882/41 and T/5291; it consists of an open, circular, concrete pit with 3ft (91cm) high wall and domed concrete roof, cantilevered off a central pillar, either cruciform or butterfly, and forming AR walls; a tubular rail, holding two movable, clamped mg mountings, is fixed below the parapet, giving a 360 degree field of fire; it was widely used for airfield defence, with well over 50 examples on 25 different airfields known.

Dimensions: diameter 13ft (4m); wall-thickness 12in (30cm)

Examples at:
SP175494, 176494 & 176495 (Long Marston, Warwickshire)
SP550372 (two) at (Hinton-in-the-Hedges, Northamptonshire)
NK079476, 074477, 073476 & 073474 (Peterhead, Grampian)
TL027972 (*272*), 020978, 021977 & 025972 (Kingscliffe, Northamptonshire)

11ni. modification of 11n
At Oakington a number of pillboxes forming a strong-point and linked by zig-zag trenches have had much of the observation slit blocked to form discrete loopholes.

Examples at:
TL416654 (*273*) & 415668

273 Oakington, Cambridgeshire (TL416654) **11ni**; F.C. Construction pillbox, in which the observation/firing slit has been extensively blocked, leaving only three small serviceable loopholes

11nii. modification of 11n to drawing number 303/41
At Peterhead, the F.C. Construction pillboxes have had their all-round embrasures blocked, two stepped mg embrasures inserted, and porches added.

Example at:
NK073473 (*274*)

11niii. pillbox based on 11n
At Penrhos, a domed pillbox has been added on the end of a Stanton shelter.

Examples at:
SH331338 & 338333 (Penrhos, Gwynedd)

11p. shell-proof mg post
This design for mg and AT rifle posts by G. Lockwood, Cumberland County Surveyor in 1941, features a central column topped by a pyramidal cairn, with circular passage, giving a spiral effect; loops are provided for different weapons at appropriate heights; only one example appears to survive; it is constructed in concrete sandbags.

Dimensions: diameter *c.*15ft (4.6m); wall-thickness *c.*12-15in (30-38cm)

274 Peterhead, Grampian (NK073473) **11nii**; F.C. Construction pillbox in which the slit has been completely blocked and two stepped pre-cast loopholes have been inserted

275 Silloth, Cumbria (NY144568) **11p**; spiral pillbox built of concrete sandbags

Example at:
NY144568 (Silloth, Cumberland) (*275*)

Refs: fieldwork, plan in Wills

11q. bullet-proof pillbox

This is the circular version of **3bi** and **9a** with an internal corridor and a central platform for an LAA mount; both inner and outer edges are scalloped; there are seven loopholes and an entrance in the outer circumference; only seen at Harrowbeer airfield, where there are two.

Dimensions: diameter 20ft (6m); wall-thickness 24in (61cm)

Example at:
SX509686 (Harrowbeer, Devon) (*276*)

Refs: fieldwork, Adrian Armishaw

276 Harrowbeer, Devon (SX509686) **11q**; circular version of RAF pillboxes with interior corridor and central, open platform for LAA mount

11r. bullet-proof pillbox

Ten-sided, rather than strictly circular, this pillbox is best included in this category; it has stepped, pre-cast loopholes in half its faces and an entrance protected by a curved stone-built blast-wall; earth is heaped up to loophole level and there is a T-shaped AR wall subdividing the interior into three compartments.

Dimensions: faces of 5ft, 6ft, 7ft & 8ft (1.5-2.4m); wall-thickness 24in (61cm)

Example at:
SC190676 (Cregneash radar site, Isle of Man) (*277*)

Ref: fieldwork, Ian Brown

11s. bullet-proof pillbox

Semi-circular on one side, and half-hexagonal on the other, this pillbox has four double rifle-loops in the seaward aspect; an L-shaped blast-wall protects the entrance.

Dimensions: half on a 9ft (2.74m) diameter, then three sides of 7ft (2.13m); wall-thickness 15in (38cm)

Two examples at:
NJ977176 (Balmedie, Aberdeenshire)

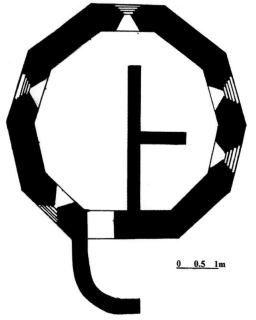

0   0.5   1m

277 Cregneash, Isle of Man (SC190676) **11r**; not circular, but 10-sided pillbox, one of several similar, built to guard a radar site

6

TYPOLOGY OF DEFENSIBLE STRUCTURES

As well as the range of pillboxes and gun-houses we have seen in the previous chapter, there are other structures which must be included in any survey of hardened defences. These include small sunken or semi-sunken structures which are here grouped together as 'turrets'; those buildings provided on airfields for the co-ordination of the defence, generally described as Battle Headquarters (BHQs); structures which range from simple concrete trenches through Seagull Trenches to elaborate section-posts forming another group; positions designed for the use of spigot mortars; a number of hybrids or structures which do not fit happily into the categories previously explored; store buildings for the use of the Home Guard; post-Second World War guard-posts; buildings converted into strong-points; and EXDO posts controlling mine-fields. This chapter seeks to make sense of these quite specialised structures.

12. TURRETS

The need, in 1940, for cheap, easily-produced defence structures produced a number of apparently ingenious solutions. Several of these consisted of sunken or semi-sunken capsules of steel or concrete. In hindsight, it is easy to regard contemporary enthusiasm for some of them as misplaced, but they served a purpose for a while.

12a. the Pickett-Hamilton retractable or disappearing fort

This was a small retractable pillbox designed in such a way that a cylindrical, concrete, loopholed drum sat inside a concentric concrete sleeve below ground-level and could be raised into a firing position by pneumatic pressure from a compressed-air bottle, or by a hand-operated oil pump. These forts were installed, usually three at a time, on airfields, in order to counter an attack by air-landing troops. In the dormant position they provided no obstacle to friendly aircraft, all that was visible was a circular concrete apron with a hatch in it, but in the raised position, they could command the landing ground. According to the planned programme, well under way in December 1940, some 335 were installed at 124 airfields in England, Scotland and Wales. Those scheduled for the Orkneys and Shetland appear to have been aborted. Each fort was manned by two riflemen, who would have sprinted across the grass, entered the fort through the hatch in the roof, and triggered the lifting mechanism, prior to engaging the enemy paratroops or gliders. The

278 Pickett-Hamilton Fort **12a**; the part which rises from below ground, here seen removed from its outer casing which stays below ground level

279 Pickett-Hamilton Fort **12a**; another example of the inner part, here set in an apron outside the D-Day Museum in Southsea

280 Pickett-Hamilton Fort **12a**; a view of the apron with the top of the inner part and the hatch, this example from Martlesham Heath airfield, now re-installed at Thorpe Abbotts airfield museum in Norfolk

fort was designed by Donald Hamilton, a London architect, based on the original idea for raising agricultural implements of Francis Pickett's, an engineer and inventor. The prototype was built in the workshop of Hamilton's friend, Malcolm Campbell, the racing driver. Production was carried out by the New Kent Company of Ashford, with 'Stanhay (Ashford) Kent' found stamped on a brass plate on a recently-excavated example from Manston. In the West Country, Marcus H. Hodges and Sons were the contractors.

Dimensions: diameter of pillbox 6ft (1.8m) and of outer sleeve 6ft 6in (2m); height above ground when raised was just under 6ft (1.8m) with the loopholes 2ft (61cm) above the ground (*278*)

There are restored examples outside the D-Day Museum, Southsea, Hampshire (*279*), Thorpe Abbotts airfield, Norfolk (*280*), and Lashenden Air Warfare Museum, Kent.

12b. Tett Turret

Designed and manufactured by Burbidge Ltd of East Horsley, Surrey; the specification mentions a rotating steel turret atop a sunken concrete pipe but the only known examples (at Hornchurch, Essex and Sudbury, Suffolk) have concrete collars; they also appear to have been used on top of existing structures where holes had been cut in the roof and a ring installed to receive the collar; there are two such structures at Ronaldsway, Isle of Man, one built into a lime-kiln and the other on the opposite headland; the manufacturers, for no immediately obvious reason, suggested sinking Tett Turrets in inter-connecting trios; the example at Sudbury, now destroyed, was mounted on a brick chamber in which the

281 Tett Turret **12b**; one of two, close together on the eastern perimeter of Hornchurch airfield (TQ535842); the recent TV series *Two Men in a Trench* discovered a number of further examples

rifleman might stand to fire through the turret; at Hornchurch some half-dozen single examples remain, only the concrete collar visible above the ground; there exists a wartime photograph of a pillbox at the west end of Cromer esplanade in Norfolk, with a steel turret on top, but by its size it would appear to be an Allan Williams turret.

Dimensions: diameter of pipe is 4ft (1.22m); height above ground is 13in (33cm)

Examples at:
TQ535842 (two+) at Hornchurch, Essex (*281*)
SC291680 & 285674 (Ronaldsway, Isle of Man) (*282*)

12c. Allan Williams turret

This two-man turret consists of a rotating steel dome over a circular pit, entered via a short tunnel; hatches in front and top were equipped with brackets for mgs and AT rifles; it was not rated highly by the military who criticised its narrow field of fire, notionally 360 degrees but inhibited by the time it took to rotate; hence, only about 200 were built, many of these on airfields. Around 30 examples survive.

Restored examples remain at IWM Duxford (*283*) and next to the War Memorial in Builth Wells, Radnorshire; a pair flank the entrance to a scrap-yard at TF221301

282 Tett Turret **12b**; an alternative way of mounting this turret was to place the upper part over a hatch cut in the roof of an existing structure. Here at Ronaldsway on the Isle of Man, there appear to be two such mountings at SC291680 and SC285674, one in the top of a limekiln, the other, pictured here, in a concrete bunker

283 Allan Williams Turret **12c**; this is the revolving top seen (upside down) during restoration. The wheels, one of the weapons mountings and hatch, and the turning handles are all visible. Photographed at IWM Duxford

284   Allan Williams Turret **12c**; a well-preserved example in situ at the Cromwellian fort at Earith, Cambridgeshire (TL393749).The entrance tunnel is visible here, as are both weapons hatches

(Gosberton, Lincolnshire); in situ examples remain at North Weald Redoubt, Essex, and Earith Bulwark, Cambridgeshire (*284*).

Refs: fieldwork, Keith Hazelwood

12ci a slightly different design which can be seen at Crail in Fife.

NB: there are reports of tank turrets being emplaced in Britain, but apparently none survived the scrap drive after the war. German use of French turrets in the Atlantic Wall fortifications both on the Continent and in the Channel Islands, and of their own turrets mounting 88mm guns in Italy, is well-documented (e.g. Neil Short).

David Wood has described a semi-sunken turret on Woodbridge airfield, possibly installed post-Second World War by the US Air Force; it has a concrete canopy with access hatch, supported on brick piers and, it appears, an underground escape tunnel (*285*).

13. AIRFIELD BATTLE HEADQUARTERS (BHQ)

This is a specialised structure which evolved through a number of different designs, until a standard design was issued by the Air Ministry in 1941 (**13b**). In addition to the early and standard designs, it is evident on many airfields that other structures were built to serve or were adapted as BHQs. This may explain, for instance, the single mushroom

285 Woodbridge, Suffolk (approx. TM333472) another type of semi-sunken turret, which may date from the post-Second World War era

pillbox (**11n**) at Wittering (Cambridgeshire), the pillbox with observation/LAA platform (**9aii**) at Windrush (Gloucestershire), or the octagonal pillbox at Lichfield, Staffordshire (**9c**). The pillbox in front of the watch office at Bicester (Oxfordshire) may have served this function prior to the construction of a dedicated standard BHQ on the opposite side of the airfield.

It would appear that some of the early fighter airfields were given experimental BHQs before 1940; Redhill (Surrey) and Hornchurch (Essex) have structures consisting of a sunken chamber with a smaller hexagonal pillbox with six loopholes on top. Further BHQs based on this concept appear elsewhere in different forms, at Waterbeach and Benson for instance. Other airfields appear to have completely unique structures, such as Hucknall with its four-storey tower, or Luton with its L-shaped air-raid-type shelter with a hexagonal, loopholed cupola in the angle. At Sywell, Northamptonshire, a field-barn (now destroyed) was adapted as BHQ.

The majority of airfields which were provided with BHQs at all had standard ones. The overriding concern was that in order to carry out its function of co-ordinating the airfield's defence when under airborne, especially air-landing, assault, the entire flying surface should be visible from the cupola. At Swinderby (Lincolnshire), Redhill (Surrey) and Baginton (Warwickshire) for instance, the BHQ is up on a hill overlooking the airfield. When airfield defence schemes moved from linear to point protection, the BHQ often became the centre of a nucleated strong-point, as at Long Marston (extant) or Bicester (now destroyed) in conjunction with pillboxes and fieldworks.

13a. BHQ to drawing number 3329/41

This is a surface structure which appears to have been sometimes converted for use as
a pillbox; at a number of airfields, such as Dunsfold and Peterhead, it was replaced by a
standard BHQ (**13b**); Dunsfold's new BHQ has an additional drawing reference of MS2779;
examples of the standard pillbox (5648/41) survive at Kingscliffe, Northamptonshire and
at Castle Camps, Cambridgeshire. It has been suggested by both Smith, and Ruddy that
the 3329/41 was a smaller version of the 11008/41, enjoying access only through the hatch,
for use on fighter stations (see also **13c**).

Refs: Simon Purcell, Austin Ruddy, Nick Catford

13b. BHQ to drawing number 11008/41

This is the standard BHQ and is found on dozens of airfields; it consists of a sunken
rectangular box, with an annexe for a pillbox and a raised concrete cupola with all-round
observation; it is accessed through a hatch next to the cupola, and a flight of stairs
descending to the messengers' room (*286*).

Dimensions: length 30ft (9.1m); width 18ft4in (5.6m); wall-thickness 19in (48cm); cupola
is 8ft (2.4m) square

Examples of the standard design survive at:
Fraserburgh and Peterhead (Aberdeenshire), Kinnell (*287*) and Montrose (Angus), Warboys
(Cambridgeshire), Harrowbeer (Devon), Hunsdon (Hertfordshire), Cark and Walney
Island (Lancashire), Market Harborough and Wymeswold (Leicestershire), Binbrook,
Hibaldstow, Wellingore and Wickenby (Lincolnshire), Bodney, Feltwell, Langham,
Methwold and West Raynham (Norfolk), Grafton Underwood, Kingscliffe and Polebrook

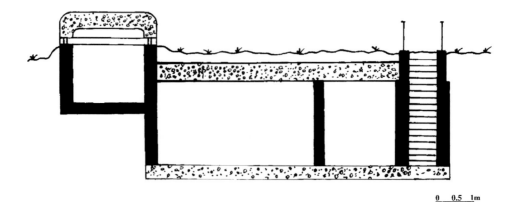

0   0.5   1m

286 Battle HQ to drawing number 11008/41, **13b**; cross-section of the standard, buried BHQ,
with the cupola and escape hatch to the left end and the stairs down to the main entrance to the
right

287 Kinnell, Angus, **13b**; the standard BHQ

(Northants), Ossington (Nottinghamshire), Carew Cheriton (Pembrokeshire), North Luffenham (Rutland), Tilstock (Shrops), Charmy Down (Somerset), Beccles, Great Ashfield and Martlesham Heath (Suffolk), Elmdon, Long Marston, Stratford-upon-Avon and Wellesbourne (Warks), Merston (W Sussex), Wigtown (Wigtownshire), Catfoss and Hunmanby (E Yorkshire).

Variations include the following:
second cupola at Ibsley (Hants)
extra level inserted in cupola at Little Staughton (Cambs) (*288*)
pillbox-type structure added on top of cupola at Goxhill (Lincs)
modified entrance at Thorpe Abbotts (Norfolk)
loophole under cupola observation slit at Baginton (Warwickshire)
inter-connecting pillbox and external shelter at Spittlegate (Lincs)

NB: the nature of the structure means that there are buried examples, e.g. at Limavady, County Londonderry, which may possibly be in good condition.

Refs: fieldwork, Simon Purcell, Mark Sansom, Adrian Armishaw, Ian Reid

Note also that at Goxhill, Lincolnshire, can be found a structure described on the official plan as 'Observation Post'. It is a combination of a Stanton shelter attached to a cupola from an 11008/41 BHQ. There are two examples at TA113223 & 121221.

288 Little Staughton, Cambridgeshire **13b**; note the heightened cupola on this otherwise standard BHQ

13c. BHQ to drawing number 11747/41

There appear to be no surviving examples of this design which, according to the Air Ministry plans, was built at Docking and Horsham St Faith, Norfolk; neither does the drawing survive. It is possible that this was the earlier version of what was to become **13b**, but originally with a larger cupola, felt to be too conspicuous (see Dobinson).

Refs: fieldwork, Colin Dobinson

13d. BHQ to local design

Consisting of an L-shaped, brick air-raid shelter type structure, with a small, hexagonal cupola, with six observation slits on the outer elbow; only one example is known, at TL126222 (Luton, Bedfordshire).

13e. BHQ to local design

Generally a sunken chamber, in some cases formed from Stanton shelter sections, with a hexagonal cupola on top.

Examples at:
TL491667 (Waterbeach, Cambs) (*289*)
Benson (Oxon) now destroyed

289 Waterbeach, Cambridgeshire **13e**; the small, hexagonal cupola of this local design of BHQ

13f. BHQ to local design drawing number RH18

The BHQ at Redhill consists of an underground chamber with a hexagonal cupola on top, reached by a steel ladder and hatch, it has six vertical observation slits.

Dimensions: sides of cupola 5ft 6in (1.7m); wall thickness 20in (50cm)

The BHQ at Hornchurch (*290*) appears to be an unremarkable hexagonal pillbox with six loopholes and a sunken entrance, but has a lower level under a hatch in the floor.

Refs: fieldwork, Simon Purcell

13g. BHQ to local design drawing number TG/1

Were this not to be marked as such on the 1946 Air Ministry plan of the airfield, as 'BHQ (Watch Tower)' then it would never have been identified; it is a four-storey brick tower, about 40ft (12.2m) high, with a door at ground-level and narrow slit windows in the upper storeys.

Example at:
SK 519475 (Hucknall, Notts)

Refs: fieldwork, Margaret and David Sibley

290 Hornchurch, Essex **13f**; the cupola of this assumed prototype BHQ

14. SECTION POSTS, SEAGULL TRENCHES AND CONCRETE TRENCHES

Most of the examples in this section share a number of common characteristics; they are all generally orientated in no more than two directions, as opposed to having all-round fields of fire; they tend to be linear features, longer and narrower than square or polygonal pillboxes; they tend to be designed to hold larger garrisons than many (but by no means all) of the pillboxes we have seen. One could argue that a number of pillboxes, **6v** or **9a**, for instance, could comfortably be included in this category. Equally, one could argue that some in this category would not be out of place in another, for instance **14g** could be grouped with **Section 6**. However, judgements relating to dominant characteristics have had to be made and, although this may not be altogether satisfactory, there are always compromises to be made in inexact sciences. This section then, includes most of those designs which feature straight lengths, in different combinations and alignments. Seagull trenches, found exclusively on airfields, get their name from the W-shaped version, which, when seen from above, resembles a flying seagull. However, back down on the ground they come in a variety of shapes.

14a. L-shaped section post
This consists of two long narrow chambers intersecting at right-angles, with an entrance in the re-entrant angle; there are five loopholes in each long outward-facing wall and another in each end wall; these are found on the north Norfolk coast and in Hampshire on the Avon Stop Line.

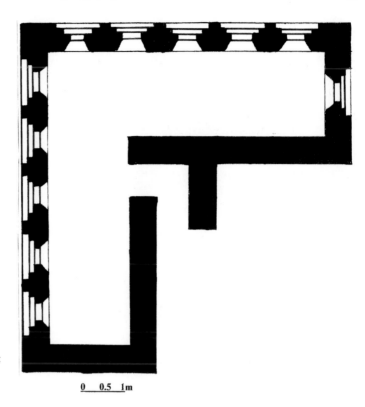

291 Cromer, Norfolk
(TG209423) **14a**; plan
of L-shaped section post
with 11 loopholes and a
protected entrance

0   0.5   1m

Dimensions: each chamber is 24ft x 9ft 6in (7.3m x 2.9m); wall-thickness 24in (61cm)

Examples:
TG209423 (Cromer, Norfolk) (*291*)
SU145137 (Fordingbridge, Hants)

14ai. L-shaped section post
As **14a** but shorter chambers with only three loopholes per side.

Example at:
SU738080 (Southleigh Park, Havant, Hampshire) (*292*)

14b. straight section post
Semi-sunken long chamber with half-hexagonal projection for mg and four rifle-loops in front wall; one loophole at each end and two in rear wall; steps down to sunken entry with steel door.

Dimensions: 28ft 6in x 8ft (8.7m x 2.4m); wall-thickness 24in (61cm)

Example at:
SZ298939 (Everton, Hants) (*293*)

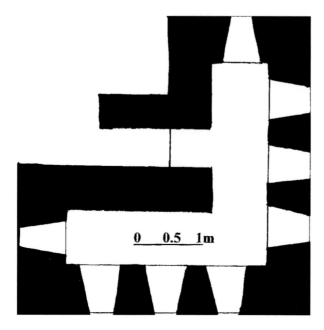

292 Havant, Hampshire (SU738080) **14ai**; shorter version of **14a**, with eight loopholes

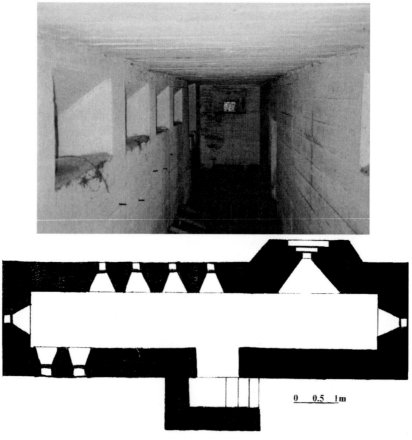

293 Everton, Hampshire (SZ298939) **14b**; straight section post with eight loopholes and a forward-facing machine-gun position

14c. boomerang-shaped section post

Each length has four loopholes on its outer face, and three on the inner, with another in each end, making 16; there is an entrance, protected by a blast-wall at each end.

Dimensions: each length is 18ft x 6ft (5.5m x 1.8m); wall-thickness 15in (38cm)

Examples at:

TA075841 (Cayton Bay, N Yorkshire) partly destroyed

NZ506253 (Cowpen Marsh, Teesside) where there are also two smaller examples; the three section posts together muster 45 loopholes.

14ci. boomerang-shaped section post

As **14c** but with short straight section inserted; loopholes on only long and end walls, totalling 13.

Example at:

NZ494363 (Hart Warren, Teesside) (*294*)

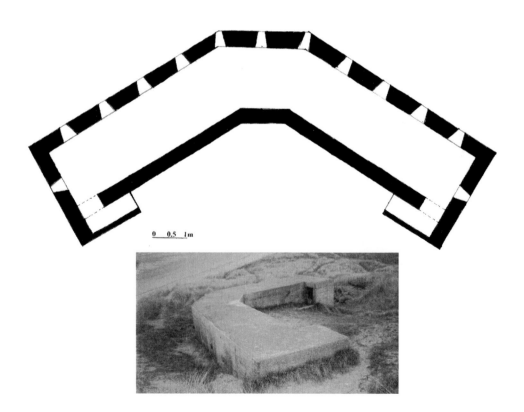

0   0.5   1m

294 Hart Warren, Teesside (NZ494363) **14ci**; section post with 13 loopholes

14cii. boomerang-shaped section post

As **14c**, but in five segments, each with a single loophole, one in each end wall, one in an inner wall and another in an outer corner, making a total of nine.

Example at:
SW 334262 (Sennen Cove) (*295*)

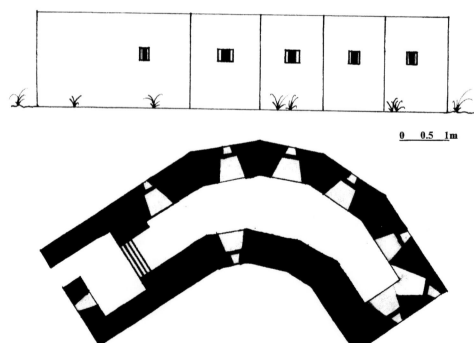

0   0.5   1m

295   Sennen Cove, Cornwall (SW 334262) **14cii**; boomerang-shaped section post

14d. shell-proof arrowhead-shaped section post

The front part has two wide, forward-facing embrasures and two rifle-loops to the side; behind is a rectangular chamber with a straight AR wall, four rifle-loops to the rear with long shelf and a side entrance, protected by a loopholed blast-wall.

Dimensions: front faces each 15ft (4.6m) long; rear chamber 13ft x 10ft (4 x 3m); wall-thickness 42in (1.07m)

Example at:
SU923015 (Bersted, W Sussex)

Refs: fieldwork, Ron Martin

14e. shell-proof boomerang-shaped concrete trench

Front faces with two loopholes in each, entrance in one end wall.

Dimensions: front walls 12ft (3.7m); end walls 8ft (2.4m); wall-thickness 36in (91cm)

Example at:
SU740591 (Hazeley, Hants)

14ei. *boomerang-shaped concrete trench*

Similar to **14e** at Bigsweir Bridge on River Wye stop line.

14f. straight-sided concrete trench

Four loopholes in each front wall, one in each end, and projecting entrance.

Dimensions: 16ft 9in x 6ft 6in (5.1 x 2m) and another similar with 13ft 6in (4.1m) front wall with only three loops; wall-thickness 24in (61cm)

Examples at:
SU733092 & 733089 (Havant, Hants)

14g. straight-sided concrete trench

Front wall with four loops, another in rear wall, entrance in one end and loophole in other.

Dimensions: 14ft x 8ft (4.3 x 2.4m); wall-thickness 15in (38cm)

Examples at:
SZ832952, 831953, 834949 & 833950 (Selsey, W Sussex)
SX600684 (Harrowbeer, Devon)

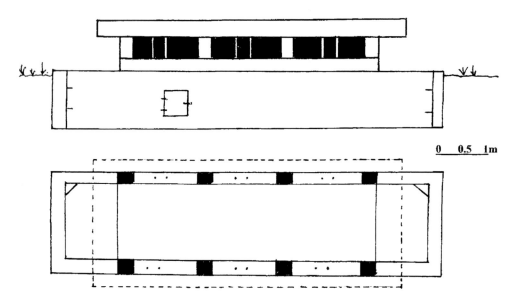

0   0.5   1m

296   Kemble, Gloucestershire (ST958961) **14h**; straight length of Seagull trench

14h. straight length of seagull trench

Middle section roofed and containing three firing bays; access down rungs set in angles of each open end.

Dimensions: 23ft 6in x 6ft (7.2 x 1.8m); roofed section 18ft 6in (5.6m); firing bays each 4ft 3in (1.3m) wide

Example at:
ST958961 (Kemble, Glos) (*296*)

14hi. straight length of seagull trench

As **14h**, but whole length roofed as at SH330340 (Penrhos, Gwynedd).

14j. L-shaped seagull trench

Two arms of unequal length, roofed but for open ends with access down rungs set in end walls; two firing bays in each roofed section.

Dimensions: 18ft 6in x 6ft (5.6 x 1.8m) and 13ft 9in x 6ft (4.2 x 1.8m); end 3ft (91cm) of each arm open; firing bays each 4ft (1.2m) wide

Example at:
ST954963 (Kemble, Glos) (*297*)

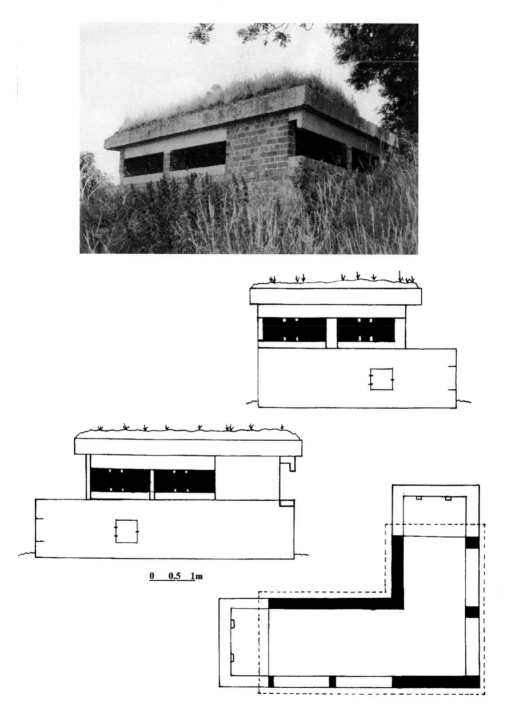

297 Kemble, Gloucestershire (ST954963) **14j**; L-shaped Seagull trench

298 Croughton, Northamptonshire (SP573332) **14k**;V-shaped Seagull trench

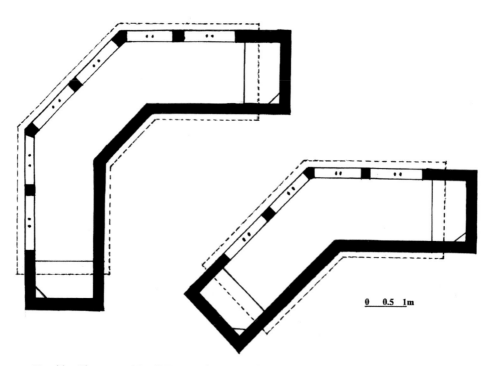

299 Kemble, Gloucestershire (ST964968) **14m** and ((ST960971) **14k**; a segmented Seagull trench (above) and a V-shaped one (below)

14k. V-shaped seagull trench

Both arms roofed except for open ends with access rungs; two firing bays in each arm.

Dimensions: each arm 13ft x 6ft (4 x 1.8m); open ends of 2ft 6in (76cm); firing bays 4ft (1.2m) wide

Examples at:
ST954963, 965962 & 967963 (Kemble) & SO933279 (Stoke Orchard) both Gloucestershire
SP597239 (two) at (Bicester, Oxon)
SP573332 (two) at (Croughton) (*298*) and SP550372 (three) at (Hinton-in-the-Hedges) both Northamptonshire

Refs: fieldwork, Adrian Armishaw

14m. segmented seagull trench

Between the two arms is a short straight; there are two firing bays in each segment; all roofed, apart from the very end of each arm; access via rungs set in end walls.

Dimensions: each segment is 10ft (3m) long and 6ft (1.8m) wide

Example at:
ST964968 (Kemble, Glos) (*299*)

14n. W-shaped seagull trench

Basically two V-shaped lengths joined together, this is the archetype.

Examples at:
SH437565 (Llandwrog, Gwynedd) (*300*)

300 Llandwrog, Gwynedd (SH437565) **14n**; fully-developed Seagull trench, overlooking the airfield

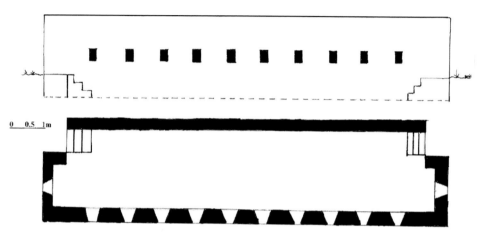

301 Bicester, Oxfordshire (SP 594244) **14p**; dual-purpose air-raid shelter and defence post facing the flying field

SN 058032 (Carew Cheriton, Pembrokeshire)
also at Cranage, Cheshire, and Rednal, Shropshire

14p. defensible air-raid shelter

There are two of these dual-purpose structures facing across the flying field in front of a hangar; each has 10 loopholes in the long forward face and one in each end; there is an entrance down steps in the back wall at each end.

Dimensions: 32ft x 9ft (9.8 x 2.7m); wall-thickness 15in (38cm)

Example at:
SP 594244 (two) at (Bicester, Oxon) (*301*)

NB: a similar structure, but with one mg embrasure in its front wall, has been reported at the nearby ordnance depot and at Kineton, Warwickshire.

Refs: fieldwork, Alec Beanse and Peter Cobb

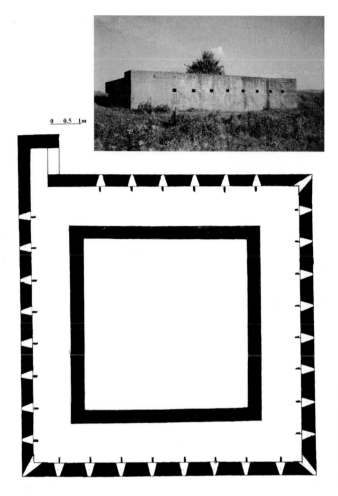

302   Cowpen Marsh, Teesside (NZ509249) **14q**; section post with 33 loopholes built round a hollow square; nearby are V-shaped section posts and other defences

Note also that there are other examples of longer structures of this type, one being the sunken 90ft x 5ft (27m x 1.5m) concrete trench at SX507686 (Harrowbeer, Devon). It has a loophole every 4ft (1.2m) or so and an entrance at each end.

14q. hollow-square blockhouse
Essentially four corridors around a blind central court; each of three corridors has eight loopholes; the fourth has six loopholes and a protected entrance; there is an extra loophole at each of three corners, giving a total of 33 loopholes.

Dimensions: 30ft (9.1m) plus 4ft (1.2m) square porch; corridors are 4ft (1.2m) wide; the inner and outer wall-thicknesses appear to be 15in (38cm)

Example at:
NZ509249 (Cowpen Marsh, Teesside) (302)

15. SPIGOT MORTAR POSITIONS

The 29mm spigot mortar or Blacker Bombard came under the category of sub-artillery for use by the Home Guard. It fired a 14lb (6.4kg) anti-personnel, or 20lb (9kg) AT projectile from a mortar. This mortar could be mounted either on a permanent concrete pedestal, or on a field tripod with spade-grips. The cylindrical concrete pedestal, the size of a large oil-drum, referred to as a *thimble*, contained a steel framework, or *spider*, whose only visible part was the protruding stainless-steel *pintle* on its domed top to receive the mortar. The *thimble* usually sat in a pit containing ready-use ammunition lockers

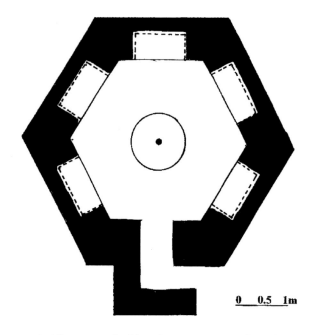

303   St Albans, Hertfordshire (TL141079) **15a**; plan of spigot mortar pit excavated in 1991, but long ago destroyed

set into the side walls. The rule was that each spigot mortar should go into action having two such prepared positions close by. Whilst there are some few instances of such provision, there are many more single ones and many more units must have relied solely on field mountings. As pits have silted up, often the only visible sign of a spigot mortar position is its domed concrete top with the steel *pintle* showing. Where the water table precluded the excavation of a pit, or the position was on an existing structure such as a bridge, then an above-ground, waist-high concrete wall was built.

15a. spigot mortar pit
Hexagonal concrete pit with central pedestal, ammunition lockers set into five sides and an entrance in the sixth; such a position was excavated by Fred Nash in St Albans in 1991(*303*), and is shown in IWM photographs of Home Guard manoeuvres.

Dimensions: pit 14ft (4.3m) across externally and 9ft (2.74m) internally; the side walls are 8ft (2.4m)

Example at:
TM127464 (Bramford, Suffolk)

15b. spigot mortar pit
Circular pit revetted in brick or concrete (but occasionally in timber palings) with central

304 Eye, Suffolk, (TG148735) **15bi**; above-ground spigot mortar emplacement with four ammunition lockers

0   0.5   1m

concrete pedestal; dug into the side of the pit are four ammunition recesses and an access trench.

Dimensions: 11ft (3.4m) internal diameter

Example at:
TQ316130 (Hertford, Herts)

Refs: fieldwork, Fred Nash

15bi as **15b**, but above ground at TG148735 & 151736 (Eye, Suffolk) (*304*)
15bii as **15b**, but only two recesses at TM477682 (Minsmere, Suffolk)
15biii as **15bii**, but octagonal pit at TL515365 (Wendens Ambo, Essex) (*305*)
15biv narrow rectangular pit with locker each end (Shrewsbury cemetery)

305 Wendens Ambo, Essex (TL515365) **15bii**; octagonal spigot mortar pit with two ammunition lockers

15c. surface spigot mortar position

Rectangular enclosure with central pedestal as used on London railway bridges, e.g. TQ195775 (Kew).

15ci as **15c**, but hexagonal enclosure as at TF865834 (Thetford, Norfolk)

15cii as **15c**, but cruciform with half-hexagonal projections as at TL825873 & TL826872 (Santon Downham, Suffolk) (*306*) on Eastern Command Line.

NB: there were different shapes of pedestal, hence they are not always accurately described as *thimbles*; most are circular, but some have irregular features such as the steeply-domed example at TF999137 (Guist, Norfolk); a large number in Norfolk and Suffolk are hexagonal, e.g. TL780864 & 781865 (Brandon, Suffolk); there are square examples at TR326420 (Dover Castle, Kent) and at SO951452 (Pershore Bridge, Worcestershire), and a 13-sided version at TQ429766 (behind Shooters Hill police station near Woolwich); at SH649643 (near Capel Curig, Conwy) there are three pedestals guarding a bridge; one has near vertical sides, a flat top and corrugated-iron shuttering; the other two are very rough, with timber centres into which a disconnected *pintle* must have been set.

16. HYBRIDS AND UNCLASSIFIABLES

16a. combination designs from two drawing numbers DFW3/22 (**1a**) and DFW3/23 (**6a**); the two are joined together, end-to-end at TM351392 (Bawdsey, Suffolk) (*307*).

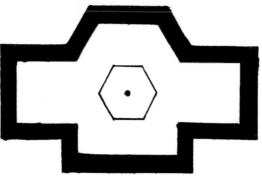

0   0.5   1m

306 Santon Downham, Suffolk (TL825873) **15cii**; above-ground spigot mortar emplacement with hexagonal thimble

16b. combination of square pillbox (**6j**) with open platform for LAA lmg attached to one side; at TM277374 (Trimley St Martin, Suffolk) (*308*).

16c. front half of a hexagonal pillbox with open annexe to rear and a double blast-wall; at SK526464 (Hucknall, Notts).

16d. nucleus of hexagonal, bullet-proof pillbox to drawing number DFW3/22 (**1a**), with long, loopholed corridors, open to the sky, extending about 90ft (27m) in two directions; located at NY121534 (Silloth, Cumbria) (*309*).

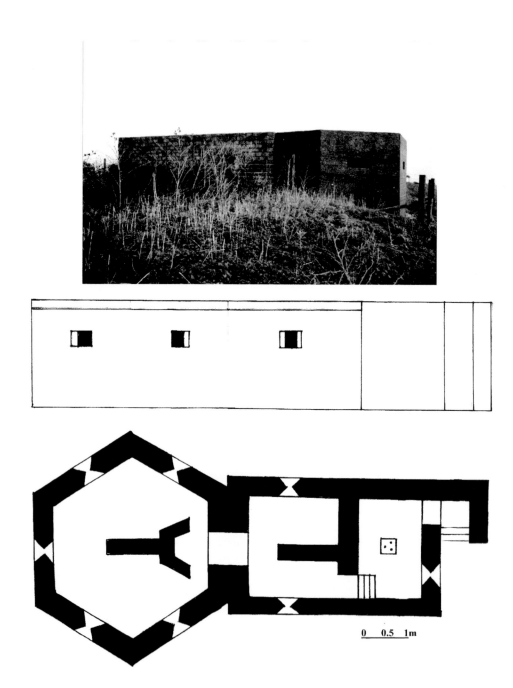

307 Bawdsey, Suffolk (TM351392) **16a**; combination of two pillboxes, one to drawing number DFW3/22 (**1a**) and the other to DFW3/23 (**6a**), joined together in line

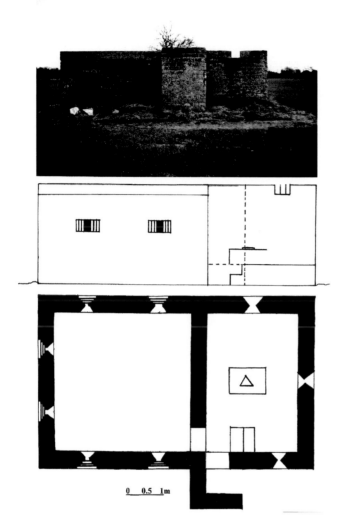

308 Trimley St Martin, Suffolk (TM277374) **16b**; a combination of two elements, one a locally-designed, square pillbox (**6j**), and the other an open platform with LAA mounting and close-defence loopholes

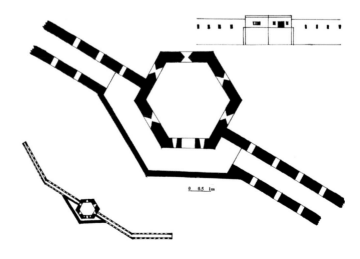

309 Silloth, Cumbria (NY121534) **16d**; a nucleus of a conventional hexagonal pillbox has added generously-loopholed wing-galleries

310 Southminster, Essex (TQ995983) **16e**; combination of three interlinked shell-proof hexagonal pillboxes (**3bii**) with tables for Vickers machine-guns and lmg-loops

16e. complex of two shell-proof, hexagonal pillboxes joined together by a rectangular chamber, with half-hexagonal open platform behind; in plan, the effect is of three **3bii** pillboxes squashed together; the front faces contain five mg embrasures, most with tables, and there are six further lmg-loops; the main chambers in the two pillboxes have V-shaped AR walls.

Dimensions: overall length 46ft (14m) & width 25ft (7.6m); wall-thickness 42in (1.07m)

Example at:
TQ995983 (Southminster, Essex) (*310* & *311*)

16f. bullet-proof pillbox (**1f**) with central open platform for LAA mounting; each of three alternating sides has a chamber with three lmg-loops added; one of the three blank sides contains an entrance.

Dimensions: furthest overall length is 30ft (9m); each of the three projecting chambers measures 9ft x 7ft (2.7 x 2.1m); wall-thickness 15in (38cm)

Example at:
TL915517 (Lavenham, Suffolk) (*312*) on Eastern Command Line

16g. a combination of three elements in line; first a hexagonal, bullet-proof pillbox with six loopholes, joined onto a featureless rectangular chamber, itself attached to an open circular

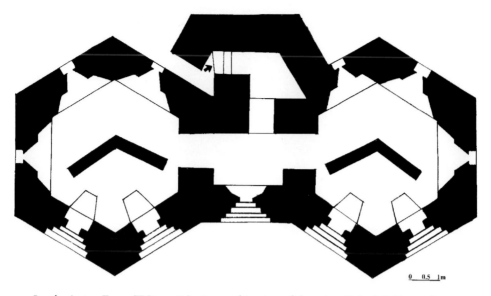

311 Southminster, Essex (TQ995983) **16e**; combination of three interlinked shell-proof hexagonal pillboxes (**3bii**)

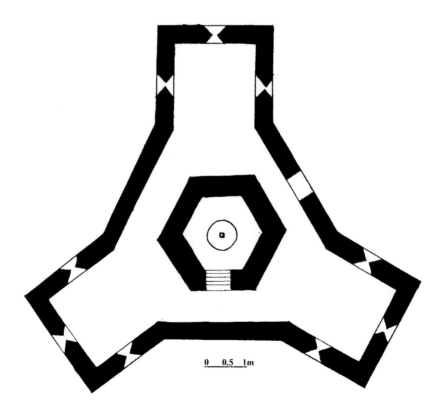

312 Lavenham, Suffolk (TL915517) **16f**; central core of bullet-proof pillbox (**1f**) with square, loopholed chambers added to alternate faces

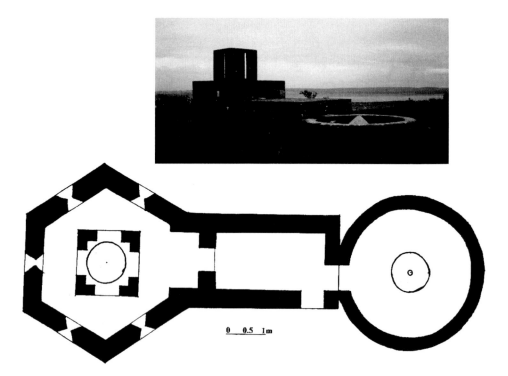

313 Bodorgan, Anglesey (SH391687) **16g**; structure of unknown purpose consisting of a hexagonal pillbox, rectangular crew-room and circular, open pit; on the roof of the pillbox, a square pillared superstructure, over a hatch

pit with a cylindrical mount with pointed conical top, in its centre; secondly, on the roof of the pillbox is a roofed structure of four L-shaped pillars over a circular hatch in the pillbox ceiling and lastly a corresponding circular plinth on the pillbox floor – a mystery object.

Dimensions: sides of pillbox 8ft (2.4m); rectangular chamber 12ft x 7ft (3.65 x 2.1m); diameter of open pit 12ft (3.65m); wall-thickness 15in-18in (38cm-46cm)

Example at:
SH391687 (Bodorgan, Anglesey) (*313*)

Refs: fieldwork, John Harding

16h. a complex of three rectangular semi-sunken buildings built into a bluff, defending a road/railway crossing outside Abergavenny; two of the buildings, each reached down steps, are joined at different levels; the third, is detached; two of the buildings each have three loopholes, the third has two.

16j. a double-decker pillbox, built onto rocks at C6638 (Magilligan's Point, Co. Donegal) (*314*); a trapezoidal lower pillbox has three loopholes; above, and set back, is the upper

314 Magilligan's Point, Co. Donegal (C6638) 16**j**; double-decker pillbox consisting of two trapezoidal loopholed chambers, offset, one above the other

pillbox, also with thee loopholes; it is entered through a hatch in the roof, with a further hatch in the floor giving access to the lower part. In concrete, shuttered in timber, with stepped, pre-cast loopholes.

16k. on Landguard Common is a defence post which appears to be composed of two back-to-back pentagonal pillboxes, now almost buried in shingle.

17. HOME GUARD EXPLOSIVES AND INFLAMMABLES STORES

At the time the Home Guard was set up there were acute problems of storage and local organisers had little choice but to grab what they could and be thankful; many must have used their own sheds and garages, and jokes about keeping grenades under the bed probably reflected the reality of the situation. By 1941, however, not only had the Home Guard been bureaucratised, but large numbers of larger weapons and quantities of munitions and other stores were accumulating. Projectiles for the Home Guard's sub-artillery – Smith guns, Northover projectors and spigot mortars – had to be stored, as did small-arms ammunition, grenades and the raw material for flame-traps and Fougasses. In August 1941, the Army Council published instructions to govern all this storage, requiring secure storehouses for explosives and, separately, for inflammables. The document laid out minimum safe distances, specifications for shelving and partitions, and the use of traverses. Clearly, purpose-built structures would have represented the optimal solution, but it was realised that this would not always be possible, or indeed necessary. Where small quantities were stored, they could safely share a building providing partitions were constructed to the prescribed thicknesses. Nissen huts could be used providing they had brick end walls and could be locked. It would appear that whilst much improvisation and opportunism occurred, there were also great efforts made to provide custom-built accommodation, several counties designing dedicated storehouses for their units. Some of these designs may derive from the Air Raid Precautions Wardens' Post as they are very similar. It must be noted that many of the examples below are found either near Home Guard HQs such as drill halls, or near defence works such as spigot mortar positions or other components of defence lines.

17a. Home Guard storehouse in Norfolk and Northamptonshire

Rectangular brick shed, roughly 10ft x 14ft (3m x 4.3m), with a flat concrete roof that had a slight overhang, a door in the front and two ventilation bricks in each of the end walls; this design was used in Norfolk and Northamptonshire. A pair may be seen side-by-side (so much for the separation distances!) behind the drill hall in Oundle (*315*) and in Bulwick village, both in Northamptonshire, and near Thorpe Station in Norwich. One of the Oundle ones has had double garage-doors installed, possibly to accommodate a Smith gun. Other examples can be seen behind the drill halls at Loddon (Norfolk) and Peterborough (formerly Northamptonshire), at Burnham Broom, Holme, Hilgay (two), Docking (two) Ludham (Norfolk), Nassington (Northamptonshire) and Newborough (formerly Soke of Peterborough).

315 Oundle, Northamptonshire (TL034883) **17a**; pair of Home Guard explosives and inflammables stores behind the drill hall on West Street

316 Sutton-St-Edmund, Lincolnshire (TF367118) **17c**; Home Guard explosives and inflammables store, located on a former Searchlight Site

17b. Home Guard storehouse in Cambridgeshire

Rectangular brick shed very similar to **17a**, but with entrance in one side near the front. This design was used in Cambridgeshire with examples in Long Stanton, Benwick, Whittlesey, North Bank and Queen Adelaide, the last named retaining wooden partitioning.

17c. Home Guard storehouse in Lincolnshire

Rectangular brick shed with shallow gable and wide door halfway along side, otherwise similar to **17a**. This design was used in Lincolnshire, with examples in Aubourn, Louth, Winterton, New Leake and Sutton-St-Edmund (*316*). There are storehouses using alternative designs at Horbling, Tattershall and Humberston.

17d. Home Guard storehouse in Nottinghamshire

Rectangular brick shed with shallow gable and door in front wall, measuring 14ft x 12ft (4.3m x 3.7m); used in Nottinghamshire with an example standing at Cromwell Lock on the Trent near a spigot mortar position.

17e. Home Guard storehouse in Bedfordshire and Leicestershire

Another rectangular shed design but different to the others in that it is clearly divided into discrete compartments accessed through separate doors. There are examples behind the drill halls in Old Bedford Road, Luton, and in Blackbird Road, Leicester. The Luton example has two doors and the Leicester one, three. They are both about 20ft (6m) long x about 8ft (2.4m) deep and both back onto boundary walls.

17f. Home Guard storehouse in Devon

Rectangular brick shed with two interconnecting compartments side-by-side, accessed through doors under a full-width open porch. This example is at Brixton, Devon.

NB: These storehouses occur all over the country but some examples, such as Nissen huts are impossible to identify without local knowledge. However some, like the pair opposite the drill hall in Victoria Road, Guiseley (West Yorkshire), one of which has double doors, and that on the banks of the Ouse below the defended Naburn Bridge, south of York for instance, or that behind a pub opposite a road-block in Reading, can be safely recognised.

18. POST-SECOND WORLD WAR GUARD-POSTS

This section looks at the natural successors to the pillbox, in use during the second half of the twentieth century, and, some of them into the twenty-first. All those structures in this category are essentially look-outs or refuges for sentries and are generally found at military facilities such as airfields, barracks and ordnance depots. Sometimes earlier structures have been adapted, as at RAF Coltishall, where a 1980s strong-point built of vertical concrete slabs is superimposed on a Second World War pillbox. At Kinloss, a Yarnold Sangar is built on top of an octagonal Second World War pillbox (**9ai**).

18a. the Yarnold Sangar

This is a pre-fabricated structure, reminiscent of the Norcon (**11g**), but made of cast concrete sections rather than pipes. It is named after its inventor and manufactured by Arc Co. (*317*). The standard model comprises five sections: floor, roof, a loopholed section and two blank wall sections. The insertion of extra sections can provide for greater height or greater loophole size. Halved wall sections can be used to provide a half-height screen around the doorway, for instance. Sometimes these sangars can be found with earth heaped up to loophole height and an access trench leading to the doorway, but they are more usually seen free-standing as sentry-posts at gateways. They may be painted white or green. The most widely-heard comment from those who regularly use them relates not to their vulnerability, but to how cold it is inside.

18b. guard-post used by the US Air Force

This square post is found on the perimeter of most of the bases used by the US Air Force in Britain. It has a loophole in each of three walls, the fourth wall containing the entrance, itself protected by a loopholed blast-wall, the whole under a slightly overhanging roof. It is usually

317 Henlow, Bedfordshire **18a**; Yarnold Sangar; a guard-post built of pre-fabricated sections painted in black, cream or in camouflage colours. The roof-slab measures 13ft 6in x 10ft (4.1m x 3m), whilst the post itself is 8ft 9in (2.7m) square. Both Bentwaters (Suffolk) and Alconbury (Cambridgeshire) have guard-posts not too dissimilar to this, but at first-floor level protecting the access to weapons-stores or to aircraft shelters. They have four steel loopholes in each face.

Examples:
Bentwaters, Suffolk (TM362534) (*318*)
Mildenhall, Suffolk (TL712762)
Lakenheath, Suffolk; see also NB to Section **12** (*285*)

Refs: fieldwork, Mark Sansom, David Wood

18c. watchtower
This was used at the Permanent Armaments Depots (PADs) of Barnham (Norfolk) and

0 0.5 1m

318 Bentwaters, Suffolk (TM362534) **18b**; guard-post used on the perimeters of US Air Force bases in Britain

319 Faldingworth, Lincolnshire **18c**; watch-tower used at atomic weapons storage sites

Faldingworth (Lincolnshire) (*319*) where nuclear war-heads were stored and armed prior to their issue to the V-Force. It consists of an octagonal observation cabin on a four-stage steel-work tower about 30ft (9m) high accessed by ladders and hatches. Four of these towers were spaced around the PAD's perimeter fence. At Coventry Air Museum at Baginton, there is an octagonal observation cabin on a circular platform on a single-stage 8ft (2.4m) high steel tower, said to have come from RAF Wellesbourne, but explained as 'for watching out for air-raids'.

18d. single- and double-height guard-posts

During the 1980s a simple square guard-post was developed by the army for barracks and other installations. It is about 8ft (2.4m) square with loopholes inserted to suit. One example at Simpson Barracks, Northampton, examined prior to demolition, had three loopholes, one across a corner and one in each of two adjacent sides. It was made of concrete blocks with a timber and corrugated-iron roof, slightly raked. The loopholes were of steel and had sliding shutters. One was served by a fire-step. The walls were 8in (20cm) thick. A similar structure guarded a training area at Fulbeck (Lincolnshire) until its demolition. At two barracks sites Oakington (Cambridgeshire) and Bovington Camp (Dorset) (*320*) there are two-storey versions with a door at ground level and four loopholes at first-floor level.

19. BUILDINGS ADAPTED AS HARDENED DEFENCES

These fall into several categories: simple loopholes inserted into existing structures in the landscape, former defence works which were refortified; military buildings which were made self defensible and civilian buildings which, by virtue of their location, were fortified.

320 Bovington Camp, Dorset
18d; two-storey version of
bullet-proof guard-post used at
British Army barracks

Loopholes

The simplest way of fortifying any structure was to insert loopholes. The War Office *Manual of Field Engineering* of 1911, shows how a house may be fortified by blocking doors and windows and inserting splayed loopholes. These ideas were developed subsequently with a significant proportion of the 1939 *Field Engineering Field Service Pocket Book* being devoted to the fortification of houses and other buildings, the adaptation of walls and hedges as defence positions and the rapid construction of obstacles to impede the enemy's progress. All over the country are examples of walls, into which loopholes have been cut, generally in order to defend a road junction or some other designated vulnerable point.

Examples include:
SH385681 (Bodorgan, Anglesey) 62 loopholes in 300 yards of wall
NO303011 (Markinch Cemetery, Fife) single loophole
NU195122 (Alnwick Cemetery, Northumberland) 6+ loopholes in wall
TM476615-6 (Sizewell, Suffolk) loops at 13ft (4m) intervals in 200 yards of wall
SE130398 (Baildon, W Yorkshire) loops in field wall covering road-block
TG393261 (Ingham Old Hall, Norfolk) several loops in boundary wall beside road
SJ930774 (Bollington, Cheshire) loopholes in parapet of canal bridge over road

SP585233 & 583233 (Bicester, Oxon) loopholes on railway bridge parapets

SP354196 (Charlbury, Oxon) 3+ loopholes in garden wall

SP162436 (Mickleton, Glos) loopholes in churchyard wall

SU638057 (Paulsgrove, Hampshire) loopholes cut in parapet of railway footbridge

SY676788 (Weymouth, Dorset) loopholes in wall overlooking harbour

ST071435 (Watchet, Somerset) loopholes in harbour wall

SX894612 (Paignton, Devon) loopholed garden wall

SX706398 (Malborough, Devon) loopholes in wall of village pound

The refortification of former defence works

Apart from the obvious places which had never relinquished their military significance
such as Dover Castle or the Victorian forts of Portsmouth, Milford Haven, Plymouth
and Chatham, these included a wide variety of historic sites ranging from the Iron Age
hill-fort of Old Bewick (Northumberland) and the Roman fort of Pevensey (East Sussex)
to the Civil War forts at Earith and Cambridge Castle (both Cambridgeshire). Many of
the Martello Towers, on both south and east coasts, were either converted into king-size
pillboxes, with mg embrasures cut into their walls, or into OPs by the addition of concrete
structures to their roofs.

Examples include:

TR324419 (Dover Castle, Kent) emplacement for 6 pounder AT gun built into curtain
    wall near the Constable's Tower

TR130321 (Dymchurch Redoubt, Kent) Second World War gun battery etc. on
    Napoleonic fort

321 Normans Bay, Pevensey, East Sussex (TQ647021); Martello Tower number 64 with stepped
lmg loops inserted on each side to enfilade the beach

Dublin, the Magazine Fort in Phoenix Park has First World War and Second World War
  pillboxes etc. on the earlier bastions of this eighteenth-century fort (*77*)

TQ647021 (Pevensey Bay, East Sussex) (*321*) Martello Tower 64 has had stepped
  loopholes inserted on two sides to allow the beach to be enfiladed by lmg fire.

TQ681053 (Normans Bay, East Sussex) Martello Tower 55 has had a loopholed
  blockhouse added to its roof.

Self-defensible military structures

Both isolated, free-standing structures, such as AA towers, and also elements of much larger
complexes such as airfields or coastal defence batteries, were often given close-defence
loopholes. This was so that, not only might they repel a local attack, by, say parachutists,
but also that they might take their place in the greater defensive scheme of things.

Examples include

ST203144 (Church Stanton, Somerset) loopholed walls to fighter-pens

TL020978 etc. (Kingscliffe, Northants) loopholed fighter dispersal pens

SK984551 (Wellingore, Lincs) (*322*) loopholed fighter dispersal pens

NT505810 (Drem, Lothian) loopholed fighter dispersal pen

ST474766 (Portishead, Somerset) loopholes in Bofors AA tower

TQ099868 (West Ruislip, London) loopholes in Bofors AA tower

NT468999 (Kincraig Bty. Fife) loopholed Battery OP

HY248079 (Ness Bty. Orkney) loopholed rear wall of 6in gun-house

ND403930 (Balfour Bty. Orkney) (*323*)
  loopholes in Twin-6 Director Tower

Civilian buildings adapted as hardened defences

These will almost always have constituted
a part of a local defence scheme, so
examples will invariably relate to other
proximate elements in the scheme, such
as road-blocks, groups of pillboxes or
fieldworks, probably all these things.
Sometimes an opportunist approach was
taken in order to exploit the camouflage
properties of, for instance, a ruined

322 Wellingore, Lincolnshire (SK984551);
view looking down on the rifle-rests
behind the loopholes of one of the
defensible fighter dispersal pens at this
airfield

323 Balfour Battery, Orkney (ND403950); director tower of this Twin-six pounder QF battery, with loopholes in the upper storey

324 Minsmere, Suffolk (TM473659); medieval chapel converted into pillbox, retaining the ancient masonry

chapel or house, but, despite the attraction of such a site, there had to be a tactical justification for the use of scant resources. A number of the examples below are on stop lines, particularly those based on canals, where waterside buildings are easily adapted.

Examples include:
TM473659 (Minsmere, Suffolk) pillbox built into medieval chapel (*324*)
NZ266965 (Low Chibburn, Northumberland) pillbox in medieval preceptory

325 Angle, Pembrokeshire (SM867019); mill converted to pillbox by the addition of an upper floor and loopholes

TG351331 (Broomholm, Norfolk) pillbox built into tower of medieval priory

SK251043 (Alvecote, Warks) medieval abbey dovecote converted to pillbox

NZ594220 (Kirkleatham, Redcar) eighteenth-century tower with (now blocked) loophole

SH237837 (Holyhead, Anglesey) lower floor of Gothic folly tower converted into a strong-point, with three loopholes, in walls of manor-house/hotel

SU517131 (Botley, Hants) two-storey polygonal gazebo converted to strong-point with loopholes on both floors, and further loops in adjoining garden wall

TQ446184 (Isfield Place, East Sussex) two gazebos/pillboxes in garden wall

TF9933339 (Thursford, Norfolk) Crawfish Pub has loopholed boundary wall

SD429125 (Burscough, Lancs) loopholed tower built onto Farmers Arms Pub

SD432124 (Burscough, Lancs) loops on two floors of former stables at Slipway Pub

SU742576 (Dipley, Hants) Old Mill Inn incorporates pillbox on GHQ Line

SP465583 (Marston Doles, Warwickshire) loopholed former pub on canal stop line

SU999475 (East Shalford, Surrey) Seahorse Pub loopholed to cover road-block

SD367083 (Haskayne, Lancs) loopholes in two sides of upper storey of house

SP354195 (Charlbury, Oxon) loopholes at two levels in side of house

SP365643 (Fosse Wharf Bridge, Warwickshire) loopholes in end wall of house

SU680706 (Burghfield, Berkshire) house converted as strong-point with at least seven loops upstairs and four down, some recently removed

TQ025475 (Chilworth, Surrey) 6 pounder Hotchkiss gun emplacement built into house

SM867019 (Angle, Pembrokeshire) (*325*) windmill converted to strong-point

Left 326 Bond End
Mill, Gloucestershire
(SO794053); alongside the
Gloucester and Sharpness
Canal, here a defence line,
the mill has had loopholes
inserted at the upper level

Below 327 Downholland
Cross, Lancashire
(SD366068); like many
other buildings along
the Trent and Mersey
Canal, this barn has had
loopholes inserted at two
levels; the upper ones are
served by brick fire-steps
reached by ladder

SO794053 (Bond End Mill, Glos) (*326*) converted to strong-point

TG442090 (Stracey Arms, Norfolk) loopholes inserted in windmill

TG372172 (Ludham, Norfolk) windmill converted to strong-point

SO573374 (Mordiford, Hereford) loopholes in two sides of water-mill

TL600266 (Tilty, Essex) rectangular pillbox built inside open barn

TR095352 (Court-at-Street, Kent) pillbox built into barn wall

SZ293933 (Lymore, Hants) pillbox built into barn wall

TG418073 (Halvergate, Norfolk) loopholes inserted in barn

SU164173 (Breamore, Hants) barn converted to strong-point with loopholes cut in three sides; on River Avon stop line

SD415124 (Burscough, Lancs) loopholes in two sides of barn

SD366068 (Downholland Cross, Lancs) (*327*) 13 loopholes in three sides of barn complex; series of brick and concrete fire-steps built inside at two levels

SD442121 (Burscough, Lancs) loopholes in three sides of former stable-block

SN373274 (Cynwyl Elfed, Carms) (*328*) two loopholes in cobbler's shop

SN373277 (Cynwyl Elfed, Carms) loophole in milking parlour

SH477629 (Carnarfon, Gwynedd) (*329*) L-shaped loopholed wall on top of Harbour-master's office on quayside

SK071427 (Alton, Staffs) railway station building converted to pillbox

SP053806 (Kings Norton, Birmingham) pillbox in base of factory chimney

328 Cynwyl Elfed, Carmarthenshire (SN373277); one of two loopholes in the village cobblers shop

20. EXDO POSTS

These structures, which developed from the Submarine-Miners' controls of the end of the nineteenth century, are included here as they were often self-defensible. Their function during the Second World War was to provide a base for the Extended Defence Officer – the naval officer in charge of inshore (up to a mile or 1.6km) minefields, anti-submarine nets, booms and hydrophones, the Royal Navy Coast Watch Service and also responsible for liaison with the other military services. These functions operated all around the coast of the British Isles, but in many places the EXDO post could either be accommodated in existing structures, such as Port War Signal Stations, forts and batteries, and harbour installations, or else incorporated into reused older structures from the First World War or even earlier. Where the EXDO post had to be isolated from other structures, then a particular, defensible design was adopted and it is that with which we will here be concerned. As a naval structure, the new design, put into effect from 1938 onwards, was loosely based on the bridge of a warship.

20a. standard EXDO post

The usual, tower, design has two or three decks, with an observation cupola on the roof. There are three main elements: the upper deck is the watch position, and a plinth allows an observer to stand with his head and shoulders inside the cupola. This is square, has a horizontal observation slit, and is often set at 45 degrees to the tower. The next element is the chart and communication room, equipped with telephone and map-table, and is reached through a hatch by a ladder from ground level. Here is the crew-room with stove, chemical toilet and hammocks. This is usually

329 Carnarfon, Gwynedd (SH477629); L-shaped loopholed firing position built on top of the harbour-master's office on the town quay

330 Coalhouse Fort, Essex (TQ691768) **20a**; EXDO post; note the diagonally-set cupola on top and porch on the left-hand corner

331 Landguard Common, Suffolk (TM283315) **20a**; EXDO post, generously provided with observation slits and close-defence loopholes; it has a partner on the other side of the estuary at Beacon Hill Fort, defended by a semi-circular pillbox

loopholed for close-defence, and has a straight diagonal, or cruciform AR wall. Towers are usually 20ft (6m) cubes, with a roofed blast-porch, often set on the diagonal at one corner.

Examples:
TQ691768 (Coalhouse Fort) (*330*), TR017958 (Holliwell Point) and TM263316 (Beacon Hill Fort, Harwich) all Essex TM283315 (Landguard Common, Suffolk) (*331*)

20b. as **20a** but the cupola is set straight as at SX923627 (Torquay, Devon) (*332*) and NZ324806 (Blyth, Northumberland)

20c. single-level linear version with all three elements in line; examples at TR052676 (Shellness, Kent) (*333*) with cupola, and Fort Bovisand, Plymouth, without

332 Torquay, Devon (SX923627) **20b**; EXDO post as **20a**, but with cupola set straight

Examples of other designs include:
a reused late nineteenth-century example at Fort Blockhouse, Gosport, Hampshire; a reused First World War example at Hoxa, Orkney Island, and one at Chapel Bay Battery. A Milford Haven example integrated into command complex at Ness Battery, Stromness Orkney Island; tower behind casemated battery at Drake's Island, Plymouth, converted example; blockhouse with frontal pointed projection and wide horizontal viewing slit at SX648440 (Burgh Island, Devon) overlooking bay, may be EXDO post (*334*).

Refs: fieldwork, Peter Cobb; newspapers August 2004 reporting sale of Burgh Island for example.

Coast-watching posts
There are networks of these structures around Britain and Ireland; they tend to be small, brick and concrete boxes with small viewing slits in the seaward-facing sides, not unlike fire-watching posts on top of factories. They should not be confused with single-storey quadrant towers used on both coastal and inland bombing and gunnery ranges.

333 Shellness, Kent (TR052676) **20c**; single-storey EXDO post with rooms set in line rather than stacked

334 Burgh Island, Devon (SX648440); a possible EXDO post

335   Fraisthorpe, East Yorkshire (TA170633); beach-light emplacement

Examples at:
NJ467687 (Portknockie, Aberdeenshire)
SX524470 (Gara Point, Devon)

Beach Light Emplacements

One specialised structure not hitherto mentioned is the Beach Light emplacement, designed to illuminate beaches under attack. There are examples, all quite different, at NO472276 (Tentsmuir, Fife), resembling a hexagonal pillbox but with larger-than-normal embrasures; TA170633 (Fraisthorpe, East Yorkshire) (*335*), which consists of a rectangular chamber and an adjoining one for the light itself, in order to enfilade the beach, and TA405113 (Spurn Head, East Yorkshire) which is a box-like structure built on top of a pillbox.

THE TACTICAL USE OF HARDENED DEFENCES

INTRODUCTION

Throughout the twentieth century, controversy has raged between those who have championed mobile warfare and those who have preferred to put their trust in fixed defences. Much has been written about the psychological conditions which might underpin either standpoint and, with benefit of hindsight, France has been pilloried for its Maginot mentality in the 1930s. However, at the same time that France was building these defences, Fuller and Liddell-Hart, the most vociferous proponents of what would eventually come to be called *Blitzkrieg*, were given little encouragement by the military establishment outside Germany and it was to be Guderian's *Panzer* divisions which vindicated them. In the battles which led to the fall of France in 1940, junior allied commanders, including both Montgomery and de Gaulle, understood the principles of armoured warfare, but had been denied the means of fully implementing them. Tanks were still, too often, deployed in twos and threes and regarded as mobile pillboxes supporting the advance of the infantry.

Warfare has always been a matter of action and reaction. As technology has advanced and new weapons have been produced, then ways have always been found to counter any, usually temporary, advantage. The plans and sections of fortifications have usually been dictated by the destructive potential of the projectile weapons arrayed against them. Chamfered parapets and rounded angle towers were found less susceptible to damage by stone-throwing catapults and, later on, the low profile of a thickened earthwork bank proved more resilient to the power of gunpowder artillery. The business of warfare has always been a subject for instruction and debate. At a tactical level, T'ai Kung, 3000 years ago, for instance, wrote about how to use chariots in war, where they would be effective and where less so. Another 500 years on and, at the strategic level, Sun Tzu advised always being prepared for war, even in times of apparent peace. Part of such preparedness meant defending frontiers, settlements and lines of communication against attack. Whilst the initiative usually lay with the aggressor, echoed in more recent times by the dictum that 'the bomber would always get through', it was usually felt that defences could delay an attacker and who knew what might go wrong for him in the meantime? Whilst wars are remembered for their battles, it must not be forgotten that they were often fought to secure territory and this within an overall context of defended lines, lands and points. The English Civil War, for example, consisted of 650 discrete actions, nearly a third of which were sieges and almost half of the War's casualties were sustained in minor skirmishes, yet it is for the four or five major battles that it is generally remembered. It is interesting that although Vauban, Louis XIV's famous military engineer, is chiefly remembered for his great fortifications all along France's lengthy frontiers, particularly in the north-east corner bordering Belgium, an area known as the cockpit of Europe, it was for being a siege engineer that he gained the Sun King's esteem. So successful had Vauban become at conducting sieges, that he even laid down a timetable for carrying out all the formal, choreographed moves which would culminate in the capitulation of the besieged fortress. He knew that once this inexorable sequence of events was in train, unless it was interrupted by unpredictable events, the siege would end in inevitable triumph for the attackers. Of the 31 major sieges carried out between 1695 and 1734 by the Duke of Marlborough's armies, 27 ended in capitulation by the garrison after sieges lasting between three and 84 days. At Belgrade, a relieving force was defeated resulting in the garrison's surrender; only at Toulon was the siege raised, whilst Turin was relieved after a siege of nearly five months; only one city, Liège, was stormed, an event to be avoided if at all possible. All that engineers like Vauban could do to counter this certainty, was to utilise the experience they had gained on the other side of the ditch, to build in structural devices for delaying the outcome. In French, the words for military engineers and genius might be the same, but the word 'impregnable' is still rendered redundant. This awareness, though, appears to have failed to prevent the construction of mighty fortresses throughout history and in all cultures, extending into modern times. The system of fortifications built to counter an invasion of Britain by Louis Napoleon in the 1860s, may have been known as 'Palmerston's Follies', but only *after* the expenditure of vast sums of money and the realisation that they had, as usual and almost immediately, been overtaken by technological advances in armaments.

THE TACTICS OF FORTIFICATION AROUND 1900

We have seen in Chapter 1 how blockhouses were used in the Boer War, and for the close-defence of coastal batteries, and these two contexts provide neat examples of two different applications of similar structures. The masonry blockhouses in South Africa were built after June 1900, until around December 1902, during the guerrilla phase of the War. From early 1902 they were generally superseded by the cheaper, more simply-constructed, octagonal or circular corrugated-iron blockhouses. Together, they constituted a key element in the strategy which was designed to deny the Boer *commandos* the freedom of movement they had previously enjoyed. At a tactical level they were intended to protect lines of communication, particularly railway bridges, and to create linear barriers to movement. These barriers both protected the railway tracks themselves and formed the perimeters of notional boxes designed to contain enemy units, forcing them to surrender through attrition. Whether Boer units were attempting to cut the lines, or to migrate into another box, the purpose was to stop them, engage in a fire-fight and destroy the enemy. The masonry blockhouses were designed to be capable of holding out for short periods of time against enemies who lacked artillery. Their walls, never more than 3ft thick, and often far thinner, would keep out rifle bullets. They were provided with shuttered loopholes through which the garrison, enjoying a fair amount of protection, could bring heavy fire upon an exposed enemy. The entrance was usually at first-floor level via a ladder which would be withdrawn in the event of an attack and the base of the wall was covered by over-hanging firing positions. The garrison had a water supply and sometimes cooking facilities within the blockhouse. The simpler model of blockhouse had walls of shingle sandwiched between sheets of corrugated iron. This, too, was bullet-proof. As the success of Kitchener's strategy became apparent, with lines of blockhouses built along the railways achieving their objectives, the scheme was rolled out across country. New lines of blockhouses were constructed by sappers travelling in convoys of ox-carts, carrying all their pre-prepared materials with them. The biggest problem was that the Boers would attempt to cross lines at night, so rifles were mounted to fire remotely along the fixed lines of the trenches if sounds were detected, or wires were tripped. To avoid one blockhouse firing on another, they were sited so as to be offset from one another, rather than in straight lines. One such line ran for 175 miles, with a garrison of over 3000 troops in around 400 blockhouses. There were over 30 such lines across the country and each of the circular iron blockhouses had space for six or seven men. They eventually became effective in restricting the Boers' movement and the only real problem for the troops manning them was the intense boredom and monotony. When action came, it was nothing like a siege, but, for a short time the garrison would be holed up in its blockhouse, fully able to repel an assault. The enemy would, at worst, be driven off having suffered casualties and expending ammunition with little hope of replacing either. It was, no doubt, the perceived success of this tactic, which led to the use of blockhouses to guard the Uganda Railway against German raiding during the East African campaign of 1915. These were built every 10 miles (16km) along the track and were used in conjunction with mobile patrols.

The blockhouses guarding Edwardian coastal batteries were designed to serve a different purpose. Their function was to defend the approaches to the coastal defence guns against attack from a raiding-force seeking to put the guns out of action prior to a landing or full-scale invasion. By 1900, many coastal batteries, particularly those in apparently vulnerable locations, had become self-contained forts, expected to repel attacks from seawards and, more especially, from the landward side. Blockhouses were equipped with machine-guns and lights intended to safeguard not only the actual entrances, but the ditches as well, many of them being sited to enfilade the ditches by firing along fixed lines. Defence plans envisaged no prolonged siege conditions, but sought to contain the attempted *coup de main*. However, the Russian experience at Port Arthur unsettled the military thinkers, to the extent that the value of fixed defences (especially if independent of field armies or, where appropriate, battle fleets) came into question. The lessons drawn appear to favour field fortifications, offering smaller targets, exploiting the element of surprise and pushed as far forward of the objective being defended as the terrain and available troops would allow. The key elements are reckoned to be howitzers bringing indirect fire onto attacking troops from hidden positions and plenty of obstacles, including electrified fences covered by machine-guns in sunken, concealed positions, using embrasures and provided with overhead cover. In contrast, the permanent forts were deemed to have little value beyond providing comfortable secure barracks and stores for the garrison, and denying some prominent locations to the enemy, forcing them into time-consuming activities such as mining. A difference might have been made had the Russian forts been equipped with artillery in iron cupolas, as were many of the French and Belgian forts at this time. However, with benefit of hindsight, it would appear that given the destructive power unleashed on them when these forts faced the German artillery bombardments in First World War, this would have made little difference. The weaknesses and limited tactical options of fortresses had been described in 1832 by von Clausewitz. Of his 11 functions of fortresses, the majority are mainly passive. He accepts the capability of the fortress to deny the enemy access, in the 'they shall not pass' sense, but points out that if only a nation's frontiers are so defended, it leaves an awful lot of interior space for exploiting a breakthrough, and it was just such ambition which was to underpin von Schlieffen's planning against France in 1914.

As applied to Britain then, the conclusions of Clarke, writing in 1907, were that important ports should be defended by coastal artillery batteries; that in order to repel raiding parties, those batteries needed to be provided with close-defence works both hardened and earthwork, making use of all the tricks of field engineering going back to classical and medieval times; a mixed economy of chains of infantry redoubts with all-round defences and permanent blinded trenches, together with mobile artillery able to put down both direct and indirect fire on attacking troops, and heavier guns in permanent emplacements able to hit predetermined target areas; but, above all, that it was up to the Royal Navy to see the enemy never got ashore in sufficient strength to threaten the integrity of the country, or for that matter parts of the Empire. Much of this was not particularly new. The professional journals of the Royal Artillery and the REs had long included articles by serving officers for whom some of Clarke's principles had long ago become givens. For example, the idea of locating guns outside forts and of hiding machine-guns in holes in the ground were presented as orthodoxy, and designs for trenches, with and without overhead cover, were easily available, along with the argument that it did not take trained sappers to construct them, for digging holes was ever a democratic activity.

TACTICS IN THE FIRST WORLD WAR

The decisive German thrust into north-eastern France, outlined in the Schlieffen Plan, had run out of steam by Christmas 1914 and a drift into static warfare had occurred with the consolidation of trench lines by both sides. These lines, which ran from the Belgian coast to the Franco-Swiss border, around 400 miles (640km) in total, were to remain fixed for most of the next three years, deviating by no more than a few miles each way, in a few specific locations. There quickly developed a predictable pattern to the attack and defence of the frontline. Any attack was preceded by an artillery barrage which was intended to flatten obstacles, destroy defence positions, particularly those mounting machine-guns, neutralise enemy artillery and demoralise the defenders. During this often lengthy bombardment, which usually failed to achieve any of those four objectives, the defenders would seek whatever cover might be available. Once the barrage ceased, signalling the imminence of an advance by infantry across No-mans-land, the defenders would emerge to man their machine-guns to lethal effect. It was in this context that the pillbox first appeared on the Western Front. The German dug-outs, constructed deep down below the frontline trench systems, were nothing less than underground barracks built to a high standard. The walls were lined with concrete and with anything up to 30 or 40ft (10-13m) of earth above, they were impervious to the constant shelling which assailed both sides. When they were sometimes captured, they impressed the allied troops, who enviously related tales of their luxury and the profusion of creature comforts within, probably to the extent of hyperbole. They certainly provided a security which was lacking in day-to-day life in the allied trenches. What was needed, in addition, was shelter against the specific shelling which heralded an attack, when it was vital to be able to resume defensive positions within a minute or so of the barrage lifting. The Germans solved this problem by constructing concrete blockhouses in the frontline, in which their machine-gun crews might shelter during the barrage, but from which they might quickly emerge on cue. These blockhouses had no loopholes and were not designed as machine-gun posts. The gun would be set up either on the roof, or in a sandbagged emplacement alongside. The importance lay in the survival of gun and crew during the bombardment phase. If, by some strange chance, attacking infantry reached such a blockhouse before its occupants emerged, then it was a simple matter of a couple of grenades through the doors to neutralise it. When the Hindenburg Line was built in 1917, concrete pillboxes furnished with embrasures were incorporated, from which it was intended that machine-guns would be operated. These could only be captured by getting close enough to throw grenades, or even shovel-fulls of earth, through the embrasure, whilst covering the rear entrance with a Lewis-gun, or a bayonet party. The British experience was that the flamethrower was not generally effective, and so tended to be avoided. More useful was the tank, arriving on the battlefield later in the War, concentrating its fire on the embrasure, allowing infantry to approach close enough to capture it in the normal way.

PILLBOXES IN THE SECOND WORLD WAR: HOW THEY WERE USED

We have seen how a defensive mentality seemed to dominate much military thought between the wars. It is interesting to note that the Dutch Army fortification manual of 1928 contained plans for a structure virtually identical to the German machine-gun crew-shelter, which was entirely lacking in firing ports. We have already seen how the Maginot Line extensions of 1939-40 in north-eastern France incorporated trios of mutually-supporting pillboxes integrated into an overall defence scheme which included AT ditches and other obstacles, emplacements for AT guns, minefields and fieldworks. Nowadays it is very easy to spot an isolated pillbox and comment on its apparently irrational and exposed situation, whilst remaining unaware of the defensive context which has largely disappeared in the 60 years since it was built. However, notwithstanding the sophistication of such defence systems, it is obvious that the British High Command was reluctant to put much faith in hardened defences. Ironside, Auchinleck and Brooke all expressed their preference for mobile forces which would operate unrestrained by fixed lines of defence. The one exception to this was the coast, where it was hoped that the defences would hold up an invasion, even if they could not prevent it. Brooke was very negative about the GHQ Line and its offshoots, pointing out the impossibility of manning it, even were that to be desirable. Once the factories were producing enough tanks, trucks and guns to make mobile forces more than a pipe-dream, everyone wanted to be part of it. General Sir James Marshall-Cornwall, GOC Western Command, for instance, felt that even the Home Guard should be trained for offensive patrolling and tank-hunting activities, or they would become 'pillbox-bound and impotent for war'. It is interesting, in this context, to note that the official history of the Home Guard in Cambridgeshire, a county through which ran the pillbox-rich GHQ Line, contains but a single reference to pillboxes in an account written in 1943. Even more interesting is the report by German Naval Intelligence, dating from the lead up to *Sealion* in the autumn of 1940, stating that 'the English [*sic*] defence is based on mobility and the concentration of all available fire-power. There is no fixed defence line with built-in defences'. This is odd given the comprehensive coverage of the defences achieved by the *Luftwaffe's* aerial photographers. It may have been that Admiral Lutjens, the officer responsible for transporting the invasion force across the Channel, his boss Admiral Raeder and Admiral Canaris of the *Abwehr*, were reluctant to be seen showing enthusiasm for an operation holding such an element of risk, particularly for the *Kriegsmarine* and saw advantage in stressing the difficulties of being up against the RAF and the Royal Navy.

This, then, was the official strategy in Britain: mobile forces, deployed to respond to invasion hot-spots and unhampered by fixed defences getting in the way physically or psychologically. The reality, however, was that several hundred miles of AT obstacles supported by thousands of pillboxes had been built as formal defence lines and thousands more pillboxes had been built to defend the coast, airfields, nodal points, and other vulnerable points – something around 28,000 pillboxes altogether. Despite the generals' misgivings, they were forced into providing, at the very least, some basic guidance as to how to use them. Therefore, in October 1940, the War Office issued their *Tactical Notes* which included *Battle Drill for using A Post in Concrete*. This begins by pointing out that the concrete pillbox can be 'a great aid to defence if intelligently used', but has the potential to 'become a death trap'. Quite! The notes go on to stress that given the limited visibility, the need to maintain external sentries and lookouts was paramount. If the pillbox were to come under attack, then it was important to man prepared positions outside the pillbox, only using the pillbox itself for light automatics if the field of fire was sufficiently wide. It is interesting to note that the contemporary London Operational Instructions issued from Horse Guards, also included injunctions to establish alternative positions for automatic weapons outside the pillbox, particularly in the LAA role, but generally as well. The evidence for this habit of siting weapons outside pillboxes rather than inside, in order to extend the field of fire and to increase the garrison's field of vision, can be found at a number of sites. On the GHQ Line in Essex there is at least one instance of the mounting pedestal for a 6 pounder Hotchkiss QF gun being placed outside the pillbox. At Lavenham on the Eastern Command Line in Suffolk and on the Norfolk coast at Heacham, spigot mortar pedestals have been placed beside AT-gun emplacements, although there is at least one example, at Barton Mills near Newmarket, where a spigot mortar *pintle* has replaced the mounting-ring of a Hotchkiss 6 pounder QF gun on its pedestal. The inference to be made most often, however, is that it was worth sacrificing an element of protection for greater effectiveness through increased vision and field of fire. When the pillbox was seen as the permanent home of an automatic weapon, then certain procedures were followed to maximise effectiveness. Weapons were ranged onto fixed points and range cards were fixed to the wall of the pillbox. These laid down tasks, including those for darkness or poor visibility, fixed lines and arcs of fire, and easily recognised aiming points. Sometimes a panorama was actually painted on the wall above the machine-gun mount and an example of such an aiming aid survives in a pillbox in Fraisthorpe, near Bridlington, as do others elsewhere.

By early 1941, the indiscriminate construction of pillboxes had stopped. The official War Office line held that concrete defences were only justified in three specific contexts:

- in vital positions to be held indefinitely and to the last round
- on airfields which would be held permanently and denied to the enemy
- at nodal points as part of in-depth defences.

It was, nevertheless, stressed that concrete and earthworks were complementary and that neither should be constructed without the other. The essential functions of the earthen fieldwork in providing the extensive observation and fields of fire which the concrete works lacked, were given particular emphasis. Many of the early pillboxes had been proof only against rifle-fire, splinters and weather, and subsequent advice continued to make this clear. The Air Ministry, however, by this time a major user of hardened defences, decided that, not only would all new builds be shell-proof (with wall thicknesses of 42in or 1.1m) but that their existing bullet-proof pillboxes would be retro-fitted with thickening to this specification. Many such structures can be seen with gaping embrasures and sometimes the original central core standing proud of its additional cladding. Particularly fine examples of these modifications may be seen at Crail (Fife) and at Jurby (Isle of Man). The Air Ministry went yet another stage further by limiting the number of loopholes in these pillboxes and also in their other designs, to just three. This may have made the garrison of the pillbox less vulnerable to incoming fire, but it also underlined the necessity for those supporting fieldworks to compensate for lost vision. Another radical shift in the tactical deployment of defensive elements on airfields was the change from linear defence to systems of defended localities, sometimes based on clusters of pillboxes, supported by fieldworks and mobile units. Some pillboxes were demoted to become dummies or decoys.

It would appear that officialdom had an expectation that the pillbox was basically a shelter for automatic weapons. Virtually all contemporary publications accept this as axiomatic. The Twelfth Battalion of the Green Howards was stationed in the Redcar and Middlesbrough area of north Yorkshire in October 1940. Battalion HQ was at Kirkleatham, where a defended perimeter was established using newly-built concrete pillboxes, converted stone lodges belonging to the Hall and extensive minefields. Standing orders stated that automatic weapons in pillboxes should be kept in gun chests during the daytime and mounted during stand-to from dusk till dawn. In the open they would be mounted for AA use, reverting to their ground bipods and tripods at night. Pillboxes would display an inventory of automatic weapons and grenades. Incidentally, although not expected to undergo long sieges, these pillboxes would always contain three days' emergency food rations and supplies of fresh water sufficient for four days.

Once the likelihood of a German invasion of Britain had receded, the likely users of the 28,000 pillboxes which had been built by mid-1941 were the part-time soldiers of the Home Guard. Training manuals, which set down the drills developed at Osterley Park, or at the zone schools such as Great Amwell (Hertfordshire), included the use and care of weapons, field-craft and street-fighting techniques, which tended to focus on AT warfare in urban settings and drew on the experiences in the Spanish Civil War of instructors such as Tom Wintringham, Hugh Slater, war correspondent John Langdon-Davies and writer John Brophy. Only Slater has much to say about fortifications at all, and hardened defences in particular. His major point is about all-round defence capability and we must remember that he was writing in late 1940, just when the notion of the nodal point was taking over from the linear defensive system to become the new orthodoxy. He extols the idea of extemporisation, accepting the reality that optimum conditions, building materials etc. will not be available. He stresses the need for clear fields of fire and makes simple points such as the need to place automatic weapons at ground level in order to maximise their killing-grounds; the need for small loopholes splayed internally to minimise the danger of admitting enemy fire whilst maintaining a wide arc of fire; the opportunity to use existing *sore thumb* pillboxes as decoys by building new, sunken, hidden ones alongside; the need to avoid symmetrically-placed loopholes; and the usefulness of constructing strong-points inside existing buildings which will not only be concealed but will gain extra strength. He has much to say about camouflage and concealment generally in both urban and countryside settings. Anyone who has searched out pillboxes will know that it is the dark rectangles of their loopholes which will always give them away. Thus Slater advocated having dummy loopholes, painting large, irregular black patches over them, dazzle-painting the whole pillbox and shrouding them under nets threaded with scrim.

It should not have been necessary for Slater, even as early as autumn 1940, to talk about his *sore thumb* pillboxes, for the principle of camouflage was well-established. Much ingenuity had gone into both disguising and concealing pillboxes. Examples of pillboxes in the guise of refreshment kiosks, public conveniences, line-side railway structures, shops, pig-sties, thatched cottages and haystacks are common, many to this day retaining false gables. More pillboxes could be seen (or preferably not) inside barns, road-side cottages, railway-stations, lodges, factory chimneys, public-houses and gazebos. They can be found on top of a broch, on the ramparts of an Iron Age hill-fort, embedded in a Roman fort, in medieval castles and on the bastion of a Civil War artillery fort. Pillboxes from Malta to Minehead and from Capel Curig to Crail can be found with an outer jacket of local stones set in mortar. In appropriate areas they were built completely in local stone. Sometimes they were painted with doors and windows, or notices, or, in at least one case, grave-stones, the better to blend with the neighbours. In at least two sites, at Tentsmuir in Fife and West Aberthaw in Glamorgan, pillboxes set in lines of AT blocks on the beach, had simulated blocks superimposed, hoping thus to become invisible from the air. Many RE officers brought enormous creativity to the problem, as did freelance inventors. The ultimate in concealed defence posts was, of course, the Pickett-Hamilton fort which could be raised hydraulically from its retracted position, flush to the ground, or the Tett Turret which stayed below ground, leaving only its concrete collar exposed.

PILLBOXES IN ACTION

One of the few locations where British-built pillboxes actually came under fire was Hong Kong. Immediately prior to the Japanese invasion of December 1941, three elements made up the defences of Hong Kong. Batteries of heavy artillery, including 9.2in guns were positioned to counter attacks from both landward and seaward approaches. On the mainland a 10-mile long defence line known as the Gin Drinkers' Line, begun in 1937, hinged on the Shing mun Redoubt, a complex of five reinforced concrete pillboxes, connected by tunnels and concrete trenches with overhead cover at one end and the heights of Devil's Peak at the other. The island was defended by more batteries, such as that at Mount Davis, and a girdle of pillboxes around the shores. The Gin Drinkers' Line was designed to be held by two divisions, with the Shing mun Redoubt, a self-contained strong-point to be garrisoned by a full company. In the event, the whole line was manned by less than three battalions, with just a weak platoon in the redoubt. This fell quickly to a night attack by Japanese troops who were directed to a route previously used in pre-War exercises. They infiltrated the sparsely-manned defences, threw grenades down the ventilation shafts and quickly overcame resistance. Although one section-post held out for a further 11 hours, this was far short of the seven days expected by HQ. Those survivors of this assault who could escape were withdrawn to Hong Kong Island. Here, the pillboxes along the coast were manned by a machine-gun battalion of the Middlesex Regiment, with their Vickers guns laid to fire on fixed lines and arcs. These fought most effectively in places under enemy attack, and it could be argued that other possible lines of attack were denied the enemy through the machine-gunners' presence. Once the Japanese were securely established on the Island, however, those Middlesex machine-gunners not hitherto committed to the battle, were redeployed to support counter-attacks. It could also be argued that although they proved vulnerable to mortar fire, the tracked Bren-gun carriers of the Volunteers were more use than the fixed concrete pillboxes. Aerial bombing was required to knock out each of the heavy batteries, and the pillboxes, both those of the Middlesex Regiment and others protecting the docks and manned by the 5/7 Rajputs, were gradually neutralised by field artillery, often after being first bypassed and isolated. Standing orders had specified that the pillboxes were to be used solely as machine-gun posts, but the complementary support fieldworks were missing as there were never enough troops to man them. The Japanese may have suffered heavy losses as they crossed to the Island, but there was never any realistic prospect of the garrison holding out beyond the first wave of troops coming ashore and establishing a bridgehead. There was one curious parallel with the French experience where troops falling back to man pillboxes in prepared positions, had found themselves locked out by previous occupants from units which had already fallen back, taking the keys with them. At the OP of the Shing mun Redoubt, personnel were unwittingly locked inside by a runner who let himself out with the sentry's key, against orders incidentally, and then took it with him. Unfortunately, those left locked inside were the Company and Platoon Commanders and the artillery Forward Observation Officer, and they were thus effectively taken out of the defence of the redoubt.

The defences of Malaya and Singapore also included a similar combination of heavy coastal defence batteries and concrete pillboxes. Despite the oft-repeated myth of the south-facing defences of Singapore, it had long been recognised that the fire-power available against a seaward invasion would, quite probably, encourage an approach from the north and, for that very reason, many of the heavy guns were capable of 360 degree arcs of fire. Unfortunately, they were not supplied with high-explosive shells. War-games had predicted that enemy forces were likely to be landed on the north-eastern coast of Malaya, or even across the border in Siam (now Thailand). The beaches of Kota Baharu near this border were fortified with mines, wire and in-depth fieldworks. There were concrete pillboxes at intervals of about 100 yards, with L-shaped slit-trenches in between and, to the rear, more Bren-gun positions, well dug-in and camouflaged. Each pillbox was garrisoned by an infantry section with at least two Bren guns. All these automatic weapons were positioned to cover the formidable barbed wire obstacles, which consisted of a sandwich with double aprons for the bread and triple Dannert concertinas for the filling, all garnished with thousands of mines. Support was provided by 18 pounder field guns, obsolete but nevertheless effective over open sights at targets trapped on the water or in the wire.

The Japanese invasion force suffered hundreds of casualties from the crossfire, so many, in fact, that once the beach-head had been established, fresh troops had to be landed for the next stage of the invasion. In the end it was a combination of sheer weight of enemy numbers, infiltrating and out-flanking the defences, the paucity of the aircraft available and the lack of a defence-boom across the river-mouth, which defeated the defenders. Heavy fire from a Japanese cruiser began to obscure the defenders' vision, becoming so bad that a build-up of blown sand and cordite fumes from the Brens inside the pillboxes was mistaken for gas, and masks were donned, thus reducing visibility even further. In spite of this gallant defence by Brigadier Key's Dogras and Baluchis, of the Eleventh Indian Division, the withdrawal of the aircraft and the abandonment of the airfield more-or-less dictated that the troops were pulled back to start the deadly leap-frogging down the Malay peninsular which culminated in the fall of Singapore itself. The commanders of the Singapore garrison may have expected an attack from the north, but it had never occurred to them that the enemy would ever be allowed to approach nearer than 25 miles (40km), i.e. the range of the big guns. Consequently, there were no fixed defences on the north side of the island covering the causeway. Even when the enemy was poised to violate this notional exclusion zone, the garrison engineers were dissuaded from building such defences, as by doing so they might cause alarm amongst the civilian population. Singapore's pillboxes, manned by a regular machine-gun battalion of the Manchester Regiment, were confined to the south coast. By the time it was obvious to all that the Japanese would be attacking across the Straits of Johore, it was far too late to construct anything, given the height of the water table and the reluctance of many local Chinese to provide the labour. The majority of Singapore's 72 miles (115 km) of coastline had no hardened defences at all, apart from the well-fortified Keppel Harbour next to Singapore City, with its heavy gun batteries and pillboxes.

WEAPONS IN PILLBOXES

Whilst pillboxes in the First World War like those we have just seen in action in Hong Kong, were designed primarily for the Vickers machine-gun, the commonest type in the Second World War, drawing number FWD3/24, was meant to hold Bren guns. Embrasures were specifically designed with this weapon in mind, with slots in the concrete cill (*336*) and timber shelves and fittings for the three feet of the raised tripod, which was sometimes used (*337*). Alternative ways of mounting the weapon included a built-in box for the bipod, or a large, flat surface for accommodating the three-legged mounting. Where provision was made for a Vickers gun, a half-hexagonal or semi-circular shelf or platform table in concrete (*338*) was built-in. Occasionally, this was replaced by either a solid triangular platform or even a skeleton triangle in brick. Where two guns might sit side-by-side, a long concrete shelf might be built. Where no specific weapon was in the designer's mind, a general-purpose monopod mount, basically a hollow tube, might

336 Ely, Cambridgeshire (TL551807); loophole in shell-proof lmg pillbox, designed with wide internal splay, and minimal external opening, to accommodate a Bren gun on any one of a number of alternative bipod and tripod mountings. A wooden shelf below the level of the brick sill would have extended the support

337 Tripod Bren mount; this could be accommodated in most of the pillboxes designed to be armed with Bren guns. This example at Newhaven Fort (East Sussex)

338 Rye Harbour, East Sussex (TQ948181) (see *162*); three of the tables for Vickers machine-guns in this shell-proof, but remarkably vulnerable, machine-gun post

339 Honington, Suffolk (TL884754) (see *221*); Turnbull mounts superseding tables which may have been intended for Bren tripods rather than Vickers guns, since the embrasures appear not to have been altered

be set in the cill of the embrasure. Eventually, Turnbull mounts (*339*) were fitted to many pillboxes, particularly those on airfields, some of them replacing the toothed, semi-circular Scarff mounting, designed for Lewis guns on First World War aircraft.

The circular, mushroom-like F.C. Construction pillbox had a tubular steel rail running around the inside just below the 360 degree embrasure, to which were clamped two fittings for Vickers guns (*340*). These could be secured to fire on fixed lines, or released to be moved freely around. Very occasionally, specific mountings were provided. For instance, a group of pillboxes near Ewshott, on GHQ Line B, were provided with a mounting for the First World War Hotchkiss lmg which had been issued to cavalry based in Aldershot in 1940. Particularly intriguing, are some pillboxes in Kent and at least two in Suffolk, which contain low-level loopholes which may have been designed for use by the Boys 0.55in (14mm) AT rifle. A number of rectangular pillboxes found on the Lincolnshire coast and the mouth of the Tees, incorporate an open concrete pit for a 2in (50mm) mortar (*204*). Both the FWD/3 design 23 and its 3-bay Lincolnshire variant contain open platforms with concrete posts for mounting lmgs in an AA role. This feature can also be seen in the large octagonal pillboxes in the London outer defences, the similar, but hexagonal, pillboxes on the Eastern Command Line, some naval guard-posts, and the gun-houses along the River Wyre in Lancashire. Gun-houses themselves were mainly designed to accommodate the 2 pounder AT gun (see *238* & *341*), or the 6 pounder Hotchkiss QF gun (see *239* & *247*) but there are also a number which could take some of the assorted field guns in use in 1940, such as the French or US 75mm guns (see *254*), or the old 13 and 18 pounders of First World War vintage. An open-backed, half-hexagonal gun-house, around a dozen examples of which are found in Sussex, is reputed to have been intended for 25 pounder gun-howitzers (see *248*). A number of gun-houses designed for 2 pounder AT guns on the GHQ and the Eastern Command Lines, as well as isolated examples elsewhere, were subsequently modified as infantry section-posts by the simple expedient of blocking up the big embrasure, and inserting two pre-cast loopholes. An example at Bonar Bridge in the far north of Scotland has a metal ladder incorporating a Turnbull mount in one of these extemporised loopholes (*341*).

During the frenetic post-Dunkirk times of maximum effort to complete defences before the Germans could invade, mass-production techniques had been used to a certain extent. Where timber was available, contractors would be issued with sets of pre-formed shuttering into which the concrete would go, generally in two pourings, each of about 3ft 6in, to achieve the usual interior height of the pillbox. Pre-fabricated concrete loopholes, many of them manufactured at railway workshops such as Ashford in Kent, were inserted into the shuttering. These methods were not always available to the builders of all the odd, isolated pillboxes defending searchlight sites or obscure road junctions. Here, loopholes were just as likely to be formed from slanting a few bricks across the wall width. Whilst the two recommended shapes for loopholes were the small exterior opening with a wide internal splay (see *336*), or the stepped, X-shaped or waisted loophole with splays to both inside and out (*342*), there were many built

340 Vickers machine-gun mounting clamped to the continuous tubular ring which ran round the inside of the F C Construction pillbox, holding two such mounts

341 Bonar Bridge, Highland (NH608913); pillbox designed for the 2 pounder AT gun to drawing number DFW3/28a (note the slots for the forward-facing split trail), subsequently converted by blocking the embrasure with brick-work and inserting a steel ladder with a Turnbull mount

which completely failed to meet the RE design criteria. Given the importance of the loophole itself, both in terms of facilitating the effectiveness of weapons and also the protection of the garrison, it is sometimes surprising how little thought has been given to its design and construction. Obviously, some tweaking went on, sometimes at a surprisingly high level. Major-General Taylor, DFW at the War Office, made his own contribution to the debate about loopholes, commenting about local modifications to the big octagonal pillboxes on the Outer London Line A. One memo from GHQ Home Forces in December 1940 almost reads like a modern-day product-recall. It points out the difficulty some units had experienced deploying a 2 pounder AT gun in combined anti-tank and Bren pillboxes, suggesting minor structural changes which could be made to facilitate moving the right trail with a handspike and sliding the gun forward in order to remove the wheels. Feedback was requested on whether these modifications should be incorporated in all new buildings.

SAFEGUARDING THE OCCUPANTS OF PILLBOXES

The precaution most obviously found in British pillboxes is the AR wall or screen. This was intended to prevent a missile entering through one loophole and then careering around inside the pillbox causing more damage. Loopholes were often stepped in order to

342 Theddlethorpe St Helen, Lincolnshire (TF476887); X-shaped or waisted loophole with internal and external splays and a wooden arm support on the steel shelf-brackets, enabling either a Bren gun or a rifle to be used

prevent a missile being funnelled into the loophole, but it was inevitable that some would get in. AR screens were usually Y-shaped, or sometimes cruciform. A very small number of pillboxes on RAF airfields had three-leaved cantilevered AR screens coming off a central column leaving spaces at ground level. This was the normal design in the majority of F.C. Construction pillboxes, so contractors may have spread the design to conventional pillboxes. Many styles of pillbox were provided with a porch, an L-shaped blast-wall, or simply a half-height blast-wall to protect the entrance from enemy fire or grenade attack. The RE manual pointed out that adequate protection from small-arms fire, i.e. 20-round bursts from automatic weapons up to 7.92mm (0.32 in), could be achieved with 18in (46cm) of brickwork in lime mortar, 12in (30 cm) of un-reinforced concrete, 30in (76cm) of sandbags, or 60in (1.5m) of earth, chalk or clay. It is thus clear why so many pillboxes had concrete walls varying in thickness between 12 and 18in (30-46cm).

We have already seen how the use of flamethrowers in the First World War was less than wholeheartedly embraced by all combatants, but those designing pillboxes for the use of the British Army felt that some attempt must be made to defend against their use. A sliding steel shutter was fitted in some cases either externally or internally, as was an asbestos screen (*343*). Another alternative was to block the loophole, albeit temporarily, with shaped concrete blocks. In France in 1939, the general commanding the garrison of Lille invented a closure device based on hexagonal boxes of gravel or sand sliding on rollers or ball-bearings set in chases in the embrasure. Known as *Bertschi's Briques*, they never got past the experimental stage. It would appear that contractors were free to

343 Hazeley, Hampshire (SU742587); a pre-fabricated concrete loophole with small external opening closed by a flip-up asbestos shutter, installed as an anti-flamethrower protection

install such devices, or not, presumably in consultation with RE officers and the units manning the pillboxes. Where a Turnbull mounting was fitted, however, the protruding muzzle precluded the installation of an external shutter. Examples survive of many of these options.

Ventilation ducts were usually fitted in emplacements designed for use by machine-guns, AT guns and field guns, in an attempt to disperse the cordite fumes which would quickly fill such a confined space. Gas was another problem entirely. It was generally believed that the use of gas in the First World War would be repeated and Britain accordingly had amassed large stocks of canisters and shells. During the invasion scare of 1940, pillboxes, along with other posts for both civil and military defence, were equipped with mustard gas detectors. Trench rattles were provided for sounding a gas alarm. It was also planned to provide gas curtains over all openings, but in the realisation that gas attack was not forthcoming this extra inconvenience was dropped. For obvious reasons, more attention had been paid to this topic in the First World War. Some pillboxes near Hazebrouck (see *36*), built in the summer of 1918, were provided with the means to remotely pump mustard-gas into them in the event of their being captured.

In the event, where pillboxes were attacked, they were usually destroyed by shell-fire. Many of the blockhouses supporting the Maginot Line in north-east France were hit by German 88mm shells, usually aimed at the embrasures. We have seen how the pillboxes in Hong Kong, Malaya and Singapore fell to artillery fire. The Atlantic Wall defences of north-west France were usually targeted by ship-borne artillery prior to amphibious landings, with varying degrees of success. Where pillboxes fell to infantry, as in the Ardennes in 1944 or on the Pacific islands and atolls, they were usually neutralised by flamethrower or by the stealthy approach of infantrymen who, under cover of machine-gun fire, would get close enough to drop grenades through the loopholes.

It would appear that little had changed since Vauban's time regarding the inevitable fall of any fortification, but much could always be done to postpone that moment. We must remind ourselves of the findings of all the recent studies of British defence positions in the Second World War, including those by William Foot of 67 such sites, DG Glover's in south-west Wales, and Gordon Barclay's in north-east Scotland. These all describe integrated in-depth systems which include both hardened and earthwork structures, grouped to provide mutual support, and a wide range of anti-personnel and AT obstacles. But it was to be the flexibility of these latter, more temporary constructions which were to spell the end for the pillbox in Britain. In February 1942 GHQ Home Forces directed that 'all experience of modern war points most strongly to the fact that the pillbox is not a suitable type of fortification for either coastal or nodal point defence'. The alternative was from now on to be field defences, capable of all-round defence, well-sited, well-concealed, and well-constructed. The reasons given related to the vulnerability of pillboxes and the problem of their restricted fields of fire. If pillboxes were to be built more strongly, then they would become more difficult to conceal, and if their fields of fire were to be increased, then their widened loopholes would become yet more vulnerable; hence the move to earthworks.

Since the end of the Second World War, conflicts around the world have seen the use of a wide variety of field fortifications, and fewer hardened defences. Field fortifications have tended to be constructed from easily portable, or locally-sourced materials: sheet steel; wire-mesh; timber; rock; and earth, gravel or sand in containers made of timber, steel or fabric. In some theatres, such as Vietnam, production of these structures by the French, the Americans and the South Vietnamese was on an industrial scale, with standardised modular systems being replicated across the country. British sangars and hedgehogs in Aden and the Arabian Gulf States appear not to have gone beyond the stage of improvisation. Albania built thousands of concrete pillboxes in the 1960s and 1970s, but is unusual in investing in such a degree of permanence. After the 1967 war, the Israelis fortified the east bank of the Suez Canal with the 26 fortress positions of the Bar Lev Line, consisting of pillboxes, gun emplacements, watchtowers and AT obstacles, all embedded in a 60ft (18m) high sand rampart. The Golan Heights were similarly fortified by the Israelis, with 17 bunker complexes holding infantry, artillery and armour. The Syrians responded with concrete gun and tank positions using designs provided by their Soviet military advisers.

Possibly the last pillbox ever to be built is at Ljubljana, where it was constructed to publicise an exhibition mounted by the National Museum of Contemporary History of Slovenia, to commemorate the Italian domination of the city from 1942-45.

BIBLIOGRAPHY

Alexander, C., 1991, 'interview with Fred Bowman', *ALDIS* 48 (Portsmouth)

Alexander, C., 1999, *Ironside's Line* (Storrington, Historic Military Press)

Anderson, R., 2004, *The Forgotten Front, E African Campaign 1914-18* (Stroud)

Armit, I., 2003, *Towers in the North, the Brochs of Scotland* (Stroud, Tempus)

Barclay, G., 2005, *The Cowie Line: a Second World War 'stop line' west of Stonehaven, Aberdeenshire,* Proceedings of the Soc. of Antiquaries of Scotland, Vol. 135

Bird, C., 1999, *Silent Sentinels* (Dereham, Larks Press)

Bogart, C., 1995, 'Fort Harrod, Kentucky', *Fort* 23

Brice, M., 1990, *Forts & Fortresses* (Oxford, Quarto)

Brophy, J., 1940, *Home Guard: a handbook for the LDV* (London)

Brooks, R.J., 2007, 'Pickett/Hamilton Fort Recovery', *After the Battle* 135 (London)

Browne, Lt Col. J.H.G., 1891, *The Artillery Combat in Siege Warfare;* Proceedings of the RA Institution Volume XVIII, Number 12, October 1891 & Volume XIX, Number 1, November 1891, Woolwich

Burridge, D., *pers. comms* 1990-present

Cambs & Isle of Ely TA Association, 1944, *We Also Served* (Cambridge)

Cave, H., *c.*1985 *papers, interview and pers. comms*

Charbonneau, A., 1990, 'The Redoubt in New France', *Fort* 18

Clark, G.S., 1907, *Fortification: its past achievements, recent developments & future progress* (2nd edn, reprinted 1989, Liphook, Beaufort)

Clayton, Lt Col. E., 1892, *Some notes on applied field fortification,* Proceedings of the RA Institution Volume XIX, Number 8, June 1892 (Woolwich)

Clements, W., 1999, *Towers of Strength, Martello towers worldwide* (Barnsley)

Clements, W., 2003, *Defending the North, Ulster 1796-1956* (Newtownards)

Cobb, P., 1991, *British-style pillboxes in Ireland* reference in *ALDIS* 47 (Portsmouth)

Cobb, P., 1994, 'EXDO Posts in British Service', *Loopholes* 7

Collier, B., 1957, *The Defence of the UK* (London, HMSO; 1995 reprinted IWM)

Cros, B., 1998, *Citadelles d'Azur* (Aix-en-Provence, Edisud)

Denfeld, DC., 1981, *Japanese Fortifications & other Military Structures in the Central Pacific* (Saipan, Micronesian Archaeological Survey)

Dobinson, C., 1996, *Twentieth Century Fortifications in England II: Anti-invasion Defences of WWII* (York, CBA)

Dobinson, C., 2000, *Twentieth Century Fortifications in England X: Airfield defences in WWII* (York, CBA)

Dorman, J, 1990, *Guardians of the Humber* (Hull)

Dunnigan, B. 1985, *History & Guide to Old Fort Niagara* (NY, Youngstown)

Evans, D., 2006, *Arming the Fleet* (Gosport, Explosion Museum & EH)

Faucherre, N., 1997, *Bastions de la Mer* (Chauray-Niort)

Field, R., 2005, *Forts of the American Frontier 1820-91, central & northern plains* (Oxford, Osprey)

Field, R., 2005, *American Civil War Fortifications 2, (land & field)* (Oxford, Osprey)

Field, R., 2006, *Forts of the American Frontier, southern plains & south-west* (Oxford, Osprey)

Fields, N, 2003, *Hadrian's Wall AD 122-410* (Oxford, Osprey)

Fields, N., 2005, *Rome's Northern Frontier AD 70-235* (Oxford, Osprey)

Floyd, D., 1991, 'United States Martello Towers', *Fortress 9*

Foot, W., 2006, *Beaches, fields, streets and hills* (York, CBA)

Forty, G., 2002, *Fortress Europe* (Hersham, Ian Allan)

Foster, J., 2004, *The Guns of the North-east* (Barnsley)

Francis, P., 1996, *British Military Airfield Architecture* (Sparkford)

Freethy, R., 2005, *Lancashire 1939-45 the Secret War* (Newbury)

Garie, F., 1995, 'Australian Colonial Forts', *Fort 23*

Glover, DG., 1990, 'A Command Stop Line on Rhos Llangeler', *Carmarthenshire Antiquary* Vol. XXVI

Green, M., 1999, *War Walks Stop Line Green* (Cheltenham)

Green, M & Plant, J., 1993 & 1994, 'The Bristol Outer Defences on the Cotswold Plateau', Dover', *Loopholes* 4 (May '93), 5 (September '93) & 7 (March '94)

Greeves, I.D., 1993, 'The Construction of the GHQ Stop-Line', *Fortress 16*

Gulvin, K & Smith, V., 1978, 'The Twydall Profile', *Fort 5*

Harding, J., 2001, *The Mini Castles of Wales, Pillboxes in Anglesey*, Transactions Anglesey Antiquarian Society & Field Club

Harris, EC., 1997, *Bermuda Forts 1612-1957* (Bermuda)

Harrison, P., 1997, 'The fortified village of Ushguli in the Georgian Caucasus', *Fort 25*

Harrison, P., 2007, 'Cuba, the provincial fortifications during the Spanish colonial era', *Casemate 78*

Hazelwood, K., 2007, 'Recovery of Allan Williams Turret', *Loopholes 37*

Hellis, J & Dawe, N., 1995, 'The Yarnold Sangar', *Loopholes 14*

Higham, R. & Barker, P., 1992, *Timber Castles* (London, Batsford)

Hill, P. & Wileman, J., 2002, *Landscapes of War* (Stroud, Tempus)

Hohnadel, A. & Truttmann, M., 1988, *Guide de la Ligne Maginot* (Heimdal)

Hope-Taylor, B., 1956, 'The Norman Motte at Abinger, Surrey, and its wooden castle' in Bruce-Mitford, R.L.S. (ed.), *Recent Archaeological Excavations in Britain* (London, RKP)

Horne, A., 1969, *To Lose a Battle* (London, Macmillan)

Hughes, Q., 1984, 'A Project for the Defence of Paris', *Fort 12*

Hughes, Q., 1974, *Military Architecture* (revd edn 1991, Liphook, Beaufort)

Hughes, Q. & Migos, A., 1995, *Strong as the Rock of Gibraltar* (Gibraltar)

Innes, G.B., 1995, *British Airfield Buildings of WWII* (Earl Shilton)

Jancovik, A., 2001, 'Rupnik Line - Yugoslavia's western front', *Fort 29*

Jarvis, R., 2002, *Fortress Lowestoft* (Lowestoft, Heritage Workshop Centre)

Kaufmann, J.E., 1989, 'Dutch & Belgian Defences 1940', *Fort 17*

Kaufmann, J.E. et al, 1999, *Fortress Europe* (London, Greenhill)

Kaufmann, J.E. et al, 2003, *Fortress Third Reich* (Cambridge MA)

Kaufmann, J.E. et al, 2004, *Fortress America* (Cambridge MA, Da Capo)

Kent, P., *pers. comms* 1980-present

Kerrigan, P., 1990, 'Fortifications in Tudor Ireland 1547-1603', *Fortress 7*

Kerrigan, P., 1995, *Castles & Fortifications in Ireland 1485-1945* (Cork)

Knight, I., 2005, *British Fortifications in Zululand 1879* (Oxford, Osprey)

Lee, E., 1985, *To The Bitter End* (Harmondsworth, Penguin)

Lindsay, O., 2005, *The Battle for Hong Kong 1941-5* (Staplehurst)

Longstaff-Tyrrell, P., 2002, *Barracks to Bunkers* (Stroud, Sutton)

Lowry, B. (ed.) *et al*, 1996, *20th Century Defences in Britain* (York, CBA)

Lowry, B., 2004, *British Home Defences 1940-45* (Oxford, Osprey)

Mace, M., 1996, *Frontline Sussex* (Storrington)

Mackenzie, S.P., 1996, *The Home Guard* (Oxford)

Mallory, K & Ottar, A., 1973, *The Architecture of Aggression* (AP)

McGovern, T., 1998, 'American Defences of the Panama Canal', *Fort 26*

Mutti, A.J., 2003, 'Pre-cast pillboxes', *Loopholes 23*

Nash, F., 1993, 'Spigot Mortar Pit at St Albans', *After the Battle 81*

Nossov, K., 2006, *Russian Fortresses 1480-1682* (Oxford, Osprey)

Oldham, P., 1995, *Pillboxes on the Western Front* (London, Leo Cooper)

Oldham, P., 1997, *The Hindenburg Line* (Barnsley, Pen & Sword/Leo Cooper)

Osborne, M., 2004, *Defending Britain* (Stroud, Tempus)

Partridge, C., 1976, *Hitler's Atlantic Wall* (Guernsey, DI Publications)

Pepper, S. & Adams, N., 1986, *Firearms & Fortifications* (Chicago, UCP)

Pfluger, H., 1977, 'The Defences of Ulm' *Fort 4*

Potochik, A., 2007, 'Defences of Ljubljana', *Casemate 78*

Prickett, N., 1994, 'British Army Field Fortifications of the New Zealand Wars', *Fort 22*

Purcell, S., 1993, 'Airfield Battle Headquarters', *Loopholes 5*

Pye, A. & Woodward, F., 1996, *The Historic Defences of Plymouth* (Exeter)

Raban, Maj., *Field Fortification*, Proceedings of the RA Institution Volume XIX Numbers 2, December 1891, and 3, January 1892 (Woolwich)

Ramm, H.G. *et al*, 1970, *Shielings & Bastles* (RCHM[E] London, HMSO)

Ramsey W. G., (ed.) 1978, After the Battle 21, *Gibraltar* (London)

Rawson, A., 2006, *British Army Handbook 1914-18* (Stroud, Sutton)

Reid, I., 1997, 'Goxhill's Battle Headquarters', *Airfield Review 74*

Reiss, G., 1993, 'Fortification in Switzerland', *Fort 21*

Rolf, R., 1983, *Der Atlantikwall* (Amsterdam, AMA-Verlag)

Rolf, R. & Saal, P., 1986, *Fortress Europe* (Shrewsbury, Airlife)

Rottman, G., 2003, *Japanese Pacific Island Defenses* (Oxford, Osprey)

Ruddy, A., 2003, *British Anti-Invasion Defences 1940-1945* (Storrington)

Saunders, Anthony, 2001, *Hitler's Atlantic Wall* (Stroud, Sutton)

Saunders, Andrew, 2004, *Fortress Builder [Bernard de Gomme]* (UEP, Exeter)

Sholl, B., *pers. comms* 1990s

Short, N., 2002, *Hitler's Siegfried Line* (Stroud, Sutton)

Short, N., 2006, *Tank Turret Fortifications* (Marlborough, Crowood)

Short, N., 2006, *German Defences in Italy in World War II* (Oxford, Osprey)

Slater, H., 1941, *Home Guard for Victory* (London, Gollancz)

Smith, C., 2005, *Singapore Burning* (London, Penguin)

Smith, D.J., 1989, *Britain's Military Airfields 1939-45* (Wellingborough)

Sneep, J. *et al*, 1982, *Vesting* ('S-Gravenhage, Stichting Menno van Coehoorn)

Spiteri, S., 1996, *British Military Architecture in Malta* (Valletta)

Stout, G., 2000, 'Pillboxes on the Boyne', *Jnl. of Old Drogheda Soc.* 12

Tomlinson, R., 1998, 'Masonry Blockhouses of the Anglo-Boer War 1899-1902', *Fort* 26

van Wieringen, J.S., 1991, 'The Grebbe Line', *Fort* 19

Walker, D., articles on Redcar area in *Loopholes* 24 (2002) & 36 (2006)

Ward, T., 'Bastle Houses of the Anglo-Scottish Borders', *Fortress* 5

Ward, W., 2005, 'A 'New' Type of Pillbox', *Loopholes* 32

War Office, 1941, *Army Council Instruction No. 1419* (London)

War Office, General Staff, 1911, *Manual of Field Engineering* (HMSO, London)

War Office, General Staff, 1916, *Notes on Trench Warfare for Infantry Officers*

Wehrmacht, 1943, *Bildheft Neuzeitlicher Stellungsbau* (reprinted 1969, Hemel Hempstead, Bellona)

Williford, G. & McGovern, T., 2003, *Defenses of Pearl Harbour & Oahu 1907-50*, (Oxford, Osprey)

Wintringham, T., 1940, *New Ways of War* (Harmondsworth, Penguin)

Wills, H., 1985, *Pillboxes, a study of UK defences 1940* (London, Leo Cooper)

Wright, G., 1983, 'Mablethorpe 1916', *Lincolnshire Life*, May issue

INDEX

Illustration numbers are shown in italics